国学经典 · 处世三奇书

汉英对照

CHINESE-ENGLISH

THE ROOTS OF WISDOM

菜根谭

[明] 洪应明 / 著

周文标 / 英译

周文标 应佳鑫 / 译注

百花洲文艺出版社

BAIHUAZHOU LITERATURE AND ART PRESS

图书在版编目（CIP）数据

菜根谭：汉英对照 /（明）洪应明著；周文标英译；周文标，应佳鑫译注. -- 南昌：百花洲文艺出版社，2020.9
ISBN 978-7-5500-3783-0

Ⅰ. ①菜… Ⅱ. ①洪… ②周… ③应… Ⅲ. ①个人 – 修养 – 中国 – 明代②《菜根谭》– 译文 – 汉、英③《菜根谭》– 注释 – 汉、英 Ⅳ. ①B825

中国版本图书馆CIP数据核字（2020）第132001号

菜根谭：汉英对照

CAIGENTAN：HAN-YING DUIZHAO

［明］洪应明 著　周文标 英译　周文标 应佳鑫 译注

出 版 人	章华荣
责任编辑	郝玮刚　蔡央扬　程慧敏
书籍设计	方　方
制　　作	黄敏俊
出版发行	百花洲文艺出版社
社　　址	南昌市红谷滩新区世贸路898号博能中心A座20楼
邮　　编	330038
经　　销	全国新华书店
印　　刷	江西华奥印务有限责任公司
开　　本	787mm × 1092mm 1/16　　印张 16.75
版　　次	2020年9月第1版第1次印刷
字　　数	268千字
书　　号	ISBN 978-7-5500-3783-0
定　　价	58.00元

赣版权登字 05-2020-106

邮购联系 0791-86895109
网　址 http://www.bhzwy.com
图书若有印装错误，影响阅读，可向承印厂联系调换。

走向世界的明清小品
——汉英对照本“处世三奇书”序

The Sketches of the Ming and Qing Dynasties Going Abroad
— Preface to the “Three Canons of Personal Cultivation”

赵丽宏

Zhao Lihong

“处世三奇书”是中国古典文学的汉英对照本。在中国传统文化的出版物中，这是一套体例新颖的双语读本。这个读本，不仅向读者展现了中国古典文学一方迷人的天地，也为对中国文化有兴趣的英语读者提供了一个学习的园圃。读者可以由中文而英文，也可以由英文而中文。研习英文的中国读者，学习中文的外国读者，都可以在其中获得阅读的乐趣。

“Three Canons of Personal Cultivation” is a Chinese-English version of Chinese classical literature. In the publications of Chinese traditional culture, this is a set of bilingual readings with new style. It not only shows the charming world of Chinese classics, but also provides a learning garden for English readers who are interested in Chinese culture. Readers can read the canons in two ways, either from Chinese to English or from English to Chinese. Both Chinese readers who are learning English and foreign readers who are learning Chinese are enabled to get the pleasure of reading them.

《菜根谭》《小窗幽记》和《围炉夜话》是明清时期流传下来的三本以修身养性、劝善励志为中心话题的清言体小品集，作者分别是洪应明、陈继儒和王永彬。因其在同类书中出众的地位和影响力，被世人誉为“处世三奇书”，颇受文人墨客和普通百姓的喜爱。

The Roots of Wisdom, *Meditative Notes in Solitude* and *Fireside Talk at Night* are the three famous books successively appearing in the Ming Dynasty (1368-1644) and the Qing Dynasty (1644-1911), with subjects mainly on moral cultivation and inspirational exhortations on doing good and working hard, and therefore known as the "Three Canons of Personal Cultivation" out of their unparalleled status in books of the same kind and influence among the intellectuals and ordinary people.

华夏文化的发展，每个历史时期都有创造性的文学形态，并在各自领域中登峰造极，成为一个时代的文化标记。明清两朝也不例外，在前后五个多世纪里，小说显然是明清时期的一个主要文化特色，其次就是那些饱蕴着智慧才情、展示着世态风情的辑录和承载着先人学说和思想的格言体小品集了。通过这些作品，我们可以清楚地了解到：优秀的文学家，是中国传统文化的脊梁，他们那些形诸文字的精神与情感结晶是中华文明最有生命力的一部分。世风日下依然能倡导并坚持孝悌，物欲横流依然能淡泊名利，仕途得意依然能心存忧患意识，遭遇不测依然能泰然处之，国家危亡依然能竭尽忠诚，温饱之余依然能不忘劳作之苦，生活清贫依然能寄情山水，凡此种种，都是这些优秀文人留给后世的宝贵精神财富。

In the long history of China, cultural development of each era has its own creative literary form and insurmountable height, thus becoming a cultural mark of the time, the same those of the dynasties of Ming and Qing. During more than five centuries, the novels and fictions are of course the primary literary identity of the dynasties, and the collections brimming with human wits and revealing the ways of the world and the compilations of previous classical works, ancestors' quotes and their developed writings must be the next. Through these works and writings, we see clearly that the excellent literati are really the backbone of Chinese classical culture, and that the crystallization of spirit and emotion they created in words is one of the most vivid parts of Chinese civilization. As the breeders of the civilization of that times, even when the general moves were getting worse and worse they would remain faithful to filial piety and fraternal duty;

even when in an acquisitive time they would remain indifferent to fame and wealth; even when content with their official careers they would remain preoccupied with the misery consciousness; even when coming across unexpected occurrences they would remain unruffled and take them calmly; even when the state was in peril they would remain loyal; even when having enough food and clothing they would remain concerned about the pain of labor; even when living a poor life they would remain disposed to bask in the poetic mood between mountains and rivers. — All these refined qualities are the precious spiritual wealth the excellent literati handed down to us later generations.

“处世三奇书”所收纳的短句小品均为清言体，风格相似，读起来朗朗上口，既有诗歌的韵律又有散文的流畅。这些编辑成集、主题鲜明的短句小品，是被柔美化了的格言，似诗非诗，似文非文，是小品文的一种，形式上是介于箴言警句和散文之间的文体，通常由前后对仗或排比的两句或两段组成，以达到均衡与和谐之美。由清言汇集而成的书籍叫清言集或清言体小品集，有分编和不分编两种，题材自由，体例松散，所收清言小品数量少则近百则、多则数百则不等，每则小品的篇幅少则七八个字，多则逾百。内容涵盖古贤经典和民俗文化，其中尤以演绎儒道释三家之言为多，形式短小精致，文风飘逸清雅，具有“小品中的小品（林语堂语）”的美称。

The short sketches contained in the “Three Canons of Personal Cultivation” are all with distinctive themes, clear-spoken, similar in style, easy to read, and full of the rhythm of poetry and fluency of prose. So far as the form is concerned, these sketches belong to a kind of maxims literarily beautified with a manner of seemingly like but actually not a poem or seemingly like but actually not a prose, normally composed of two sentences or two paragraphs adorned with antitheses, couplets and other rhetoric devices to achieve the beauty of balance and harmony, and with its writing style lying between maxim and prose. The collections with such writings are called clear-and-upright sketches, usually there being two ways of compilation, classified or non-classified, either freely with subject matter or loose in layout, in which the pieces collected vary from nearly one hundred to several hundreds, and Chinese characters used in different pieces vary from seven or eight to more than a hundred, and the contents arranged cover Chinese classics and folk culture, mostly related to the sayings derived from the theories of Confucianism, Taoism and Buddhism. They are short in length, vivid in format and elegant in expression, and therefore praised by Mr. Lin Yutang (a famous modern Chinese scholar) as "a mini-sketch of sketches".

"处世三奇书"的可贵之处在于：三位作者皆以其丰富的学养、渊博的知识、明敏的思辨、冷隽的文字、促人深省的儆诫、益人心智的启迪，以及豁达如禅的觉醒，从古贤经典和民俗文化中撷取菁华但又不简单地复述这些原文，而是在赋予它们一定的情景衬托后将其锻造成一个个既养眼又养心的段子，于寥寥隽语中将经典所含的意旨优雅地展现在读者面前，充分诠释了中国传统文人的文化底蕴和人文情怀，为世人展现了一幅古人修身养性的清晰图景，让读者在诵读这些金科玉律时多了一份愉悦感和亲近感。

The praiseworthiness of the "Three Canons of Personal Cultivation" is as obvious as this: instead of simply quoting the original sayings, the three authors, by applying their rich learning and cultivation, profound knowledge, dialectical thinking, grave and stern expressions, thought-provoking warning, meditative enlightenment and self-awareness, turned out their sketches in the least paradoxes to exemplify the extracts from the classical works and folk culture, and gave prominence to the pieces well matched with relevant scene, sight, circumstances, background or landscape, thus achieving the effect of being pleasant to readers' eyes and minds. Their endeavors fully annotate the cultural deposits and humanistic sensibilities of the traditional literati, and thus enable us to have the opportunity to see a clear picture of the personal cultivation of the ancients, and make us feel more pleasure and intimacy than ever in reading the famous aphorisms of ancient classics.

十年前，周文标先生在上海人民出版社出版发行《菜根谭》汉英对照本时，我曾为他写过一篇序。据我所知，十余年来，他一直不懈地致力于用英文翻译和编撰中国传统典籍，并在呈现方式上做了积极的探索。这次他与百花洲文艺出版社共同成套推出“处世三奇书”汉英对照本，足见他这些年在这方面所倾注的时间和精力。周文标先生是上海市作家协会的会员，我为我们作协有这么一位孜孜不倦向世界推广中国传统文化的同仁感到骄傲。衷心祝贺他的“处世三奇书”汉英对照本成功出版，这是明清小品走向世界的一次积极尝试。期待他有更多新著在不久的将来问世。

10 years ago, when Mr. Zhou Wenbiao's *The Roots of Wisdom* in Chinese-English version was about to be published by Shanghai People's Publishing House, I wrote a preface for him. As I know, Mr. Zhou has been unceasingly spending most of his spare time on translating and compiling Chinese classics in English for more than ten years, and has made an active scrutiny into the modes of presentation. This time, he and Baihuazhou Literature and Art Press jointly plan to issue the "Three Canons of Personal Cultivation" in the form of three-in-one packing, which shows how much time and energy he has devoted in this respect. Mr. Zhou is a member of Shanghai Writers Association, and I am proud to have such a colleague who has been working so tirelessly to introduce Chinese traditional culture to the world. Here I'd like to extend my hearty congratulations on his successful publication of the Chinese-English

"Three Canons of Personal Cultivation", thinking that it is a positive attempt for the sketches of the Ming and Qing Dynasties to go abroad. Furthermore, I'll look forward to seeing his more new works to be published in the near future.

是为序。

It's my pleasure to write this preface as above.

2018 年 7 月 31 日于四步斋

Four-Pace Study in Shanghai
July 31st, 2018

《菜根谭》序

Introduction to *The Roots of Wisdom*

赵丽宏
Zhao Lihong

《菜根谭》为明人洪应明所著，是一部内容丰富、充满智慧和哲理的奇书。其形式是格言体，三百余段，每段篇幅简短，语言精湛生动，深入浅出，耐人寻味。作者通晓中国古代哲人的学说和思想，孔孟老庄，儒道佛法，取其精义，归于禅宗。书中的内容，涉及人世万象，劝善，立志，处世，修身，养性，品尝天地间形形色色的美妙景象，可谓无处不达、无所不包。因其睿智的思想、豁达的心境、清新的语境，并描绘出种种令人向往的人生佳境，数百年来流传于民间，不仅被文人赞赏，也被普通百姓喜欢，成为一本广受欢迎的书。所谓“咬得菜根，百事可做”“布衣暖，菜根香，读书滋味长”。这些民间俗语，其实都是对这本书的赞扬。

The Roots of Wisdom, written by Hong Yingming in the Ming Dynasty, is a rare book which contains abundant perspectives, wisdom and philosophy. With its literary form embodied in maxim, the book is composed of more than three hundred short writings, from which there can be seen striking expressions, simply-explained profoundness and thought-provoking substances. By reading the book, we will be strongly impressed by the author's rich accumulation of the theories of the ancient sages in Chinese history, his knowledge ranging from the thoughts of Confucius, Mencius, Lao Zi and Zhuang Zi to the relevant doctrines involved in Confucianism, Taoism, Buddhism and Legalism, as well as his successful exploits in extracting the essences therein and putting them into meditation in the way of Chan. So what he presented in his book are mostly related to the substantial issues regarding myriad affairs of the human world, exhortations on people's doing good and enlightenment for them on how to determine their will, regulate their conduct, cultivate their inner power and refine their personal dispositions. In addition, the book also unfolds before our eyes a big variety of subtle views existing between the heaven and earth. It can be said that it stops at nothing and nothing is left out. It is because of the fantastic features manifested in its context such as intelligent ideology, broad-mindedness, fresh extent of wording and phrasing and enormous desirable braveries of life that the book, during the hundreds of years of circulation, has been not only appreciated by men of letters but also cherished by the common people, thereby coming out as a rare book universally welcomed. As a matter of fact, the proverbs like "One who can endure chewing vegetable root will find nothing is difficult." and "Course clothes give warmth and vegetable roots fragrance, while indulgence in study brings about lifelong benefit." are all considered to be the plaudits for the book.

对这本奇书，历来有不少解读，原著的文字，衍生出很多后人心得，古老的文字，历久弥新，被不同时代的读者读出新的意味。此书的影响，不仅在国内，也流传到了国外，日本、韩国、东南亚，都有《菜根谭》引发的回声。现在，这本中英文对照的《菜根谭》即将出版，我想，这对学习英文的中国读者是一件幸事，对正在学习中文、对中国文化有兴趣的英文读者，更是一件意义非凡的事情。

There have been many different annotations and interpretations on the words and expressions contained in this rare book since its appearance. The dictions used in it have been evolved into numerous understandings all through the ages. The implied meanings of the vocabulary have been renewed from time to time and yet remain new to the readers of the coming generations. Its influence has flowed widely not merely within China but also without, wherefrom its echoes have been now and then sounding from Japan, South Korea and Southeast Asia.Now *The Roots of Wisdom* in the version of Chinese-English is about to be published soon. I would like to take this chance to say that the publication of the translation is a piece of good news to Chinese readers who are now engaged in English learning and also an event even more significant to those English-speaking people who are interested in Chinese culture.

本书的译者周文标先生，很多年前曾领衔将篇幅浩瀚的英文版《世界名言博引词典》（伯顿 · 史蒂文森主编）翻译成中文，并以一己之力根据中文习惯重新编列分辑，成为翻译出版界的一个壮举。这次，周文标选择将《菜根谭》转译成英文，有眼光，也有勇气。把这样一本古书翻译成英文，对一个中国人来说，绝非易事，除了精通英文，还必须对博大精深的中国传统文化有深入准确的理解。将数百年前的涵义幽深的中国古语转换成异国文字，会遇到多少障碍，可以想象，但是周文标没有被难倒。呈现在读者眼前的这本汉英对照《菜根谭》，是周文标先生多年心血的结晶。我相信，在品读此书时，读者会对这位为中国文化搭建沟通桥梁的翻译家产生由衷的敬意。

Many years ago, Mr. Zhou Wenbiao, the translator of *The Roots of Wisdom*, lead an English-to-Chinese translation of *The Home Book of Quotations* (compiled by Burton Stevenson) and recompiled it single-handedly in accordance with Chinese phonetic alphabet, and thus created a remarkable precedent for the dictionaries of this kind in China. This time Mr. Zhou takes *The Roots of Wisdom* as his new rendering which manifests again the sense of his exertion and confidence. For having such an ancient book translated from Chinese into English is no easy matter for an unadulterated Chinese. To do it well there must come into play a good command of English language and a deep, precise understanding of Chinese traditional culture as well. So it can be imagined that Mr. Zhou must have encountered many difficulties in his rendering into English those old Chinese with profound meanings of several centuries prior. Be that as it was, he was not baffled and what he contemplated three years ago has now come true in the very publication he presents to us. No wonder when readers have the book in their hands there would surely well up in their hearts the appreciation for the translator who has done his part in putting up a bridge to connect Chinese and English cultures.

是为序。

It's my pleasure to write this preface for the book as above.

2008 年 6 月 12 日于上海四步斋

Four-Pace Study in Shanghai
June 12th, 2008

译者按：

以上是上海市作家协会副主席赵丽宏先生 2008 年 6 月为本人的《菜根谭》汉英对照单行本所赐的《序》，此次百花洲文艺出版社出版合装“处世三奇书”汉英对照本，仍沿用作《菜根谭》的序，谨以此再次表示本人对赵丽宏先生的感谢和敬意。

Translator's Note:

Above is the preface written by Mr. Zhao Lihong, vice president of Shanghai Writers Association, in June 2008. It's my honor to have his preface reused as the introduction to *The Roots of Wisdom* in the publication of Chinese-English version of "Three Canons of Personal Cultivation" issued by Baihuazhou Literature and Art Press, and hereby to express again my heartfelt gratitude and respect to him.

1. 栖守道德　毋阿权贵 /001

1. Rather stick to moral integrity than be attached to the powerful and influential.

2. 与其练达　不若朴鲁 /001

2. Better be honest and straightforward than scheming and calculating.

3. 心地光明　才华韫藏 /002

3. The mind of a man should be made open and broad, but his talents carefully concealed.

4. 近纷华而不染　知机巧而不用 /003

4. Not be sullied by extravagance even if close to it nor resort to intrigues even if acquainted with them.

5. 闻逆耳言　怀拂心事 /003

5. It is helpful to hear words unpleasant to the ear and meditate on things unpleasant to the mind.

6. 和气喜神　天人一理 /004

6. Harmony and happiness are agreeable to both Nature and human beings.

7. 真味是淡　至人如常 /005

7. Genuine flavor only lies in light and mild food; and a man of perfect morality is no different from ordinary people.

8. 闲时吃紧　忙时悠闲 /005

8. Keep the sense of imminence while at leisure and while busy, be at ease.

9. 静坐观心　真妄毕现 /006

9. Sit quietly in meditation, and you will perceive both the true character and the distracting thoughts.

10. 得意早回头　拂心莫停手 /007

10. Stop seeking more in times of contentment but keep going on even if suffering setbacks.

11. 志从澹泊来　节在肥甘丧 /007

11. Aspiration is attained in natural simplicity while moral integrity spoiled in extravagance.

12. 田地放宽　恩泽流长 /008

12. In dealing with people, better be large-minded and tolerant; and in bestowing favors, better let them spread far and wide.

13. 路留一步　味减三分 /008

13. Step aside one pace for others when the path is narrow and when you are fine fed, share three-tenths of your food with others.

14. 脱俗成名　减欲入圣 /009

14. Get rid of vulgarity, and you will become a man of celebrity; decrease

the desires for fame and wealth, and you will enter sainthood.

15. 侠气交友　素心做人 /009

15. Be chivalrous in getting along with friends and unadorned in conducting yourself.

16. 利毋居前　德毋落后 /010

16. Never anticipate others in seeking wealth nor lag behind in dispensing charities.

17. 忍让为高　利人利己 /011

17. Forbearance means superiority and is beneficial to both others and yourself.

18. 矜则无功　悔可减过 /011

18. Arrogance spoils contributions and repentance counteracts faults.

19. 美名不独享　责任不推脱 /012

19. When winning a good name, do not reap it all alone and when at fault, do not shift responsibility onto others.

20. 功名不求盈满　做人恰到好处 /012

20. Seek no perfection in personal achievement and do just to the point in human relationships.

21. 诚心和气　胜于观心 /013

21. Even temperament is superior to meditation.

22. 有动有寂　动寂相宜 /014

22. Movement harbors in stillness and stillness in movement, and both give rise to each other.

23. 责恶勿太严　教善勿太高 /014

23. Be not too severe when reproaching someone with his faults, nor too demanding when initiating someone into righteousness.

24. 洁常自污出　明每从暗生 /015

24. Cleanliness often derives from dirt and brightness always from gloom.

25. 伸张正气　再现真心 /016

25. Only when healthy trends are encouraged can there emerge the true characters from within.

26. 事悟痴除　性定动正 /016

26. Ex-post repentance dispels infatuations and nature well preserved begets appropriate action.

27. 志在林泉　胸怀廊庙 /017

27. Keep in mind the ambition and statecraft to serve the country while lodging your aspiration in the forests and fountains.

28. 无过是功　无怨是德 /018

28. To go without blame is creditable and without others' enmity, grateful.

29. 忧勤勿过　待人勿枯 /018

29. In performing your duties, not be overstrained; and in dealing with people, not be indifferent.

30. 原其初心　观其末路 /019

30. To judge a man is to look into his initial intention; and to comment on a man is to examine his integrity in his later years.

31. 富宜宽厚　智宜敛藏 /019

31. Be generous even if you are rich and honorable and keep your talents obscured even if you are replete with wisdom.

32. 登高思危　少言勿躁 /020

32. Think of danger when ascending a height and talk less to avoid vexation.

33. 放得功名　即可脱俗 /021

33. One who can sever himself from fame and wealth will overcome worldly thoughts.

34. 偏见害人　聪明障道 /021

34. Self-willedness harms man's notion, and smart aleck hinders man's virtue.

35. 知退一步　加让三分 /022

35. Step backward for others when on a narrow path and give way for them even if on an open road.

36. 不恶小人　有礼君子 /022

36. Treat a base man with no hatred and a worthy man with etiquette.

37. 正气清名　留于乾坤 /023

37. It is better to leave both righteousness and untainted name to the world.

38. 降魔先降心　驭横先驭气 /024

38. To vanquish monsters, first vanquish the wicked thoughts in mind; to control absurdity, first control the internal rashness in heart.

39. 教育子弟　要严交游 /024

39. To educate disciples, it is better to do so by setting rigid rules on their social intercourse.

40. 欲路勿染　理路勿退 /025

40. Do not act willfully in pursuing material gains, nor shrink back in seeking the truth.

41. 不可浓艳　不可枯寂 /025

41. In everyday life, one should be neither too particular nor too casual-minded.

42. 超越天地　不入名利 /026

42. Transcend the mundane world by not being tempted into fame and wealth.

43. 高一步立身　退一步处世 /027

43. Stand on a higher plane in pursuit and for the sake of security, learn how to compromise.

44. 修德忘名　读书深心 /027

44. Do away with fame when striving for virtue and be wholly devoted when resolving upon study.

45. 一念之差　失之千里 /028

45. A momentary slip gives occasion to a permanent loss.

46. 有木石心　具云水趣 /029

46. A rock-firm will is indispensable in moral cultivation, so is a natural temperament in dedication to the country.

47. 吉人和气　凶人杀气 /030

47. A good man is always imbued with composure, and a bad man with a murderous look.

48. 君子无祸　勿罪冥冥 /030

48. An accomplished man should do no evil on the sly if he wants to distance calamities.

49. 多心为祸　少事为福 /031

49. It is a misfortune to be sunk in excessive exertions, but a fortune to have few cares.

50. 当方则方　当圆则圆 /032

50. Be upright whenever needed and slick, when it is necessary.

51. 己功不念　人恩不忘 /032

51. Bear not in mind the favors we have done to others but the bounties

others might have bestowed on us.

52. 施之不求　求之无功 /033

52. Never seek return for the benefaction we have given, otherwise winning no reputation.

53. 相观对治　方便法门 /034

53. It is good for one to take mutual examination and contrast others' position with one's own.

54. 心地干净　方可学古 /034

54. Only when the heart is made clear and pure can one start to model after ancient sages and men of virtue.

55. 崇俭养廉　守拙全真 /035

55. Frugality makes honesty and dullness brings sincerity.

56. 学以致用　立业种德 /036

56. Studying for the purpose of application conduces to both moral cultivation and career development.

57. 扫除外物　直觅本来 /037

57. Only by clearing away outside enticement can one find a straight path to the essence of his nature.

58. 苦中有乐　得意生悲 /037

58. As pleasure grows in suffering, so frustration forms in contentment.

59. 富贵名誉　来自道德 /038

59. Riches and honor should be derived from the cultivation of morality.

60. 花铺好色　人行好事 /038

60. As flowers would bloom a riot of color, so should one do good turns so long as one lives.

61. 兢业的心思　潇洒的趣味 /039

61. Unrestrained interest for life is as vital as assiduous thoughts in learning.

62. 立名者贪　用术者拙 /040

62. Those who seek reputation are greedy and clumsy, those who resort to craft.

63. 宁虚勿溢　宁缺勿全 /040

63. Emptiness is better than spillage, and so is incompletion than completion.

64. 拔去名根　融化客气 /041

64. Uproot the lust for fame within and dispose of influences without.

65. 心体光明　暗室青天 /042

65. An open, aboveboard mind makes a dark room bright.

66. 无名无位　无忧无虑 /042

66. Without fame and rank one will be free from worldly cares.

67. 阴恶恶大　显善善小 /043

67. Vice concealed is more harmful than that revealed, but benevolence known by all inferior to that known to none.

68. 居安思危　天亦无用 /043

68. Get prepared for danger in times of peace, and Providence can do nothing against you.

69. 偏激之人　难建功业 /044

69. Those who are liable to go to extremes can hardly make any contributions.

70. 愉快求福　去怨避祸 /045

70. Keep a happy mood so as to seek good fortune and to avoid disasters, discard grudge and hatred.

71. 宁默毋躁　宁拙毋巧 /045

71. Rather keep silence than act on impulse; and rather look dull than clever.

72. 热心之人　其福亦厚 /046

72. Those willing to help others will be requited with boundless fortune.

73. 天理路广　人欲路窄 /047

73. The path for pursuing the Heavenly principles is wide and narrow is that for following human desires.

74. 磨练福久　参勘知真 /047

74. The fortune attained through hardship is everlasting and true, the knowledge acquired after test and verification.

75. 虚心明理　实心却欲 /048

75. Be open-minded so as to attain righteousness and to dispel mundane desires, be solid-hearted.

76. 宽宏大量　胸能容物 /048

76. Tolerance breeds breadth of mind.

77. 多病未羞　无病是忧 /049

77. It is not a shame to have made many mistakes, but a worry to deny the mistakes ever made.

78. 一念贪私　坏了一生 /050

78. A selfish desire will spoil the virtue one has accumulated over lifetime.

79. 心不所动　焉受诱惑 /050

79. An unswerving heart helps to guard against exterior temptations.

80. 保已成业　防将来非 /051

80. Better keep the exploits already gained and prevent mistakes in the future.

81. 气象高旷　心思缜密 /052

81. As a man's makings must be dignified, so must his thoughts be deliberate.

82. 风不留声　雁不留影 /052

82. No sound will be heard when the wind is gone; no shadow will remain when a wild goose has passed.

83. 君子懿德　中庸之道 /053

83. It is an admirable virtue for an accomplished man to adopt the doctrine of the mean.

84. 穷当益工　不失风雅 /053

84. It is a grace not to give up but to try harder in face of destitution.

85. 未雨绸缪　有备无患 /054

85. Repair the house before it rains and get prepared against want.

86. 念头起处　切莫放过 /054

86. Never let off a vicious thought the moment it evolves.

87. 静闲淡泊　观心证道 /055

87. Only by preserving tranquility, leisure and simplicity can one properly examine man's nature and comprehend the Way of the world.

88. 动中真静　苦中真乐 /056

88. That attained amid noise is tranquility indeed and so is delight that gained in adversity.

89. 舍己勿疑　施恩勿报 /056

89. Do not hesitate when you are to sacrifice your own interests and to bestow favors, do not anticipate return.

90. 厚德载福　逸心补劳 /057

90. Great virtue carries fortune with it, while a leisurely mind remedies

weariness in body.

91. 天机最神　智巧何益 /058

91. The magic power of Providence is so supernatural that the resources of human beings can do nothing to it.

92. 人生态度　晚节更重 /058

92. To judge a man's life attitude, it is best to look at his moral integrity in his later years.

93. 种德施惠　无位公相 /059

93. Cultivating morality and bestowing favors make an ordinary person a duke without rank.

94. 积累念难　倾覆思易 /060

94. Keep in mind both the hardships to accumulate wealth and the aptness to ruin it.

95. 君子诈善　无异小人 /060

95. An accomplished man pretending to be virtuous is no more than a villain.

96. 家人有过　春风解冻 /061

96. In dealing with the faults of family members, one should act like the spring breeze thawing the frozen land.

97. 看得圆满　放得宽平 /061

97. Regard the world as perfect, and the world in the heart will be open and fair.

98. 坚守操履　不露锋芒 /062

98. Seek no limelight while persevering in moral cultivation.

99. 逆境砺志　顺境杀人 /063

99. Adverse circumstances whet aspirations, while favorable ones snap willpower.

100. 富贵如火　必将自焚 /063

100. Lust for riches and honor is like raging flames; whoever has it will get burned in the end.

101. 精诚所至　金石为开 /064

101. Complete sincerity of a man can affect metal and stone.

102. 文章恰好　人品本然 /065

102. A piece of writing which attains the right extent is the best, and so is the moral character which reflects a man's inborn nature.

103. 能看得破　才认得真 /065

103. Only by seeing through the world of illusions can one understand the world of realities clearly.

104. 美味快意　享用五分 /066

104. Foods agreeable to the taste and things pleasant to the mind are all desirable if only half assumed.

105. 忠恕待人　养德远害 /067

105. Whoever is faithful and tolerant in getting along with others can refine his morality and keep clear of calamities.

106. 持身勿轻　用心勿重 /067

106. Not be frivolous in personal behaviors nor be too rigid in attaining personal objectives.

107. 人生百年　不可虚度 /068

107. A man's life-span is only a hundred years long, so one should not idle away his time.

108. 德怨两忘　恩仇俱泯 /068

108. Better make others forget both gratitude and resentment and let both bounties and enmities fall into oblivion.

109. 持盈履满　君子兢兢 /069

109. A worthy man should be circumspect in his heyday.

110. 扶公却私　种德修身 /070

110. Be selfless by rendering assistance to the public and cultivate your moral integrity by accumulating benevolence.

111. 公论不犯　权门不沾 /070

111. Never go against a popular verdict nor be associated with those from a circle of bigwigs.

112. 直躬不畏人忌　无恶不惧人毁 /071

112. Fear no jealousy when keeping upright nor slander when having no vicious deeds.

113. 从容处变　剀切规友 /071

113. Be calm and unhurried while facing an unforeseen event and while admonishing a friend, be firm and pertinent.

114. 大处着眼　小处着手 /072

114. Set your mind on the general goal but put your hand to minor details.

115. 爱重为仇　薄极成喜 /073

115. Love taken to its maximum may convert to enmity, while a trivial kindness may result in heart-felt contentment.

116. 藏巧于拙　以屈为伸 /073

116. Hide ingenuity in clumsiness and take recoil as extension.

117. 居安虑患　处变当坚 /074

117. Beware of danger at a time of peace and stick it out in face of disasters.

118. 奇人乏识　独行无恒 /075

118. A man fascinated by novelties lacks profound knowledge and that inclined to isolation has no perseverance.

119. 放下屠刀　立地成佛 /075

119. A butcher becomes a Buddha the moment he drops his cleaver.

120. 毋形人短　毋忌人能 /076

120. Do not counter others' demerits with your own merits, nor make yourself jealous of others' talents for your own incompetence.

121. 己所不欲　勿施于人 /077

121. Do not impose on others what you yourself do not desire.

122. 阴者勿交　傲者勿言 /077

122. Never befriend an insidious fellow nor talk too much to an arrogant guy.

123. 调节情绪　一张一弛 /078

123. A man's mood should be timely adjusted by alternating tension with relaxation.

124. 君子之心　毫无障塞 /079

124. The heart of an accomplished man should go freely without a momentary blockade.

125. 智慧识魔　意志斩妖 /079

125. To discern the inner demons depends on wit and to decapitate them, on willpower.

126. 宽而容人　不动声色 /080

126. Be tolerant towards the folly of others and stay calm and collected when offended.

127. 英雄豪杰　经受锤炼 /080

127. Heroes must be tempered in hardships.

128. 天地父母　万物敦睦 /081

128. Heaven and earth, by acting like father and mother, can harmonize myriad things.

129. 戒疏于虑　警伤于察 /082

129. Advisable are admonition to negligence and counsel to overcaution.

130. 明辨是非　大局为重 /082

130. Distinguish clearly between right and wrong, and take the interests of the whole into account.

131. 亲善杜谗　除恶防祸 /083

131. Prevent slanders when befriending good men and avoid curse when getting rid of vicious men.

132. 培养节操　磨炼本领 /084

132. A man's morality should be cultivated through hardships and his ability fostered in the process of surmounting difficulties.

133. 父慈子孝　伦常天性 /084

133. Fathers' kindness to their sons and sons' filialness to their fathers are one of the natural bonds and ethical relationships between the members of a family.

134. 不夸妍洁　谁能丑污 /085

134. Boast of your beauty and cleanliness not, and nobody can call you ugly or dirty.

135. 富多炎凉　亲多妒忌 /085

135. Fickleness is common among the rich and so is jealousy between kinsfolk.

136. 功过要清　恩仇勿明 /086

136. Merits and demerits should be distinctly demarcated, while bounties and enmities should not.

137. 位盛危至　德高谤兴 /087

137. Rank of nobility too elevated is easy to bring about dangers and so is virtue too outstanding to court slanders.

138. 阴恶祸深　阳善功小 /087

138. Evil deeply hidden produces more harm, while good widely advertised brings less benefit.

139. 以德御才　恃才败德 /088

139. Rule your talent with virtue, knowing that unduly relying on talent spoils your virtue.

140. 穷寇勿追　投鼠忌器 /088

140. Not press the enemy at bay and in order to save the dishes, spare the rat.

141. 有过归己　有功让人 /089

141. One should have the merit to put on himself the blame for faults and give others the credit for accomplishment.

142. 警言救人　功德无量 /090

142. To help others by submitting a sincere advice is also a sort of beneficence beyond measure.

143. 趋炎附热　人之通病 /090

143. To fawn upon the rich and powerful is one of the common failings of human nature.

144. 冷眼观物　轻动刚肠 /091

144. Observe the world with cool detachment and show your uprightness with deliberation.

145. 德量共进　识见更高 /091

145. A man's knowledge increases along with the improving of his virtue and broadening of his mind.

146. 人心惟危　道心惟微 /092

146. Human heart is unfathomable and power of virtue negligible.

147. 反省从善　尤人成恶 /093

147. Self-reflection guides one to good while blame shifted onto others breeds the root of evil.

148. 功名一时　气节万古 /093

148. Honor and rank are only in fashion for a time, but the integrity of aspiration will ever be immortal.

149. 机里藏机　变外生变 /094

149. An unknown skilful contrivance always hides in another and a new event often crops up unexpectedly.

150. 诚恳为人　灵活处世 /095

150. Be sincere in conducting yourself and in dealing with the world, be flexible.

151. 去混心清　去苦乐存 /095

151. There emerges a tranquil mind the moment one discards his distracting thoughts and a joy the moment one is apart from pains.

152. 一言一行　切戒犯忌 /096

152. When you speak or act, do your utmost to avoid violating taboos.

153. 宽之自明　纵之自化 /096

153. As things might be clear of themselves if more time is spared, so people might be moved to action if less binding is laid.

154. 不能养德　终归末技 /097

154. Without moral cultivation man's skill can only be a small trick.

155. 急流勇退　与世无争 /098

155. Retire at the height of your official career and hold yourself aloof from the world.

156. 细处着眼　施不求报 /098

156. Adhere to morality by starting with trivialities and bestow favors without expecting for return.

157. 清心去俗　趣味高雅 /099

157. Clear your heart by banishing vulgarity and hold your interest by acting with elegance.

158. 修身种德　事业之基 /100

158. Virtue is the foundation of a career.

159. 心善子盛　根固叶荣 /100

159. Mercy gives birth to the prosperity of our descendants and sturdy root brings about luxuriant foliage.

160. 勿昧所有　勿夸所得 /101

160. Not belittle what we have possessed nor boast of what we have gained.

161. 真理学问　人皆可求 /101

160. Everyone is entitled to seek truth and engage in learning.

162. 信人己诚　疑人己诈 /102

162. He who has trust in others is sincere and deceitful is he who has a distrust of others.

163. 春风催生　寒风残杀 /103

163. Spring breeze hastens the growth of life, while piercing cold wind brings life to ruin.

164. 善根暗长　恶损潜消 /103

164. The benefit of good deeds grows without being noticed and the harm of evil ones vanishes from sight secretly.

165. 愈隐愈显　愈淡愈浓 /104

165. The more esoteric the thing, the more we should be open-minded; the less associated the one, the more we should be warm-hearted.

166. 君子立德　小人图利 /105

166. Accomplished men pay attention to moral cultivation, while petty ones are only keen on seeking material gains.

167. 意气用事　难有作为 /105

167. Men of easy temperament can scarcely make great achievements.

168. 律己宜严　待人宜宽 /106

168. Better be strict with ourselves and lenient to others.

169. 为奇不异　求清不激 /106

169. To be outstanding is not the result of a queer deed, nor is that of an extreme one to be noble and unsullied.

170. 恩宜后浓　威宜先严 /107

170. Favors should be bestowed from small to great while authority go first with severity and then with tolerance.

171. 心虚性现　意净心清 /108

171. The true nature emerges when internal distracting thoughts are banished; the heart becomes clear when the mind is purified.

172. 我自为我　物自为物 /108

172. I am but my self; all the things I have are only my possessions.

173. 慈悲心肠　繁衍生机 /109

173. Kind-heartedness ensures endless procreation.

174. 心体天体　人心天心 /110

174. Man's heart and the cosmos resemble each other in essence.

175. 无事寂寂　有事惺惺 /111

175. Preserve tranquility while unoccupied and keep a clear head while occupied.

176. 议事任事　明晓利害 /111

176. Before making comments on a matter he has nothing to do with, one should first endeavor to find out all the right and wrong causes in it.

177. 操履严明　但毋偏激 /112

177. In preserving moral principles one should be strict rather than drastic.

178. 浑然和气　居身之珍 /112

178. To preserve an easy-going manner is the golden rule of getting on in the world.

179. 诚心和气　激励陶冶 /113

179. Nobody cannot be roused and molded with sincerity and gentleness.

180. 一念慈祥　寸心洁白 /114

180. A thought of kind-mindedness makes the heart pure and clean.

181. 异行奇能　涉世祸胎 /114

181. Unusual behaviors and queer talents are the sources of disasters in social relations.

182. 忍得耐得　自在之境 /115

182. Endurance is the gateway to the realm of freedom.

183. 心体莹然　本来不失 /116

183. A pure heart enables one to retain his true characters.

184. 一张一弛　事先安排 /116

184. Alteration of work and relaxation should be arranged beforehand.

185. 为民固本　造福子孙 /117

185. Ensure the lifeblood of the people so as to benefit the coming generations.

186. 为官公廉　居家恕俭 /118

186. Be impartial and white-handed when holding office and when managing a household, be lenient and frugal.

187. 富贵知贫　少壮念老 /118

187. Be aware of poverty when rich and wealthy and think of being old when young and strong.

188. 气量宽厚　兼容并包 /119

188. Be large-minded so as to tolerate people of different qualities.

189. 勿仇小人　勿媚君子 /119

189. Never be the enemy of mean fellows nor curry favor with gentlemen.

190. 疾病易医　魔障难除 /120

190. Physical diseases are easy to cure, while mental barriers set up by a demon are hard to remove.

191. 百炼成金　轻发无功 /120

191. Gold can only be made with great effort.

192. 戒小人媚　愿君子责 /121

192. Better be blamed by a worthy man than be flattered by a mean fellow.

193. 好利害浅　好名害深 /121

193. He who is greedy for wealth brings less harm but more does he who is eager for fame.

194. 忘恩报怨　刻薄之极 /122

194. To forget others' kindness and requite it with ingratitude is a thing most contemptible in the world.

195. 不畏谗言　却惧蜜语 /123

195. Fear no slanders, but beware of flattery.

196. 清高褊急　君子重戒 /123

196. An accomplished man should attentively guard against being too stiff and narrow-minded.

197. 虚圆建功　执拗偾事 /124

197. Modesty and flexibility lead to success, while stubbornness avails nothing.

198. 处世之道　不同不异 /125

198. In dealing with the world, do not totally act in accord with the social mores, nor totally go against them.

199. 烈士暮年　壮心不已 /125

199. The heart of a hero in his old age is as stout as ever.

200. 聪明不露　才华不逞 /126

200. A wise man should never show off his intelligence nor parade his talent.

201. 过俭者吝　过谦者卑 /126

201. Undue thrift is regarded as miserliness and over-modesty as lowliness.

202. 喜忧安危　勿介于心 /127

202. Not turn a hair in the face of joy and worry, safety and danger.

203. 声华名利　非君子行 /127

203. An accomplished man should not sink himself in sensual pleasures nor seek fame and wealth.

204. 乐极生悲　苦尽甜来 /128

204. Extreme pleasure ends in sorrow, and after suffering comes happiness.

205. 过满则溢　过刚即折 /129

205. Overfullness begets spillage and overrigidness induces fracture.

206. 冷眼观人　冷心思理 /129

206. Be sober-eyed when observing the people around you and when pondering the reasons in things, be sober-minded.

207. 心宽福厚　量小福薄 /130

207. Open-mindedness brings in profound happiness, while narrow-mindedness only slight one.

208. 闻恶防谗　闻善防奸 /131

208. Guard against the slanderous when hearing someone has done evil and when hearing someone has done good, watch out for the treacherous.

209. 躁急无成　平和得福 /131

209. Rash-temperedness ends in failure, while calm-heartedness brings about good fortune.

210. 用人不刻　交友不滥 /132

210. Not be too fastidious in choosing a person for a job and in making friends, not be too indiscriminate.

211. 立得脚定　著得眼高 /132

211. Get your foothold firm and let your gaze roam afar.

212. 和衷少争　谦德少妒 /132

212. Amiability evokes no dispute and modesty arouses no jealousy.

213. 居官有节　居乡有情 /133

213. Be moderate when on an official position and when in retirement, be amiable and easy of approach.

214. 事上警谨　待下宽仁 /134

214. Be careful when attending upon your superiors and in dealings with your inferiors, be generous.

215. 逆境消怨　怠荒思奋 /134

215. When in adversity, try to dispel the grievances from your heart; and when becoming indolent, think about how to rouse yourself.

216. 轻诺惹祸　倦怠无成 /135

216. Promise lightly made courts disasters and indolence makes previous work undone.

217. 读书得其要领　观物达其实质 /136

217. When reading a book, try to understand its essence; when observing an object, try to reach its substance.

218. 勿以长欺短　勿以富凌贫 /136

218. Do not humiliate others with your strong points, nor bully the poor with your wealth.

219. 中才之人　高低难成 /137

219. A medium-gifted man is fit for neither a higher post nor a lower one.

220. 守口应密　防意应严 /138

220. The mouth should be closely guarded and the minds well controlled.

221. 责人宜宽　责己宜严 /138

221. Better be lenient when censuring another for a fault but strict when

making self-reproaches.

222. 幼时定基　少时勤学 /139

222. Characters should be tempered from childhood and diligent study begins in youth.

223. 君子忧乐　亦怜茕独 /140

223. A man of virtue will be consumed with circumspection in a time of joy and with pity when together with the abandoned and helpless.

224. 浓夭淡久　大器晚成 /140

224. Gaudy colors and rich flavors are inferior to light but constant ones and early flourish is not as good as late maturity.

225. 静中真境　淡现本然 /141

225. The true realm of a man's life exists amid tranquility and his natural characters emerge from simplicity.

226. 乐者不言　言者不乐 /141

226. Those who understand happiness may not talk about it; those who talk about happiness may not understand it.

227. 省事为适　无能全真 /142

227. Less engagement leads to leisureliness; incompetence keeps man's nature intact.

228. 艳为虚幻　枯为胜境 /143

228. The reality of Nature is revealed by decay instead of brilliance which is nothing but an illusion.

229. 天地之闲　因人而异 /143

229. The realization of whether the world is of leisure or not varies from man to man.

230. 盆池竹屋　意境高远 /144

230. Even a basin-sized pool or a bamboo house can bring in profound subtleties.

231. 静夜梦醒　月现本性 /145

231. The sound of a temple bell on a still night wakens the dream of life; the moon reflection in the pool reveals the origin of man's nature.

232. 天地万物　皆是实相 /145

232. Everything in the world has its own way to express itself.

233. 知无形物　悟无尽趣 /146

233. To apprehend a thing by its essence instead of its form leads to boundless subtlety.

234. 淡欲有书　神仙之境 /146

234. Books help to weaken men's material desires and guide them into the fairyland.

235. 盛宴散后　兴味索然 /147

235. When a grand feast comes to an end, flatness appears.

236. 得个中趣　破眼前机 /148

236. Ascertain the subtlety of Nature and perceive the deceptions and trickeries before your eyes.

237. 非上上智　无了了心 /148

237. Only with supreme wisdom can one make a thorough comprehension of Nature and human life.

238. 人生苦短　宇宙无限 /149

238. Man's life is transient while the cosmos is boundless.

239. 极端空寂　断不可取 /150

239. Extreme void is absolutely undesirable.

240. 休无休时　了无了时 /150

240. Take a rest when time allows; if you wish to do so till all the works in hand are completed, then you will never meet your wishes.

241. 从冷视热　从冗入闲 /151

241. In times of calm, reflect on the boisterousness; while being busy, try to take a moment's respite.

242. 轻视富贵　不溺酒中 /151

242. Wealth and rank are what men should despise and wine is what they should not wallow in.

243. 不嫌人醉　不夸己醒 /152

243. Not cold-shoulder others if they are infatuated with fame and wealth, nor brag that you are the only one who is above the worldly considerations.

244. 心闲日长　意广天宽 /153

244. To a leisurely-minded person, a single day is longer than enough; to a broad-minded person, a tiny hovel seems as a large space.

245. 栽花种竹　去欲忘忧 /154

245. Raising flowers and planting bamboos are conducive to removal of material desires and mundane worries.

246. 知足则仙　善用则生 /154

246. Those content with their lot are happy; those good at making use of opportunities are prosperous.

247. 附势遭祸　守逸味长 /155

247. Fawning upon the influential and powerful brings disaster, while preserving ease of mind produces durable taste.

248. 松涧望闲云　竹夜见风月 /156

248. At day, watch the floating clouds along the side of a pine-covered rivulet and at night, view the scene of the wind and moon in a bamboo shed.

249. 欲时思病　利来思死 /156

249. When lust rages in your mind, think of the trouble; and when benefit comes to you, think of the calamity.

250. 退后一步　清淡一分 /157

250. A pace back makes a road more spacious，lightly seasoned food gives more taste.

251. 忙不乱性　死不动心 /158

251. Be steadfast and composed when occupied and fearless when facing death.

252. 隐无荣辱　道无炎凉 /158

252. To live as a hermit, give no thought to personal honor and disgrace; to seek morality, pay no heed to the fickleness of human nature.

253. 心静自然凉　乐观无穷愁 /159

253. Free from vexation, and one will feel cool of oneself; be optimistic, and one will have no distress about poverty.

254. 进时思退　得手思放 /159

254. Think out a way to retreat when progress has been made, and consider how to let go when you set about a task.

255. 贪者常贫　知足常富 /160

255. Avarice of wealth begets poverty in morality; contentment leads to spiritual enrichment.

256. 隐者多趣　省事心闲 /161

256. To be obscure is to invite more pleasures, and to save trouble is to breed leisure in mind.

257. 自得之士　逍遥自适 /161

257. Self-composed persons are always leisurely and carefree.

258. 孤云出岫　朗镜悬空 /162

258. Be as free as the solitary cloud floating from the valley and as elegant as the bright moon hanging in the night sky.

259. 浓处味短　淡中趣真 /162

259. Rich and pungent dishes only create a transient taste, while simplicity and plainness make a true delight.

260. 高寓于平　难出于易 /163

260. Just as the loftiest and most profound truth dwells in the most inconspicuous place, so the most difficult things originate from the easiest.

261. 处喧见寂　出有入无 /164

261. Tranquility is attainable in a noisy environment and from Existence there emerges Nothingness.

262. 心无系恋　乐境仙都 /164

262. Not set your mind on the worldly gains, and so the place you live in will then become a land of immortals.

263. 静躁稍分　昏明顿异 /165

263. A slight distinction made between clamor and tranquility brings different consequence of either muddle-headedness or clear-headedness.

264. 卧雪眠云　绝俗超凡 /166

264. Keep away from the vanity of the world by preserving a cool and quiet mind.

265. 浓不胜淡　俗不如雅 /167

265. Richness and gaudiness are not as good as plainness and lightness, nor is vulgarity a match for refinement.

266. 出世涉世　了心尽心 /167

266. To transcend the mean world, go through it first; to comprehend the essence of man's inherent quality, put your whole brains onto it.

267. 身放闲处　心安静中 /168

267. Stand aloof from the place of conflict and preserve your mind in a state of stillness.

268. 云中世界　静里乾坤 /169

268. From clouds there emerges the wonderland of leisure; in silence there is a different world.

269. 不忧利禄　不畏仕祸 /169

269. Disregard wealth and rank, and you will be free from the fear for the vicissitudes in officialdom.

270. 山泉去凡心　书画消俗气 /170

270. Cast aside mundane thoughts by roaming among mountains and springs; dispel vulgar interest by reposing feelings in calligraphy and painting.

271. 秋日清爽　神骨俱清 /171

271. The clarity and brightness of autumn brings freshness to man's body and spirit.

272. 得诗真趣　悟禅玄机 /171

272. To write a poem, it is best to seek the subtlety to do so; to meditate on Zen Buddhism, it is best to perceive the mystery of it.

273. 好用心机　杯弓蛇影 /172

273. A person of sensitive imagination mistakes the shadow of a bow in his wine cup as a snake.

274. 身心自如　融通自在 /173

274. Let the body and heart be as free and unrestrained as the air.

275. 皆鸣天机　皆畅生意 /173

275. The crying of animals and the vitality of vegetation are all the expressions of natural instincts.

276. 盛衰始终　自然之理 /174

276. The vicissitudes of life are the course destined by Nature.

277. 无欲则寂　虚心则凉 /174

277. One can find both tranquility and cool when he is free from worldly desires.

278. 贫则无虑　贱则常安 /175

278. Poverty gives no rise to fear, while humbleness brings more safety.

279. 晓窗读易　午案谈经 /175

279. Read *The Book of Changes* against the window at dawn and at noon, expound Buddhist Scripture by the desk.

280. 花失生机　鸟减天趣 /176

280. A pot-planted flower is bereft of vitality and a caged bird lacks natural amusement.

281. 诸多烦恼　因我而起 /177

281. Many of the vexations are incurred by the sense of self-centeredness.

282. 少时思老　荣时思枯 /177

282. When you are young, think about the time of old age; when you go prosperous, ponder on the declining days.

283. 人情世态　倏忽万端 /178

283. The ways of the world are changing all the time.

284. 热中取静　冷处热心 /179

284. Be sober-minded on the occasions of bustle and excitement, and preserve a positive attitude in times of dejection and desolation.

285. 寻常人家　最为安乐 /179

285. The most carefree life can only be found in an ordinary family.

286. 乾坤自在　物我两忘 /180

286. Untrammeled Nature makes man ignorant of the existence of the world and the self.

287. 生死成败　任其自然 /181

287. Let life and death, success and failure take their own course.

288. 水流境静　花落意闲 /181

288. However swift the water flows, its surroundings are quiet; however frequently the flowers bloom and fade, the scene remains leisurely and carefree.

289. 自然乐曲　乾坤文章 /182

289. Most wonderful are the melody and spectacle created by Nature.

290. 豁壑易填　人心难满 /183

290. Gullies are easy to fill up, but men's desires are hard to fulfill.

291. 心无风涛　性有化育 /184

291. Get rid of the distracting thoughts from your mind and nurse the charity in the depth of your heart.

292. 贵贱高低　自适其性 /184

292. Everyone should conform himself to his own nature, whatever his social status.

293. 处世忘世　超物乐天 /185

293. Rise above the world though you live in it, and you will enjoy the natural amusement.

294. 盛衰无常　强弱安在 /186

294. Prosperity and decline are not constant, nor everlasting are the strong and weak.

295. 宠辱不惊　去留无意 /187

295. Remain indifferent whether granted favors or subjected to humiliation and give no heed to whether demoted or promoted from the present post.

296. 高天可翔　万物可饮 /187

296. The vast sky allows a soaring flight, and produces of Nature are open to all living beings.

297. 求心内佛　却心外法 /188

297. Plead with yourself for enlightenment by shaking off the bonds of external things.

298. 冷情当事　如汤消雪 /188

298. Handling affairs with a cool mind is like thawing the snow by pouring hot water on it.

299. 物欲可哀　性真可乐 /189

299. It is lamentable to be trammeled by material desires but joyful to preserve the genuine character.

300. 胸无物欲　眼自空明 /190

300. As soon as you cast aside the material desires, your eyes will be brightened up.

301. 林岫江畔　诗兴自涌 /190

301. Amidst the forests and hills or beside the rivers and lakes, the exalted, poetic mood will spring up of itself.

302. 伏久飞高　开先谢早 /192

302. The longer the bird rests in concealment, the higher it flies; the earlier the flower blooms, the sooner it fades.

303. 花叶徒荣　玉帛成空 /192

303. The flourishing flowers and leaves are nothing but brilliance in vain; the multitude of wealth is only a brief dream of grandeur.

304. 真空不空　在世出世 /193

304. To preserve internal emptiness does not mean to expel all the sensations; only by living in the mundane world can one transcend it.

305. 欲有尊卑　贪无二致 /194

305. The respected and the humble are different in desires, but are much the same in cravings.

306. 覆雨翻云　不介于怀 /195

306. Take no heed to the changes of the world, however frequent.

307. 前念后念　随缘打发 /196

307. The distracting thoughts, previous or present, are better to be dismissed as circumstances would allow.

308. 偶会佳境　自然真机 /196

308. A casually grasped apprehension leads to the realm enjoyable, and a thing arising in accord with Nature bares its mystery.

309. 性天澄澈　何必谈禅 /197

309. A pure-natured person needn't explicate the Buddhist tenets.

310. 人有真境　即可自愉 /197

310. In everyone's heart there is a wonderland, leisurely and comfortable.

311. 幻以求真　雅不离俗 /198

311. Truth cannot but be obtained through illusions, nor can but nobility be derived from vulgarity.

312. 俗眼观异　道眼观常 /199

312. View with a mundane eye, things are different one another; but with a super-mundane eye, all the same.

313. 布被神酣　藜羹味足 /199

313. Even a quilt of coarse cloth can bring a sound sleep and a scanty meal produce sufficient flavor.

314. 了心悟性　俗即是僧 /200

314. A layman is called a monk if he can discard the worldly desires and realize the essence of the Way.

315. 万虑都捐　一真自得 /201

315. Clear off all the worldly vexations, and one will feel quite oneself.

316. 性天未枯　机神触发 /201

316. The instincts of all nature never wither and the tendency of life stops at nothing.

317. 把柄在手　收放自如 /202

317. Obtain a firm hold so as to feel free whether to be restrained or unrestrained accordingly.

318. 造化人心　混合无间 /203

318. Nature's creation and human feelings often blend as one.

319. 文以拙进　道以拙成 /204

319. It is only on the basis of plainness that progress can be made in writings and accomplishment be effected in moral cultivation.

320. 以我转物　大地逍遥 /204

320. A good control over exterior things breeds boundless freedom and unrestrainedness.

321. 形去影去　心空境空 /205

321. When the shape is removed, its shadow disappears; when the heart is made void, its surroundings become void, too.

322. 处世任事　总在自适 /206

322. In dealing with the world or doing something, one should always suit them to oneself.

323. 思及生死　万念灰冷 /207

323. Think about life and death, and all the thoughts and ambitions will be blasted.

324. 福祸生死　须有卓见 /207

324. There needs supreme wisdom to understand happiness and calamity, life and death.

325. 妍丑胜负　今又安在 /208

325. Where now are the beautiful and ugly on the stage or the victory and defeat on the checkerboard?

326. 风花竹石　静闲得之 /209

326. The wind, the flowers, the bamboos and the rocks are only enjoyable at tranquility and leisure.

327. 天全欲淡　人生至境 /209

327. It is the acme of human life to keep the nature intact and get along with few desires.

328. 观心增障　齐物剖同 /210

328. To undertake self-examination is to add more barriers to self-cultivation; to integrate the myriad things is to disintegrate the organic whole.

329. 悬崖撒手　苦海离身 /211

329. Rein in at the brink of the precipice so as to avoid falling into the sea of bitterness.

330. 修行绝尘　悟道涉俗 /212

330. To conduct self-cultivation, it is best to cut loose from the worldly affects; to perceive the way of the world, it is best to merge into the world of mortals.

331. 人我一视　动静两忘 /213

331. Regard the multitude and yourself as one and let both quietude and clamor fade into oblivion.

332. 山居清洒　入尘即俗 /214

332. When dwelling in mountains one feels fresh and relaxed but becomes vulgar when returning to worldly society.

333. 野鸟作伴　白云相留 /215

333. So long as your mind is set at leisure, even the wild birds and white clouds will come to accompany you.

334. 念头稍异　境界顿殊 /216

334. A minor shift of mind can immediately bring about a quite different world in front of our eyes.

335. 水滴石穿　瓜熟蒂落 /216

335. A stone can be worn away by drops of water; when a melon is ripe, it falls off its stem.

336. 机息有风月　心远无喧嚣 /217

336. The mind free of intrigues and maneuvers brings natural subtlety; the heart far apart from the mundane world has no room for distractions and confusions.

337. 生生之意　天地之心 /218

337. Boundless vitality of myriad things is the fruit of the charity of Nature.

338. 雨后山清　静中钟扬 /219

338. After a shower of rain the hills look so fresh and so melodious sounds the bell tone in stillness.

339. 雪夜读书　神清气爽 /219

339. Reading a book on a snowy night helps to refresh the spirit and comfort the heart.

340. 万钟一发　存乎一心 /220

340. The value of a thing, big or small, is decided by the conception of value.

341. 以我转物　驾驭欲念 /220

341. Control the external things and be master of your internal desires.

342. 就身了身　以物付物 /221

342. Understand your true self through meditation, and let things go in accord with their natural bent.

343. 抱身心忧　耽风月趣 /222

343. Just as beware of untoward happenings to the body and heart, so try to understand how to take the pleasure to enjoy the mysteries of Nature.

344. 一念不生　处处真境 /222

344. Banish the distracting thoughts from your mind, and you will find paradise everywhere.

345. 顺逆一视　欣戚两忘 /223

345. Extend equal treatment to both fortune and adversity, and remain unswayed by either joys or worries.

346. 空谷巨响　过而不留 /224

346. The whistling wind blowing through an open valley leaves no sound behind when it passes.

347. 世亦不尘　海亦不苦 /225

347. The world is not a land of pomp and vanity, nor is the human life a sea of bitterness.

348. 花看半开　酒饮微醉 /226

348. To enjoy flowers, it is best to enjoy them when they are in half bloom; when drinking wine, drink only until you are tipsy.

349. 坚守故我　不受点染 /226

349. Keep your nature intact by remaining unspotted by the mundane affairs.

350. 玩物自得　不在物华 /227

350. To ride a hobby is not to enjoy the superficial brilliance, but to attain enlightenment from it.

351. 清名沦丧　生不如死 /228

351. A depraved person would be better off to die than to live.

352. 着眼要高　不落圈套 /228

352. Be far-sighted and high-minded so as to avoid falling into a snare.

353. 根蒂在手　不受提掇 /229

353. Stick to the crucial points by not being manipulated by the outside force.

354. 无事为福　雄心冰融 /230

354. To be involved in nothing is happiness in which ambitions vanish like the melted ice.

355. 茫茫世间　矛盾之窟 /231

355. The vast world is like a den of motley crowd.

356. 身在事中　心超事外 /231

356. When engaged in something one should let his heart stay aloof from it.

357. 不减求增　桎梏此生 /232

357. Those who do not seek to save the troubles but strive to increase them instead are simply fettering themselves.

358. 满腔和气　随地春风 /233

358. Fill the heart with auspiciousness, and wherever you go you will have the spring breeze for company.

359. 嗜欲无碍　纯朴就好 /234

359.Personal addictions and desires bring no harm so long as they are kept in a simple and honest way.

360. 万事随缘　随遇而安 /235

360.Comply with fate and Nature in doing everything and accommodate yourself to circumstances.

1. 栖守道德　毋阿权贵

1. Rather stick to moral integrity than be attached to the powerful and influential.

栖守道德者，寂寞一时；依阿[①]权势者，凄凉万古。达人观物外之物[②]，思身后之身[③]；宁受一时之寂寞，毋取万古之凄凉。

【中文注释】 ① 依阿：依附讨好。
② 物外之物：物质之外的东西。此处指精神财富或精神价值。
③ 身后之身：人死后留在世上的名声。

【今文解译】 谨守道德的人，也许会寂寞一时；而依附权贵的人，则必然会凄凉一辈子。豁达的人看重的是精神层面的东西以及自己身后的名声。所以，他们宁肯忍受寂寞于一时，也不愿意凄凉孤寂一辈子。

【English Translation】
Those who stick to their moral integrity might be lonesome for a time. Whereas, those who cling to the powerful and influential will surely become desolate for good and all. To a well-cultivated person, the worthiest are the gains beyond material and the name after him. It is because of this that he had rather endure momentary loneliness than receive endless desolation.

2. 与其练达　不若朴鲁

2. Better be honest and straightforward than scheming and calculating.

涉世浅，点染[①]亦浅；历事深，机械[②]亦深。故君子与其练达[③]，不若朴鲁[④]；与其曲谨[⑤]，不若疏狂。

【中文注释】 ① 点染：熏染。此处指受社会不良风气的影响。
② 机械：巧诈，机巧。
③ 练达：阅历丰富而通晓人情世故。
④ 朴鲁：朴实鲁钝。此处指不谙人情世故。

⑤ 曲谨：指过于谨小慎微。

【今文解译】 涉世尚浅的人，受不良风气的影响也少；而阅历丰富的人，心里的算计也多。所以：君子与其精明老到，不如纯朴愚鲁；与其谨小慎微，不如狂放不羁。

【English Translation】

A man who is less experienced in the world will equally be less stained with its undesirable trends. A man who has seen more of the world will equally be more trickery and crafty. It is therefore worthwhile for the man of moral integrity to remain honest and straightforward rather than become scheming and calculating, and remain large-minded and unrestrained rather than become overcautious and fainthearted.

3. 心地光明　才华韫藏

3. The mind of a man should be made open and broad, but his talents carefully concealed.

君子之心事，天青日白，不可使人不知；君子之才华，玉韫珠藏，不可使人易知。

【今文解译】 君子的心事，要像青天白日那样光明磊落，不可对人有所隐瞒。
君子的才华，要像珠宝玉器那样深藏不露，不可让人轻易得见。

【English Translation】

The heart of a worthy man should be as clear as the blue sky and the bright sunshine, so that everybody can lightly feel it. But on the contrary, his talents should be carefully concealed like jade and pearls, so that nobody can easily find them out.

4. 近纷华而不染　知机巧而不用

4. Not be sullied by extravagance even if close to it nor resort to intrigues even if acquainted with them.

势利纷华①，不近者为洁，近之而不染者为尤洁；智械机巧，不知者为高，知之而不用者为尤高。

【中文注释】 ① 势利纷华：势利，权力和财势；纷华，繁华富丽。二者泛指一切具有诱惑力的物质。

【今文解译】 权势和奢华，不去接近的是人品高洁，接近了但不受其影响的，则人品尤为高洁。
计谋和巧诈，不知道的堪称人品高贵，知道了但从不使用的，人品堪称尤为高贵。

【English Translation】

It is decent for one not to be close to power, influence and extravagance, the more so for him not to be sullied even if being close to them.
It is noble for one not to be acquainted with intrigues and plots, the more so for him not to resort to them even if having such acquaintances.

5. 闻逆耳言　怀拂心事

5. It is helpful to hear words unpleasant to the ear and meditate on things unpleasant to the mind.

耳中常闻逆耳之言，心中常有拂心之事①，才是进德修行的砥石②。若言言悦耳，事事快心，便把此生埋在鸩毒③中矣。

【中文注释】 ① 拂心之事：不顺心或不如意的事情。
② 砥石：磨刀石。此处指磨炼品德的逆耳之言和拂心之事。
③ 鸩毒：鸩，传说中的一种毒鸟。用鸩的羽毛制成的酒叫鸩毒，即饮即亡。

【今文解译】 耳朵常常听些不中听的话，心里常常有些不顺心的事，这样才有利于我们德行的磨砺和提高。如果听到的每句话都悦耳，遇到的每件事都顺心，这无异于将自己的一生都浸泡在毒酒中了。

【English Translation】

Constantly hearing words unpleasant to the ear and constantly meditating on things unpleasant to the mind are worth a whetstone, upon which we cultivate our moral characters and refine our temperaments. If we contemplate every word we hear being pleasant to the ear and everything we come into contact with pleasant to the mind, it would be no more than soaking ourselves in poisoned wine.

6. 和气喜神　天人一理

6. Harmony and happiness are agreeable to both Nature and human beings.

疾风怒雨，禽鸟戚戚[①]；霁日光风[②]，草木欣欣。可见天地不可一日无和气，人心不可一日无喜神[③]。

【中文注释】 ① 戚戚：忧愁悲哀之状。
② 霁日光风：雨过天晴的明朗景象。
③ 喜神：喜悦的神态，欢快的心情。

【今文解译】 狂风暴雨中，鸟兽都凄惨无比；天气晴朗时，草木都生机勃勃。由此可见，天地间没有一天是可以不安宁的，人的心情没有一天是可以不愉悦的。

【English Translation】

When the wind rages and the rain pours down, even the birds and animals are caught in tragedy. But when the sun comes out shining and the wind turns mild, the very grasses and trees are all immersed in delightfulness. Thus it can be seen that in Nature — not a single day could pass peacefully if celestial and terrestrial forces fail to go in harmony; and in the world of men — not a single day could be spent well if people are deprived of happy mood.

7. 真味是淡　至人如常

7. Genuine flavor only lies in light and mild food; and a man of perfect morality is no different from ordinary people.

醲肥辛甘[①]非真味，真味只是淡；神奇卓异[②]非至人[③]，至人只是常。

【中文注释】 ① 醲肥辛甘：泛指丰盛的酒菜。
② 神奇卓异：标新立异，与众不同。
③ 至人：修为和学识达到最高境界的人。俗称高人。

【今文解译】 美酒佳肴并不是真正的美味，真正的美味是清淡甘平。标新立异并不是高人的作为，高人的作为与常人无异。

【English Translation】
Genuine flavor is derived not from good wine and delicious food, but from that which tastes light and mild.
The man of perfect morality is not such a one who is peculiar in action, but the one who is similar to ordinary people.

8. 闲时吃紧　忙时悠闲

8. Keep the sense of imminence while at leisure and while busy, be at ease.

天地寂然不动，而气机[①]无息稍停；日月昼夜奔驰，而贞明[②]万古不易。故君子闲时要有吃紧的心思[③]，忙处要有悠闲的趣味。

【中文注释】 ① 气机：指天地有规律的内部运动。
② 贞明：谓日月能固守其运行规律而常明。
③ 心思：此处指精神或意识。

【今文解译】 天地表面上看似平静，但其内部有规律的运动却一刻不曾停歇；日月不分白昼黑夜地运转着，然而它们的光芒却万古未变。同理，君子闲暇时精神上不能放松自己，忙碌时则要有一点闲情逸致。

【English Translation】

The heaven and earth seem to be motionless, but their vital energy within never stops breathing and moving. The sun and moon run in cycles day and night, emitting eternal, immutable beams. Similarly, the accomplished man should keep the sense of imminence while at leisure and maintain a leisurely mood when occupied.

9. 静坐观心　真妄毕现

9. Sit quietly in meditation, and you will perceive both the true character and the distracting thoughts.

夜深人静独坐观心①，始觉妄穷②而真③独露，每于此中得大机趣④；既觉真现而妄难逃，又于此中得大惭忸。

【中文注释】 ① 观心：观察自己的心性，即反省自悟。佛教主张的修为之法。

② 妄穷：妄，非分或越轨的念头；穷，穷尽，消失。

③ 真：本性中真实自然的东西。亦作本真。

④ 大机趣：自然的乐趣。

【今文解译】 夜深人静，独坐观心，一开始总会感觉到心里的非分之想都消失了，而本性中真实自然的东西流露出来了。每当于此，心中就深受鼓舞，仿佛悟得了人生的真谛。可是，继而发现自己并未因为本真的流露而摒弃那些非分之想时，心中又不免十分惭愧。

【English Translation】

When you sit alone introspecting in the quiet of late night, you will first, from the bottom of your heart, perceive the disappearance of the distracting thoughts and then the appearance of the true character. Every time at this moment you will be rejoiced to find that you have comprehended the real meaning of life. But when you are aware that the true character can not take the place of the distracting thoughts, you will feel quite ashamed of yourself.

10. 得意早回头　拂心莫停手

10. Stop seeking more in times of contentment but keep going on even if suffering setbacks.

恩里由来生害，故快意时，须早回首；败后或反成功，故拂心处，切莫放手。

【今文解译】 接受别人的恩惠往往会招来祸害，所以得意时须懂得早早回头。
遭受挫败反而有助于获得成功，所以做事不顺时切莫轻言放弃。

【English Translation】

Given favors are often followed by calamities. Therefore, one should deliberate how to stop when one's desires are fulfilled.
Failure sometimes indicates success to come. Therefore, one should keep going on even if suffering setbacks.

11. 志从澹泊来　节在肥甘丧

11. Aspiration is attained in natural simplicity while moral integrity spoiled in extravagance.

藜口苋肠①者，多冰清玉洁；衮衣玉食②者，甘婢膝奴颜。盖志以澹泊③明，而节从肥甘④丧也。

【中文注释】 ① 藜口苋肠："藜"和"苋"均为一年生草本植物，其茎叶可食。此处喻粗茶淡饭或简朴的生活。
② 衮衣玉食：衮衣，古代天子及上公穿的绘有卷龙图案的礼服；玉食，泛指山珍海味。此处喻吃穿讲究或生活奢华。
③ 澹泊：不追逐名利、清心寡欲之意。
④ 肥甘：美味。此处指奢华淫逸。

【今文解译】 甘于粗茶淡饭的，大多具有冰清玉洁的品格；耽于锦衣玉食的，一般都唯唯诺诺，低头哈腰。由此可见，人的志节可以在淡泊中得以彰显，也可以在奢华淫逸中丧失殆尽。

【English Translation】

Those willing to take plain tea and simple fare are mostly provided with pure and noble sentiment. Those craving for beautiful dresses and nice food mostly tend to resign themselves to humiliation led by subservience. It can be therefore recognized that high aspirations can only be seen in plainness and simplicity while moral fortitude is often spoiled in extravagance and luxury.

12. 田地放宽　恩泽流长

12. In dealing with people, better be large-minded and tolerant; and in bestowing favors, better let them spread far and wide.

面前的田地①要放得宽，使人无不平之叹；身后的惠泽②要流得久，使人有不匮③之思。

【中文注释】 ① 田地：处所，境地。此处喻为人处世。
② 惠泽：恩泽，德泽。
③ 匮：空乏，穷尽。

【今文解译】 为人处世要得体大方，不要让人因你而哀叹世道不公。身后的德泽要流传得越久越好，要让人永远感念不尽。

【English Translation】

In dealing with people, better be as large-minded and tolerant as you can, thus you will not make them sigh with complaint.

In bestowing bounties, better let them spread as far and wide as they may, so that the bestowed will owe an endless debt of gratitude even after your death.

13. 路留一步　味减三分

13. Step aside one pace for others when the path is narrow and when you are fine fed, share three-tenths of your food with others.

径路窄处，留一步与人行；滋味浓的，减三分让人尝。此是涉世一极安乐法。

【今文解译】 道路狭窄的地方，要想着让一步给人行走；遇有好吃的东西，要想着匀三分与人共享。这些都是立身处世最安全、最令人愉快的方法。

【English Translation】

Step aside one pace for others when you are on a narrow path. Share three-tenths of your food with others when you are fine fed. This is the best way for you to ensure safety and attain happiness in social intercourse.

14. 脱俗成名 减欲入圣

14. Get rid of vulgarity, and you will become a man of celebrity; decrease the desires for fame and wealth, and you will enter sainthood.

作人无甚高远事业，摆脱得俗情便入名流；为学无甚增益功夫，灭除得物累①便入圣境②。

【中文注释】 ① 物累：心为外物所累。
② 圣境：至高无上、超凡脱俗的境界。

【今文解译】 做人并不需要建立什么了不起的功业，只需摆脱庸俗之气，人便可以跻身名流。做学问没什么奥秘和诀窍，只要不为功名利禄所累，人便可以进入圣贤的境界。

【English Translation】

A good personhood does not count on how terrific one's exploits are; so long as doing away with vulgarity, one will surely become a man of great celebrity. The pursuit of knowledge needs no help of magic means; so long as shaking off the yoke of fame and wealth, one will certainly enter sainthood.

15. 侠气交友 素心做人

15. Be chivalrous in getting along with friends and unadorned in conducting yourself.

交友须带三分侠气，做人要存一点素心。

【今文解译】 交朋友要有些豪爽仗义的气概，做人要有点不张扬的平常心态。

【English Translation】

Be somewhat chivalrous when you get along with friends.

Be a bit unadorned when you conduct yourself in society.

16. 利毋居前　德毋落后

16. Never anticipate others in seeking wealth nor lag behind in dispensing charities.

宠利[①]毋居人前，德业[②]毋落人后，受享[③]毋逾分外[④]，修为毋减分中[⑤]。

【中文注释】 ① 宠利：恩宠和利禄。此处可理解为利益或名利。

② 德业：乐善好施的行为。

③ 受享：得到并享用。

④ 分外：超出自己该得的范围，喻不该得的东西。

⑤ 修为毋减分中：修炼德行要有始有终，决不半途而废。

【今文解译】 有利可图时，不要抢在别人前面；行善立德时，不要落在别人后面；获享成果时，不要超过自己应得的那一份；修身养性时，不要分心也不要半途而废。

【English Translation】

Never anticipate others in the face of fame and wealth. Never fall behind in doing good turns and dispensing charities. When reaping benefit, never intend to receive what you do not deserve to. In cultivating your moral character, never slack off before accomplishment.

17. 忍让为高　利人利己

17. Forbearance means superiority and is beneficial to both others and yourself.

处世让一步为高，退步即进步的张本[①]；待人宽一分是福，利人实利己的根基。

【中文注释】　① 张本：为事态发展预先所做的安排。

【今文解译】　处世忍让是品德高尚的表现，后退一步是为了更进一步。待人宽厚一些会给自己带来福祉，利人也即利己的根本。

【English Translation】

To make a concession to others in social intercourse is a sign of wit where lies a flight of anticipatory stairs, from which more progress can be made in the future.

To be tolerant towards others is a sort of felicity where lies the foundation of social courtesy, on which things can be done to benefit both others and yourself.

18. 矜则无功　悔可减过

18. Arrogance spoils contributions and repentance counteracts faults.

盖世功劳，当不得一个"矜[①]"字；弥天罪过，当不得一个"悔"字。

【中文注释】　① 矜：傲慢自大，骄横。

【今文解译】　即使立下了不世之功，如果居功自傲，功劳也会付之东流。

即使犯下了弥天大罪，只要能悔过自新，最终将得到救赎。

【English Translation】

Contributions, however unparalleled, will be eventually spoiled by arrogance.

Crimes, however monstrous, will be finally counteracted by repentance.

19. 美名不独享　责任不推脱

19. When winning a good name, do not reap it all alone and when at fault, do not shift responsibility onto others.

完名美节，不宜独任，分些与人，可以远害[1]全身；辱行污名，不宜全推，引些归己，可以韬光[2]养德。

【中文注释】 ① 远害：远离祸害。
② 韬光：敛藏光彩。此处可理解为自我收敛或自我约束。

【今文解译】 完美的名声和高尚的节操，不可自己一人独占，分些给别人，可以远离祸害，自保无虞。
遇到令人不齿的事情，名声遭人诟病，不可将责任全推给别人，主动承担点，有助于自律和提高自己的修为。

【English Translation】
When a person has won a good name for his moral integrity, it is better for him not to reap it all alone, but to mete out some of it to others, so as to keep possible harm at a distance.
When a person falls accidentally into a thing shameful in deed or fame, it is better for him not to shirk all duty onto others, but to undertake some of it, so as to discipline himself and nourish his own virtue.

20. 功名不求盈满　做人恰到好处

20. Seek no perfection in personal achievement and do just to the point in human relationships.

事事留个有余不尽的意思，便造物不能忌我，鬼神不能损我。若业必求满、功必求盈者，不生内变，必召外忧。

【今文解译】 凡事都留个余地，造物主便无法忌恨我，鬼神便无法伤害我。如果事事都要求十全十美，功德圆满，即使身边的人不说什么，外界也一定会有人议论纷纷。

【English Translation】

If we can leave adequate leeway in doing things, the Creator will not frown on us, nor will the ghosts and spirits be able to hurt us. If we insist on seeking perfection in handling affairs and completion in personal achievement, we will surely become an object of external wild comments even if there is no internal complaint.

21. 诚心和气　胜于观心

21. Even temperament is superior to meditation.

家庭有个真佛①，日用有种真道②。人能诚心和气，愉色婉言，使父母兄弟间形骸两释③，意气交流，胜于调息④观心⑤万倍矣！

【中文注释】

① 真佛：可理解为“真信仰”。
② 真道：可理解为“真准则”。
③ 形骸两释：此处喻相互间没有误解和隔阂。形骸指人的形体。
④ 调息：根据意念调整呼吸，进行练气。
⑤ 观心：静坐审视内心。

【今文解译】

一个家庭不能没有可以尊奉的信仰，日常生活不能没有可以践行的准则。如果居家时人们都能一团和气，彼此以诚相待，和颜悦色，相敬如宾，父母兄弟亲密无间，意气相投，这一切都要比闭目调息、静坐观心好过千万倍。

【English Translation】

There should be true faith for a family and genuine principles in daily life, abiding by both, people become even-tempered, good-humored and gentle-behaved. Such atmosphere enables the parents and brothers to clear up their mutual misunderstandings and become congenial to each other. This is ten thousand times better than only regulating breath or sitting in meditation.

22. 有动有寂　动寂相宜

22. Movement harbors in stillness and stillness in movement, and both give rise to each other.

好动者云电风灯[1]，嗜寂者死灰槁木。须定云止水[2]中，有鸢飞鱼跃气象，才是有道的心体[3]。

【中文注释】　① 云电风灯：划破云层的闪电和风中摇曳的灯光。
② 定云止水：（看似）不动的云彩和静止的河水。
③ 有道的心体：整个句子都围绕动与寂展开陈述，所以此处的"有道的心体"就是对前述的一个总结，与道德二字无关。

【今文解译】　好动的人像云里的闪电和风中的油灯，而喜静的人则像燃尽的死灰和没有生机的枯木（此二者皆不可取）。我们应该学点鹰翔定云、鱼跃止水的样子，真正做到：静中有动，动中见静。

【English Translation】

A man fond of movement is like lightning fleeting through the clouds or an oil lamplight flickering in the wind, while a man fond of stillness is like dead ashes of fire or a withered tree bereft of vitality. It is only by acting like an eagle flying through the stationary clouds or fish leaping in the still water that one can come up to the point: movement harbors in stillness and stillness in movement.

23. 责恶勿太严　教善勿太高

23. Be not too severe when reproaching someone with his faults, nor too demanding when initiating someone into righteousness.

攻人之恶毋太严，要思其堪受；教人以善毋过高，当使其可从。

【今文解译】　批评别人的过错，言语不宜过激，要顾及他们是否能够承受。
教人学做善事，要求不可太高，而应考虑他们是否能够做到。

【English Translation】

Not be too severe when you reproach others with their faults; it is better to consider how much they can endure.

Not be too demanding when you initiate others into righteousness; it is better to make them feel easy to keep up.

24. 洁常自污出　明每从暗生

24. Cleanliness often derives from dirt and brightness always from gloom.

粪虫[1]至秽，变为蝉而饮露于秋风；腐草无光，化为萤[2]而耀彩于夏月。因知洁常自污出，明每从晦生也。

【中文注释】

① 粪虫：尘芥中所生的蛆虫。此处指蛴螬（金龟子的幼虫），古人认为蝉是从蛴螬演变而来的。

② 化为萤：萤火虫产卵在水边的草根处，多半潜伏在土中，次年草蛹化为萤火虫。古人不明白其中原理，误以为萤火虫是由腐草变化而成。

【今文解译】

粪土里的蛆虫是最肮脏的东西，可一旦蜕变成蝉，它就能在秋风中啄饮洁净的甘露。腐烂的草垛黯然无光，可它孕育出的萤火虫却能在月色溶溶的夏夜里发出耀眼的光亮。由此可知，世上洁净的东西常常出自污秽，而光明的东西则每每形成于晦暗。

【English Translation】

There is none as filthy as the beetle waggling in muckheap, yet it sips pure dewdrops in the autumn wind after having transformed into a cicada. Lusterless are rotten weeds, yet the fireflies bred thereby glitter fluorescent light under the moon at summer night. These natural givens show that cleanliness usually derives from dirt and brightness from gloom.

25. 伸张正气　再现真心

25. Only when healthy trends are encouraged can there emerge the true characters from within.

矜高倨傲，无非客气[①]，降服得客气下，而后正气伸；情欲意识，尽属妄心[②]，消杀得妄心尽，而后真心[③]现。

【中文注释】 ① 客气：客气是相对于后面的正气而言的，所以此处可理解为人的不良气性或不良习气。
② 妄心：妄念，非分或越轨的想法，虚妄之心。
③ 真心：真正的本心，善良的本性。即儒家所说的真性。

【今文解译】 居高临下、目空一切是人的一种不良气性，只有把不良气性克服了，正气才会得到伸张。
七情六欲、意想识见都是人的妄心造成的，只有将妄心去除了，真正的本心才会显现。

【English Translation】

The reason why a man is arrogant is just because of the existence of undesirable dispositions in his heart; only when the undesirable dispositions are choked can the healthy ones prevail.
All the mundane intentions and desires in the mind are nothing but improper thoughts; only when the improper thoughts are dislodged can the true characters come out from within.

26. 事悟痴除　性定动正

26. Ex-post repentance dispels infatuations and nature well preserved begets appropriate action.

饱后思味，则浓淡之境都消；色后思淫，则男女之见尽绝。故人常以事后之悔悟，破临事之痴迷，则性定[①]而动无不正[②]。

【中文注释】 ① 性定：保持纯真的本性。
② 动无不正：做事无不符合道德规范。

【今文解译】 酒足饭饱后若还想着美味佳肴，就再也无法体味出食物的滋味；男欢女爱后若还想着床笫之事，就再也感觉不到肌肤之亲的甜蜜。所以，人们只要常常能用事后的悔悟来破除自己对当前之事的痴迷，就能不失本性，行为举止也就不会违背天理人伦。

【English Translation】

If someone were to tell the flavor of more food right after having eaten his fill, his palate would let him down. If someone were to seek more pleasures of the flesh right after having been sated with his carnal appetites, the mysteries of love-making would become extinct. Therefore, if people can take a habit of repenting their folly in the past and relieving infatuations for the time being, they will undoubtedly have their true natures well preserved and their actions morally regulated.

27. 志在林泉　胸怀廊庙

27. Keep in mind the ambition and statecraft to serve the country while lodging your aspiration in the forests and fountains.

居轩冕之中①，不可无山林的气味②；处林泉之下，须要怀廊庙③的经纶④。

【中文注释】 ① 居轩冕之中：轩冕，古代卿大夫的轩车和冕服；居轩冕之中，喻身居高位、俸禄丰厚的官员。

② 山林的气味：山林，与此后的“林泉”二字同义，喻指与世无争；气味，气息。山林的气味，可理解为与世无争的意趣或情调。

③ 廊庙：朝廷。此处表示治国安邦的意思。

④ 经纶：本意为经过整理的蚕丝。此处喻规划、管理政治的才能。结合前面的“廊庙”二字，可理解为“治国安邦的抱负和才能”。

【今文解译】 身居要职的，不可没有山林居士那种淡泊名利的闲情逸致。

以林泉为伴的，不可没有胸怀天下、经济国家社稷的才志。

【English Translation】

Those who enjoy high positions and handsome salaries should not dispense with the plain makings of the hermit in mountains and forests. Contrarily, those who live in seclusion far from the earthly world must be always provided with ambitions and talents to serve the country and people.

28. 无过是功　无怨是德

28. To go without blame is creditable and without others' enmity, grateful.

处世不必邀功，无过便是功；与人不求感德，无怨便是德。

【今文解译】　做事不必讨功邀赏。所作所为没有过错，这本身就是最大的犒赏。

助人不要求回报。做到别人对你没有怨言，也就是最好的回报。

【English Translation】

In conducting yourself, do not desire for merit and reward; it is quite desirable to go without making any mistakes.

When helping others, do not expect gratitude in return; it is grateful enough to go without inviting enmity from them.

29. 忧勤勿过　待人勿枯

29. In performing your duties, not be overstrained; and in dealing with people, not be indifferent.

忧勤是美德，太苦则无以适性怡情；澹泊是高风，太枯则无以济人利物。

【今文解译】　工作勤勉是一种美德，然而一味地讲求苦干则不利于自己性情的调适。

淡泊名利是一种高风亮节，然而过于清心寡欲则对人类社会毫无助益。

【English Translation】

To spare no effort in performing one's duties is a good virtue; but if overstrained, it will be of no help to cheering the mind and pleasing the feelings.

Being indifferent to fame and wealth is a noble character; but if overdone, it will be of no worth for the benefit of the humans and the world.

30. 原其初心　观其末路

30. To judge a man is to look into his initial intention; and to comment on a man is to examine his integrity in his later years.

事穷势蹙之人，当原其初心；功成行满之士，要观其末路。

【今文解译】 当一个人事业受挫、处境落魄时，我们应当看他开始做事时的初心究竟是怎样的。

当一个人事业有成、功德圆满时，我们应当观察他能否将这个势头一直保持到最后。

【English Translation】

To judge a man who has suffered failure and is now down and out, it is better to look into his original intentions at the outset.

To comment on a man who has come to a successful issue, it is better to examine if he can maintain his success to the end of his life.

31. 富宜宽厚　智宜敛藏

31. Be generous even if you are rich and honorable and keep your talents obscured even if you are replete with wisdom.

富贵家宜宽厚，而反忌刻[1]，是富贵而贫贱其行矣！如何能享？聪明人宜敛藏[2]，而反炫耀，是聪明而愚懵[3]其病矣！如何不败?

【中文注释】 ① 忌刻：对人忌妒刻薄。

② 敛藏：收敛锋芒之意。

③ 愚懵：愚昧。

【今文解译】 富贵人家处世要宽容大度些，不要刻薄挑剔。刻薄挑剔是贫贱者的行为，富贵人家若此岂能安享富贵？！
聪明人平时最好低调些，不要炫耀自己的才华。炫耀自己的才华是愚蠢的毛病，聪明人染此毛病岂有不败的道理？！

【English Translation】

A family of wealth and rank should be magnanimous, and should not be harsh and stingy; otherwise it will be no more than the poor and the lowly. How could it enjoy its wealth and rank?
An intelligent man should have his wisdom and talents obscured, and should not parade them; otherwise he will make the same mistake as the ignorant do. How could he not be defeated?

32. 登高思危　少言勿躁

32. Think of danger when ascending a height and talk less to avoid vexation.

居卑①而后知登高之为危，处晦而后知向明之太露②；守静而后知好动之过劳，养默而后知多言之为躁。

【中文注释】 ① 卑：低处或地位低下。
② 露：云气。此处可理解为“晃眼”或“显眼”等。

【今文解译】 到了低矮的地方才知道攀高登顶是那么危险。
身处晦暗的地方才知道亮光底下是那么扎眼。
安静下来了才知道四处奔波是那么辛苦。
习惯沉默了才知道多嘴多舌是那么浮躁。

【English Translation】

Only when a person comes to a low place can he realize the danger of ascending a height.
Only when a person is placed in obscurity can he realize that the things in brightness are too dazzling.
Only when a person knows how to live in peace can he realize the hardship to toil and moil.

Only when a person knows how to keep silence can he realize that overtalking is the root of vexation.

33. 放得功名　即可脱俗

33. One who can sever himself from fame and wealth will overcome worldly thoughts.

放得功名富贵之心下，便可脱凡；放得道德仁义之心下，才可入圣[1]。

【中文注释】　① 才可入圣：在中国古代，能按仁义道德要求去处世为人的是君子，而思想行为不受其束缚却又能时时处处为人师表的则是至人或圣人。

【今文解译】　能放下功名富贵之心的，便可以摆脱凡俗的束缚。
能摆脱仁义道德桎梏的，便可以达到圣贤的境界。

【English Translation】

It is only by discarding the desire to seek riches and honor that one will be able to transcend the mundane world.
It is only by finding freedom from the sermon of justice and virtue that one will be able to enter sainthood.

34. 偏见害人　聪明障道

34. Self-willedness harms man's notion, and smart aleck hinders man's virtue.

利欲未尽害心，意见[1]乃害心之蟊贼[2]；声色未必障道，聪明乃障道之藩屏[3]。

【中文注释】　① 意见：此处指刚愎自用或自以为是。
② 蟊贼：专吃禾苗的两种害虫。《诗·小雅·大田》："及其蟊贼。"传："食根曰蟊，食节曰贼。"此处喻祸害或祸端。
③ 藩屏：篱笆和屏风。比喻障碍。

【今文解译】 名利欲望未必能伤害人的心智，真正伤害心智的是"刚愎自用"这个蟊贼。

声色犬马未必能妨碍人的德行，真正妨碍德行的是"自作聪明"这种毛病。

【English Translation】

Material desires may not necessarily do harm onto man's notion, but self-willedness, by acting like a pest, will do.

Sensual pleasures may not necessarily hinder man's virtue, but smart aleck, by acting like an obstacle, will do.

35. 知退一步　加让三分

35. Step backward for others when on a narrow path and give way for them even if on an open road.

人情反覆，世路崎岖。行不去处，须知退一步之法；行得去处，务加让三分之功。

【今文解译】 世间人情反复无常，世间道路崎岖不平。路窄过不去时，要知道还有退一步这种走法；即使路宽好走，也一定要有让出三分便利给人的胸襟和公德。

【English Translation】

Human relationships are inconstant. The road of life is rugged and rough. When there is no enough room ahead on a path, you should have the sense to take a step back for others. Furthermore, even when you come to an open road, you should also take it as your merit to make way for them.

36. 不恶小人　有礼君子

36. Treat a base man with no hatred and a worthy man with etiquette.

待小人不难于严，而难于不恶；待君子不难于恭，而难于有礼。

【今文解译】 以严厉的态度对待劣迹斑斑的小人，这不难，难的是去除内心对他们的鄙夷。
以恭敬之心对待谦谦君子，这不难，难的是对待他们要礼数周全，不失体统。

【English Translation】

It is easy to be severe with a base man, but difficult to treat him without disgust.
It is easy to be respectful to a worthy man, but difficult to treat him with proper etiquette.

37. 正气清名　留于乾坤

37. It is better to leave both righteousness and untainted name to the world.

宁守浑噩①而黜②聪明，留些正气还天地；宁谢纷华而甘澹泊，遗个清名在乾坤。

【中文注释】 ① 浑噩：混沌无知的样子。此处指朴实无邪。
② 黜：去除，摒弃。

【今文解译】 宁可朴实愚鲁也不要玩弄小聪明，这样至少还可以给这个世界留下点正气。
宁可选择清贫也不要涉足名利场，这样至少还可以留个清廉的名声在人间。

【English Translation】

It is better to preserve natural instincts and forsake astuteness, so as to save some righteousness for the world. Likewise, it is better to decline extravagance and be content with a simple life, so as to leave behind an untainted name in history.

38. 降魔先降心　驭横先驭气

38. To vanquish monsters, first vanquish the wicked thoughts in mind; to control absurdity, first control the internal rashness in heart.

降魔者先降自心，心伏则群魔退听；驭横者先驭此气，气平则外横不侵。

【今文解译】 要想降伏恶魔，首先要降伏自己内心的邪念，唯有如此，形形色色的恶魔才会乖乖地退避三舍。
要想制服乱象，首先要控制自己的焦躁情绪，控制住了自己的焦躁情绪，乱象也就于你无害了。

【English Translation】

To vanquish monsters, one should first vanquish the wicked thoughts in one's own heart; only when the wicked thoughts are vanquished could all the monsters be obedient at one's command.

To control external absurdity, one should first have control over the impetuosity of one's own; only when the impetuosity of one's own is well under control could the external absurdity not invade.

39. 教育子弟　要严交游

39. To educate disciples, it is better to do so by setting rigid rules on their social intercourse.

教弟子①如养闺女，最要严出入、谨交游。若一接近匪人②，是清净田种下一不净的种子，便终身难植嘉禾③矣！

【中文注释】 ① 弟子：此处系指学生或追随者。
② 匪人：本指非亲非故之人。现指品行不端的人。
③ 嘉禾：长势喜人的庄稼。

【今文解译】 教书育人如同养育待字闺中的姑娘，最要紧的是要求她们日常起居要有规矩，与人交往要小心谨慎。一旦不小心接触了不该接触的人，就好比在干净的田地里撒下了不良的种子，一辈子休想种出好的庄稼。

【English Translation】

Educating disciples can be compared to bringing up daughters. The most important thing thereby is to set rigid rules on their daily life and social intercourse. In case they make any acquaintance of ill-behaved ones, it would be like sowing a bad seed in the clean farmland. Consequently, no good crops can be expected over there for a lifetime.

40. 欲路勿染　理路勿退

40. Do not act willfully in pursuing material gains, nor shrink back in seeking the truth.

欲路上事①，毋乐其便而姑为染指，一染指便深入万仞；理路上事②，毋惮其难而稍为退步，一退步便远隔千山。

【中文注释】 ① 欲路上事：物质上的追求。
② 理路上事：对真理的探索。

【今文解译】 追求物质利益时，切不可为图一时之便而姑妄为之，一旦放纵涉事就会跌入万丈深渊。
在探索真理的过程中，切不可因为有畏难情绪而退缩，一旦退缩就会和真理相去千山万水。

【English Translation】

When you pursue material gains, do not act willfully for the love of convenience. If you do, you will surely fall into an abyss of one hundred thousand feet.
When you seek the truth, do not flinch for fear of difficulties. If you do, you will inevitably be separated from the truth by a thousand mountains.

41. 不可浓艳　不可枯寂

41. In everyday life, one should be neither too particular nor too casual-minded.

念头浓者①，自待厚，待人亦厚，处处皆浓；念头淡者②，自待薄，待人亦薄，事事皆淡。故君子居常嗜好，不可太浓艳，亦不宜太枯寂。

【中文注释】 ① 念头浓者：凡事总图个讲究的人。

② 念头淡者：凡事皆不讲究的人。

【今文解译】 做事上心的人，善待自己，也善待别人，做什么都十分讲究，非尽善尽美不肯罢休；做事不上心的人，对自己马虎，对别人也马虎，做什么都随随便便，心不在焉。由此我们得以明白：君子平素的喜好，既不可太过讲究，也不可太不讲究。

【English Translation】

A man striving for exquisiteness has a habit to be considerate towards himself and towards others as well; wherever he goes, he intends to go in an exquisite manner. Whereas, a casual-minded man has a habit to be indifferent to himself and to others as well; whatever he does, he just does it with casualness. Therefore, a smart gentleman should be neither too particular about exquisiteness nor too casual-minded in his daily life and personal addictions.

42. 超越天地　不入名利

42. Transcend the mundane world by not being tempted into fame and wealth.

彼富我仁，彼爵我义，君子固不为君相[①]所牢笼；人定胜天，志一动气[②]，君子亦不受造化之陶铸[③]。

【中文注释】 ① 君相：国君的大臣。此处喻高官厚禄。

② 志一动气：意志专注才能形成强大的力量。

③ 陶铸：范土曰陶，熔金曰铸。比喻造就，培养。

【今文解译】 人有富贵我有仁德，人有爵禄我有义理：君子因此而不为高官厚禄所束缚。

人定胜天，关键在于齐心协力：君子若意志坚强，造物主对他也无可奈何。

【English Translation】

Others have riches while I cherish benevolence. Others have official titles while I value righteousness. He that is noble-minded will never be restrained by the high position and its advantages.

The feat that human efforts prevail over heaven's will can only be achieved through the constancy of a concentrated mind. He that is strong-willed will never be constrained by the Creator.

43. 高一步立身　退一步处世

43. Stand on a higher plane in pursuit and for the sake of security, learn how to compromise.

立身不高一步立，如尘里振衣，泥中濯足，如何超达？处世不退一步处，如飞蛾投烛，羝羊触藩[1]，如何安乐？

【中文注释】　① 羝羊触藩：羝羊，公羊；触，抵撞；藩，篱笆。指公羊抵撞篱笆时，羊角缠在了篱笆上，进退不得。

【今文解译】　安身立命的目标定得不高，就仿佛在尘埃中抖衣，在泥水里洗脚，如何能做到超凡脱俗？

为人处世若不能做到恭敬礼让，就如同飞蛾扑火、公羊触藩一般，如何能安享平安快乐？

【English Translation】

If a man cannot stand on a higher plane in his pursuit, it is similar to dusting his clothes in the dust and washing his feet in the muddy water. How can he rise above the general run of people?

If a man does not know how to make compromises in social intercourse, he would resemble a moth darting into flame or a ram rushing against fences. How can he rest his life on peace and ease?

44. 修德忘名　读书深心

44. Do away with fame when striving for virtue and be wholly devoted when resolving upon study.

学者[1]要收拾精神，并归一路。如修德而留意于事功名誉，必无实诣[2]；读书而寄兴于吟咏风雅，定不深心。

【中文注释】 ① 学者：做学问的人。
② 实诣：实实在在的造诣。

【今文解译】 为学者修身治学贵在全神贯注，心无旁骛：如果一边修身一边却又惦记着事功名誉，就很难取得实实在在的成效；如果一边读书一边却又耽于吟咏风雅，就一定沉不下心来刻苦钻研。

【English Translation】
One who persuades virtue and knowledge should be of concentration and wholeheartedness. If he cares too much about success and honor while undertaking self-refinement, there would be no real attainment. And by the same token, if he is too interested in chant and elegance while learning, there would be no whole devotion.

45. 一念之差　失之千里

45. A momentary slip gives occasion to a permanent loss.

人人有个大慈悲，维摩[1]屠刽[2]无二心也；处处有种真趣味，金屋茅檐非两地也。只是欲闭情封[3]，当面错过，便咫尺千里矣。

【中文注释】 ① 维摩：即“维摩诘”，与释迦牟尼同时代的著名居士。
② 屠刽：屠夫和刽子手。
③ 欲闭情封：意为“无欲无情”。

【今文解译】 每个人的心里都有一颗菩萨心，在这一点上，维摩居士和屠夫刽子手是一样的。世界虽大但真趣味无处不在，在这一点上，富贵之家和贫贱之家是没有区别的。如果因为无动于衷而当面错过了菩萨心和真趣味，即使近在咫尺也好似远隔千里。

【English Translation】

Everyone is born with Buddha-nature, in which respect, the saint Vimalakirti and butchers and executioners are all the same. Everywhere is a genuine mood, which can be found both in a golden mansion and in a thatched cottage. But it is much to be regretted that Buddha-nature is often obscured by the craving for fame and fortune and the genuine mood always obstructed by sensual desires. Should a person let slip Buddha-nature and the genuine mood when coming face to face with them, then this would be the result: a short distance away, yet poles apart.

46. 有木石心　具云水趣

46. A rock-firm will is indispensable in moral cultivation, so is a natural temperament in dedication to the country.

进德修道，要个木石①的念头，若一有欣羡，便趋欲境；济世经邦，要段云水②的趣味，若一有贪著，便堕危机。

【中文注释】 ① 木石：喻坚定。
② 云水：禅林称行脚僧为云水，以四海为家，有如行云流水。此处含飘逸洒脱之意。

【今文解译】 进德修道要有木石般坚定的意志，稍有对名利的艳羡，就会陷入物欲缠身的境地。
济世经邦要有云水般洒脱的情怀，稍有对权势的贪恋，就会坠入危机四伏的深渊。

【English Translation】

One determined to cultivate his moral character and temper his virtue should do so with a rock-firm will. Once laid in admiration for fame and gain, one would be snared by material desires.
One committing himself to serving his people and benefiting his country should do so with a natural temperament. Once becoming greedy for power and rank, one would fall into a crisis.

47. 吉人和气　凶人杀气

47. A good man is always imbued with composure, and a bad man with a murderous look.

吉人无论作用[1]安详，即梦寐神魂，无非和气；凶人无论行事狠戾[2]，即声音咲语[3]，浑是杀机。

【中文注释】 ① 作用：作为，行为。
② 狠戾：凶狠残暴。亦可写作“狼戾”，同义。
③ 咲语：含带笑容所说的话。咲，同“笑”。

【今文解译】 心地纯良的人无论做什么都一派吉祥，即使是在梦里，其神情也和蔼可亲。
心狠手辣的人做什么都一副凶相，即使在谈笑间，也透着咄咄逼人的杀气。

【English Translation】
A good man looks serene not only in his speech and deportment, even in his dreams there can be seen a state of harmony imbued with composure and ease. An evil man looks ferocious not only in his actions, even amidst his voice and smiling countenance there can be discerned an aggressive design.

48. 君子无祸　勿罪冥冥

48. An accomplished man should do no evil on the sly if he wants to distance calamities.

肝受病，则目不能视；肾受病，则耳不能听。病受于人所不见，必发于人所共见。故君子欲无得罪于昭昭[1]，必先无得罪于冥冥[2]。

【中文注释】 ① 得罪于昭昭：此处的“罪”意为“侮辱”。昭昭，明亮，此处指“人所能见的地方”。
② 得罪于冥冥：此处的“罪”意为“罪过”。冥冥，晦暗，昏昧，此处指“人所不见的地方”。

【今文解译】 肝脏有病则眼睛的视力就会下降，肾脏有病则耳朵的听力就会衰退。发生在人所不见的地方的毛病，最终都会暴露在有目共睹的地方。由此我们认识到：作为一个堂堂正正的君子，要想在公众面前表现得清白坦荡，他必须首先在私底下不做任何有失体面的事情。

【English Translation】

A person will be unable to see clearly in case his liver goes wrong, and will be unable to listen distinctly in case his kidneys are disordered. A disease is usually contracted in a place where nobody can see, but in the end the symptoms will come to light. Therefore, the accomplished man must conduct himself properly in private if he does not want to be disgraced in public.

49. 多心为祸　少事为福

49. It is a misfortune to be sunk in excessive exertions, but a fortune to have few cares.

福莫福于少事，祸莫祸于多心①。唯苦事者，方知少事之为福；唯平心者，始知多心之为祸。

【中文注释】 ① 多心：此处指多余的操劳，与前半句的“少事”形成对照。

【今文解译】 人生最大的幸福是无事打扰，最大的不幸是牵肠挂肚。只有每天苦于奔命的人，才知道无事打扰是一种清福；只有神闲气定的人，才知道整天牵肠挂肚实在是一种煎熬。

【English Translation】

Of man’s lot, the greatest fortune is to have few cares, and the greatest misfortune is to be sunk in excessive exertions. Only the person who has been busy all the time realizes that it is a joy to have few cares. And only the person who is in a tranquil state realizes that it is a suffering to go with excessive exertions.

50. 当方则方　当圆则圆

50. Be upright whenever needed and slick, when it is necessary.

处治世宜方，处乱世宜圆，处叔季之世[①]当方圆并用；待善人宜宽，待恶人宜严，待庸众之人[②]当宽严互存。

【中文注释】 ① 叔季之世：喻国家衰乱将亡的时代。
② 庸众之人：才智平庸无奇的人。

【今文解译】 处在治世，为人要刚正；处在乱世，为人要圆通；处在由盛转衰的时代，则要刚正圆通并济。
对待善良的人要宽容；对待凶恶的人要严厉；对待才智平庸无奇的人，则既要宽容又要严厉。

【English Translation】
In times of peace and order, one should be upright; at turbulent days, one should be slick; and in declining times, one needs to be both upright and slick. In dealing with good people, one should be generous; in dealing with bad people, one should be severe; and in dealing with mediocre people, one needs to be both generous and severe.

51. 己功不念　人恩不忘

51. Bear not in mind the favors we have done to others but the bounties others might have bestowed on us.

我有功于人不可念，而过则不可不念；人有恩于我不可忘，而怨则不可不忘。

【今文解译】 自己对别人有恩，不可念念不忘；自己做事对不起别人，就应当反躬自省。
别人对自己有恩，不可不记在心；别人有事冒犯了自己，就不可耿耿于怀。

【English Translation】

We should not bear in mind the good turns we have done for others, but should reflect on the offences we might have given to them. Contrarily, we should bear in mind the bounties others have bestowed on us, but should forget the displeasures they might have caused to us.

52. 施之不求　求之无功

52. Never seek return for the benefaction we have given, otherwise winning no reputation.

施恩者，内不见己，外不见人，则斗粟①可当万钟②之惠；利物者③，计己之施，责人之报，虽百镒④难成一文之功。

【中文注释】 ① 斗粟：斗，十升，约合十五公斤；粟，谷子。斗粟形容极少。

② 万钟：钟，古代量器，六石四斗为一钟，约合二百五十升。万钟表示极多。

③ 利物者：以财物帮助别人的人。

④ 百镒：镒，古代重量单位，一镒为二十四两。百镒喻重或多。

【今文解译】 有恩于人，施恩者自己不能老记在心里，更不能四处宣扬。如此，即使一斗粟的恩惠也抵得上万斗重的恩泽。

一个资助过别人的人，老在盘算自己的付出并期待别人有所回报，这样的资助即使价值万金也无一文之功德。

【English Translation】

A true benefactor should neither bear in mind nor give publicity to the good turns he has done to others. Thus, a wee bit of alms will result in boundless gratitude. But if a donator harps on the largess he has given to others and seeks for return, then his merits will not be worth a cent even though he has spent millions of gold to help.

53. 相观对治　方便法门

53. It is good for one to take mutual examination and contrast others' position with one's own.

人之际遇，有齐[①]有不齐，而能使己独齐乎？己之情理，有顺有不顺，而能使人皆顺乎？以此相观对治[②]，亦是一方便法门[③]。

【中文注释】　① 齐：通“济”，意喻顺利，成功。
② 相观对治：相互对照修正。此处有将心比心的含义。
③ 法门：佛教用语。修行者入道的门径。泛指途径或方法。

【今文解译】　每个人的境遇是不尽相同的，有的顺有的不顺，有谁能保证自己的境遇一直是顺的？人的心智是不断变化的，时而畅明时而瘀滞，有谁能要求别人的心智始终都保持畅明？为人处世能有这样换位思考的心态，倒也不失为一种修身立德的好方法。

【English Translation】

Men's lots are different from each other. Among them, some are commendable, and some are not. How can a man claim that he himself is the only one whose lot is commendable? The state of a man's heart and mind changes accordingly from time to time. Now he may be sensible, now may not. How can he demand that others hold on to a sensible state of heart and mind without any change? Empathy as considerate as such is quite a way fit for refining our moral behaviors.

54. 心地干净　方可学古

54. Only when the heart is made clear and pure can one start to model after ancient sages and men of virtue.

心地干净，方可读书学古。不然，见一善行窃以济私，闻一善言假以覆短[①]，是又藉寇兵[②]而赍盗粮[③]矣。

【中文注释】　① 覆短：掩盖自己的短处或过失。

② 藉寇兵：借给敌人武器。藉，借；寇，敌人；兵，武器。
③ 赍盗粮：送给强盗粮食。赍，输送，送与。

【今文解译】 一个人只有摒除了心中的私心杂念，方才可以读书学古。不然，一见到别人的某个善举就用来美化自己，一听到别人的某句善言就用以掩饰自己的劣迹，这岂不成了借武器给敌寇、送粮草给盗贼了吗？！

【English Translation】

Unless all the distracting thoughts are removed from the mind, one can never set out his studying classics and emulating sages and worthies of antiquity. Otherwise, upon having a good deed at sight he will exploit it to beautify himself, or upon hearing a good word he will use it to disguise his own ignominious actions. Such doings are equivalent to lending weapons to enemies and supplying provisions to bandits.

55. 崇俭养廉　守拙全真

55. Frugality makes honesty and dullness brings sincerity.

奢者富而不足，何如俭者贫而有余？能者劳而府怨[①]，何如拙者逸而全真[②]？

【中文注释】 ① 劳而府怨：一边辛劳地付出一边却又牢骚满腹，怨恨不已。府，聚集之处。怨，怨恨。
② 逸而全真：安逸而又不失真性情。

【今文解译】 生活追求奢华的人，对已经获得的财富仍然不知满足，这样的人怎比得上那些虽然贫穷但却因为节俭而有盈余的人呢？
有能耐的人一边埋头干活一边却牢骚满腹，怨恨不已，这样的人怎比得上那些虽然笨拙但却悠闲而不失真性情的人呢？

【English Translation】

A man lapped in luxury and extravagance always feels dissatisfied though he is rich enough. Would it be better for him to be like that than to be a frugal man

who is poor, and yet surplus?
A gifted man often stores up complaints in his heart while working hard. Would it be better for him to be like that than to be a dull man who is incapable, and yet sincere and leisurely-minded?

56. 学以致用　立业种德

56. Studying for the purpose of application conduces to both moral cultivation and career development.

读书不见圣贤，如铅椠佣①；居官不爱子民，如衣冠盗；讲学不尚躬行，为口头禅②；立业不思种德，为眼前花。

【中文注释】 ① 铅椠佣：古代雇来抄写文字的人。铅椠，古人书写文字的工具。

② 口头禅：古代为宗教用语，本意指未经心灵证悟就把一些现成的经言和公案挂在嘴边，装作很得道的样子。通俗说就是指一个人在有意或无意间常讲的说话语句。

【今文解译】 读圣贤书但却不领会书中的思想精髓，这与写字匠何异？官职在身但心里却不装着黎民百姓，这与衣冠盗贼何异？讲授圣贤思想但却不身体力行，这与只会说口头禅何异？注重建功立业但却忽略修为的积累，这与昙花一现何异？

【English Translation】

If a man keen on learning does not gain an insight into the essence of the classics written by sages and men of virtue, he will be not any more than a hired copyist.
If a man with official title cannot take good care of his people, he will be no less than a bandit clad in court attire.
If a man giving lectures on moral principles cannot earnestly practice what he advocates, he is merely a Buddhist monk reciting scriptures.
If a man absorbed in his career development does not pay heed to self-cultivation, he is nearly a flash in the pan.

57. 扫除外物　直觉本来

57. Only by clearing away outside enticement can one find a straight path to the essence of his nature.

人心有一部真文章[①]，都被残篇断简封锢了；有一部真鼓吹[②]，都被妖歌艳舞淹没了。学者须扫除外物，直觉本来，才有个真受用。

【中文注释】　① 真文章：此处喻人的行为准则。

② 真鼓吹：鼓吹，代指乐曲。此处隐喻人心底里的美妙乐谱。

【今文解译】　每个人的心里都有一篇关于行为准则的好文章，可惜被那些乌七八糟的乱章杂句给充斥了；也都有一首美妙动听的好乐曲，可惜都被那些妖歌艳舞的声音给淹没了。为学者只有排除外界的干扰，坚持本性，才能真正地学有所获。

【English Translation】

In everyone's heart there is a book on code of conduct, but it is crammed with miscellaneous fragments; and also there is a music score of innermost feelings, but it is inundated with indecent melodies. As a learner, one must do his utmost to clear away external enticement and come straightway to the perception of the essence of his nature. Only by doing like this will he be really able to benefit from his learning.

58. 苦中有乐　得意生悲

58. As pleasure grows in suffering, so frustration forms in contentment.

苦心中，常得悦心之趣；得意时，便生失意之悲。

【今文解译】　人在苦心追求一样东西的时候，常会有愉悦之情泛自心底。

人有所获而沾沾自喜的时候，失意的悲情往往会悄然而生。

【English Translation】

In the course of hard pursuit joys may often spring from the bottom of the heart; while at the time of contentment the sorrow of frustration may arise beyond expectation.

59. 富贵名誉　来自道德

59. Riches and honor should be derived from the cultivation of morality.

富贵名誉，自道德来者，如山林中花，自是舒徐繁衍；自功业来者，如盆槛中花，便有迁徙兴废；若以权力得者，如瓶钵中花，其根不植，其萎可立而待矣。

【今文解译】　财富、地位、名声和荣誉若由道德而得来，自会像山林中的野花，舒展从容，繁衍不绝；若由功业而得来，就会像盆栽的花朵，迁徙得法则盛开，迁徙不得法则凋敝；若由权势而得来，就会像插在瓶钵里的花朵，因为没有根基而很快枯萎。

【English Translation】

Man's riches and honor, if derived from the cultivation of morality and virtue, are like wild flowers in the mountains and forests, and will naturally flourish and multiply; if obtained by the means of personal exploits, are like flowers in discs, and might flourish when well transplanted and wither when not; and if seized by force of political power or trickeries, are like rootless flowers in vases, and will die down before you get tired by standing.

60. 花铺好色　人行好事

60. As flowers would bloom a riot of color, so should one do good turns so long as one lives.

春至时和，花尚铺一段好色，鸟且啭几句好音。士君子①幸列头角②，复遇温饱，不思立好言，行好事，虽是在世百年，恰似未生一日。

【中文注释】 ① 士君子：士君子的含义在古代可有三种解释：一是指上层统治人物，如周制中的卿、大夫或士；二是指有学问且品德高尚的人或学者；三是泛指读书人。
② 列头角：头顶左右的突出处，比喻才华出众。此处指科考榜上有名。

【今文解译】 春天来临，万物复苏，花草都纷纷争奇斗艳，鸟儿都一个个婉转啼鸣。读书人一旦有幸金榜题名，温饱不再发愁，若不想着写出几篇像样的好文章，做几件像样的好事，即使苟活百年，也如未到人世一日。

【English Translation】
When spring comes together with fine weather, flowers will bloom a riot of color and birds sing beautiful songs. If a scholar, who is lucky enough to have cut a splendid figure and now has adequate days, makes no attempt to lay store on good words and deeds, it would be as if he had never lived a single day in this world even though he were to live a century.

61. 兢业的心思　潇洒的趣味

61. Unrestrained interest for life is as vital as assiduous thoughts in learning.

学者要有段兢业①的心思，又要有段潇洒的趣味。若一味敛束②清苦，是有秋杀无春生，何以发育万物?

【今文解译】 ① 兢业：兢兢业业。
② 敛束：收敛约束。

【今文解译】 为学者不仅要有刻苦钻研、积极向上的心志，而且还要有寄情山水、潇洒开放的情趣。如果只是一味地克制自己，清苦度日，生命就只有秋天的肃杀而没了春天的生机，万物何以生长发育呢?

【English Translation】
A scholar should have both assiduous thoughts in learning and unrestrained interest for life. If he restrains himself blindly by merely living under the

plain and harsh circumstances, both his thoughts and his interest would seem wrecked by the decay of autumn and bereft of the vigor of spring. How can he be expected to nourish the world?

62. 立名者贪　用术者拙

62. Those who seek reputation are greedy and clumsy, those who resort to craft.

真廉无廉名，立名者正所以为贪；大巧无巧术，用术者乃所以为拙。

【今文解译】 真正的廉洁不需廉洁为其名：为自己树立廉洁的名声，其实就是一种贪图名声的行为。
真正的才智不需机巧为其术：靠玩弄机巧来施展才智，其实就是为了掩饰自己的无能。

【English Translation】

True honesty has no reputation to seek; the person who seeks reputation for himself is called greedy.

Great wisdom needs no craft to resort to; the person who resorts to craft is called clumsy.

63. 宁虚勿溢　宁缺勿全

63. Emptiness is better than spillage, and so is incompletion than completion.

欹器①以满覆，扑满②以空全。故君子宁居无不居有，宁处缺不处完。

【中文注释】 ① 欹器：古代一种倾斜易覆的盛水器皿。没盛水时，它呈倾斜状；盛水一半时则呈直立状；而装满水时则立刻翻倒。古人将此物置于案头右侧引以为戒，后来的“座右铭”一说即源于此。孔子常以此物对其弟子进行教诲。
② 扑满：储钱罐。过去的储钱罐大多是陶制的，顶部有一个小小的放入口，等里面装满了硬币，主人要用钱时就会把罐子砸了。所以，就储钱罐本身而言，里面没有硬币

才是最安全的。

【今文解译】 欹器装满水就会倾覆；扑满空无一文反倒安全。所以，君子宁可一无所有也不愿意竞长争短，宁可有所不足也不愿意完美无缺。

【English Translation】

An inclined vessel is easy to topple when it is filled to the brim. A piggy bank is safe to be its self so long as it remains empty. Accordingly, the genuine person would rather have nothing than compete for advantages, and rather be contented with incompletion than with completion.

64. 拔去名根　融化客气

64. Uproot the lust for fame within and dispose of influences without.

名根未拔①者，纵轻千乘②甘一瓢③，总堕尘情；客气④未融者，虽泽四海利万世，终为剩技。

【中文注释】 ① 名根未拔：心里依旧怀着追求名声的欲望。
② 千乘：也即千乘之国，指古代拥有战车千乘的国家。此处喻巨大财富。
③ 一瓢：一瓢清水。常喻清贫、淡泊之意。
④ 客气：此处喻指来自外界的不良影响。

【今文解译】 名利心没有祛除干净的人，纵能蔑视一国之富而甘受一瓢之清贫，说到底也还是名利心在作怪。
不能抵挡外界不良影响的人，虽能慷慨解囊，利泽四海，惠及万代，最终还是处世的小伎俩而已。

【English Translation】

If a person has not yet uprooted the lust for fame from within, he will remain frail in the long run even though he himself claims to despise riches and rank and be willing to live a scanty life.
If a person cannot stem the torrent of the harmful influences from without, his benefaction will consequently become an uncalled-for trick even though he

has done a lot to benefit both the world and the generations of all coming ages.

65. 心体光明　暗室青天

65. An open, aboveboard mind makes a dark room bright.

心体光明，暗室中有青天；念头暗昧，白日下有厉鬼。

【今文解译】 心胸光明磊落的，即使呆在黑暗的屋子里，也会觉得头顶有一片蓝天。
心里阴暗蒙昧的，即使在正午的太阳底下，也会感觉有厉鬼出没左右。

【English Translation】
The man of open and aboveboard mind, even if in a dark room, would feel as if there were a blue sky overhead.
The man of wicked and sinister mind, even if in the sunshine, would feel as if there were a ferocious ghost beside him.

66. 无名无位　无忧无虑

66. Without fame and rank one will be free from worldly cares.

人知名位为乐，不知无名无位之乐为最真；人知饥寒为虑，不知不饥不寒之虑为更甚。

【今文解译】 人人都知道名分和位分能给人带来快乐，殊不知没有名分和位分的逍遥之乐才是最实在的快乐。
人人都知道饥饿和寒冷会给人带来忧虑，殊不知不愁吃穿、终日不思忧患才是更加令人担忧的。

【English Translation】
People only know that it is a pleasure to have fame and rank, but know not that having no fame and rank is the truest pleasure.
People only know that it is a worry to live in hunger and cold, but know not

that the state carefree from food and clothing is worse than a worry.

67. 阴恶恶大　显善善小

67. Vice concealed is more harmful than that revealed, but benevolence known by all inferior to that known to none.

为恶而畏人知，恶中犹有善路；为善而急人知，善处即是恶根。

【今文解译】　做了坏事但怕人知道，这是良知尚未泯灭、虽恶犹善的表现。
做了好事却急于示人，这是为善动机不纯、沽名钓誉的行为。

【English Translation】
If one has done evil and is afraid of being found out, it can be understood that, in spite of his wickedness, he still entertains a clear conscience to return to the right track.
If one has done good and is anxious to make it known to others, it can be understood that, amidst his benevolence, there lies a seminary of vice.

68. 居安思危　天亦无用

68. Get prepared for danger in times of peace, and Providence can do nothing against you.

天之机缄①不测，抑而伸，伸而抑，皆是播弄②英雄、颠倒豪杰处。君子只是逆来顺受，居安思危，天亦无所用其伎俩矣。

【中文注释】　① 机缄：唐成玄英《疏》："机，关也；缄，闭也。"此处指推动事物运动发展的造化力量。
② 播弄：掌管。此处喻捉弄。

【今文解译】　上天的造化之功是深不可测的，它忽而叫人背运忽而叫人走运，忽而又反之，那些所谓的英雄豪杰都一个个被它玩弄于股掌之间。有鉴于此，真正的君子应该学会逆来顺受和居安思危，这样就连上天对他都无计可施了。

【English Translation】

The power of Providence can never be outguessed. It now sets people out of luck and now favors them with good fortune, and then does the same the other way round. However, no matter what it does, it does it purposely to make fools of the so-called heroes who consider themselves no ordinary beings. In light of this, what a true gentleman should learn to do is to resign himself to adversity when out of luck and get prepared against danger in times of peace. That way, even Providence is unable to play a trick on him.

69. 偏激之人　难建功业

69. Those who are liable to go to extremes can hardly make any contributions.

燥性者火炽，遇物则焚；寡恩者冰清，逢物必杀①；凝滞②固执者，如死水腐木，生机已绝。俱难建功业而延福祉。

【中文注释】　① 逢物必杀：意即遇到什么就加害什么。
② 凝滞：呆板且缺乏活力。

【今文解译】　性情暴躁的人就像炽热的火焰，遇到什么就焚毁什么；寡恩薄义的人就像冷酷的冰块，遇到什么就扼杀什么；呆板固执的人就像一潭死水或一块朽木，毫无生的气息。这三种人都难以建立功业，也不足以承传福祉。

【English Translation】

Those who have irascible temperament are as fierce as raging flames; whatever they come across they burn it up. Those who grudge bestowing favors on others are as cold as ice; whatever they run into they do it harm. Those who are idiotic and obstinate are like dead water or rotten wood, without any vitality. Such people mentioned above can hardly make contributions to the society and carry forward good fortune.

70. 愉快求福　去怨避祸

70. Keep a happy mood so as to seek good fortune and to avoid disasters, discard grudge and hatred.

福不可徼[1]，养喜神[2]以为召福之本而已；祸不可避，去杀机[3]以为远祸之方而已。

【中文注释】 ① 福不可徼：徼，求。意为“福气是刻意求不来的”。
② 养喜神：保持快乐的心情。
③ 去杀机：去除心中的怨恨。

【今文解译】 福祉不可设计强求，保持愉快的心情也即把握住了祈福的根本。
祸害不可侥幸回避，去除心中的仇恨也即寻找到了避祸的良方。

【English Translation】

Good fortune cannot be seized with scheme; to keep a happy mood is a wise policy to invite good fortune.
Disaster cannot be shunned by a fluke; to remove hatred from the heart is a good way to avoid disasters.

71. 宁默毋躁　宁拙毋巧

71. Rather keep silence than act on impulse; and rather look dull than clever.

十语九中，未必称奇，一语不中，则愆尤骈集[1]；十谋九成，未必归功，一谋不成，则訾议[2]丛兴。君子所以宁默毋躁，宁拙毋巧。

【中文注释】 ① 愆尤骈集：愆尤，过失和罪过。此处引申为指责。骈集，接二连三而至。
② 訾议：诋毁他人的言论。

【今文解译】 十句话有九句说到点子上，这不足为奇；只要有一句话说不到位，众人便会横加指责，不依不饶。十条计策有九条奏效，这未必讨得了好；只要有一条计策失败，诋毁的声音就会此起彼伏，不绝于耳。这就是为什么君子宁可缄默也不鼓噪多言、宁可笨拙也不自作聪明的缘故。

【English Translation】

You will not necessarily be praised for your prophetic vision even if nine of your ten remarks turn out to be correct. But once you make one incorrect remark, you will be universally condemned. By the same token, you will not necessarily be commended for your brilliance even if you mastermind ten schemes, out of which nine prove effective. But once you put up one ineffective scheme, you will have to face numerous accusing fingers. That is why the accomplished man would rather keep silence than have a loose tongue, and rather look dull than clever.

72. 热心之人　其福亦厚

72. Those willing to help others will be requited with boundless fortune.

天地之气，暖则生，寒则杀。故性气清冷者，受享亦凉薄；惟和气热心之人，其福亦厚，其泽亦长。

【今文解译】 大自然中的气候是不断变化的，温暖的时候则万物生长，寒冷的时候则万物萧条。同理：一个人若是孤傲冷漠的，别人对他也一定是不屑一顾的；只有那些为人和气、做事热心的人，才能享受到厚福，且福泽绵长久远。

【English Translation】

When the substance of heaven and earth is warm it speeds up the growth of all living beings; and when cold it suppresses. Thus we know that if a man gives cold shoulder to others, he will surely receive the same in return. Only those who are brimming with enthusiasm and ready to lend a hand could enjoy boundless fortune and endless gratitude.

73. 天理路广　人欲路窄

73. The path for pursuing the Heavenly principles is wide and narrow is that for following human desires.

天理①路上甚宽，稍游心，胸中便觉广大宏朗；人欲路上甚窄，才寄迹②，眼前俱是荆棘泥涂③。

【中文注释】 ① 天理：自然之理。此处可以理解成为“自然规律”。
② 寄迹：涉足。
③ 泥涂：泥泞的道路。

【今文解译】 探索自然规律的路十分宽广，只需稍稍地用心其中，人的胸怀就会豁然开朗。
追求物质利益的路非常狭窄，双脚刚刚踏入其中，眼前就充满了荆棘和泥泞。

【English Translation】
The path for exploring the laws of nature is wide; so long as you set your mind on it, even a bit, you will find your heart suddenly broadened and enlightened. The road for following human desires is narrow; as soon as you start off, you will find yourself confronted with brambles and mud everywhere.

74. 磨练福久　参勘知真

74. The fortune attained through hardship is everlasting and true, the knowledge acquired after test and verification.

一苦一乐相磨练，练极而成福者，其福始久；一疑一信相参勘，勘极而成知者，其知始真。

【今文解译】 人是需要经过吃苦和享乐交替磨炼的，只有磨炼到了极致，才会有源远流长的福报。
知识是需要反复质疑和验证的，只有验证做到了极致，所学的知识才能转化为真理。

【English Translation】

A person should temper himself by repeatedly experiencing both hardships and enjoyment; only in this way and when it has been done to the utmost can the fortune he attains remain long.

A person should testify his researches by being open to belief and doubt over and over again; only in this way and after every bit of effort has been made can the knowledge he acquires become true.

75. 虚心明理　实心却欲

75. Be open-minded so as to attain righteousness and to dispel mundane desires, be solid-hearted.

心不可不虚，虚则义理①来居；心不可不实，实则物欲不入。

【中文注释】　① 义理：正义，道理。

【今文解译】　要学会听得进别人意见，这样，正确的东西才会在我们心里扎根。要有坚定信念，这样，物质的诱惑才不至于攻破我们的心理防线。

【English Translation】

The heart should be made open to conviction so that righteousness can root over there. Meanwhile, it should also be made solid so that material desires cannot penetrate.

76. 宽宏大量　胸能容物

76. Tolerance breeds breadth of mind.

地至秽者多生物，水至清者常无鱼。故君子当存含垢纳污之量，不可持好洁独行之操。

【今文解译】　越是污秽不堪的地方生物也就越多；过于清澈的水里常常见不到鱼儿。由此可见，一个真正的君子应该要有容人过失的雅量，切不可因独善其身而孤芳自赏。

【English Translation】

Where the place is extremely dirty there likely breed organisms aplenty. Where the water is too clear there are always no fish. So the accomplished man should be tolerant of others' mistakes, and should not merely content himself with his own purity and moral integrity.

77. 多病未羞　无病是忧

77. It is not a shame to have made many mistakes, but a worry to deny the mistakes ever made.

泛驾之马①可就驰驱，跃冶之金终归型范。只一优游不振②，便终身无个进步。白沙③云："为人多病未足羞，一生无病是吾忧。"真确论也。

【中文注释】

① 泛驾之马：泛驾，翻车。泛驾之马，此处喻野性十足、难于驾驭的马。

② 优游不振：即游手好闲，萎靡不振。

③ 白沙：陈献章，广东新会人，明代学者。晚年隐居新会东白沙里，被世人称为"白沙先生"。

【今文解译】

野性十足的马匹驯服后就可以供人驱驰，溅出熔炉的金属溶液收集起来还可以重新回炉。做人游手好闲，不思进取，就必然一辈子庸庸碌碌，无所建树。白沙先生说得好："一个人有这样那样的毛病并不可怕，可怕的是这个人觉得自己没毛病。"真是一语中的！

【English Translation】

A wild horse can be tamed for ride. Spattered metal can be picked up and put back into the mould again. As for a man, if he passes his days just in idleness and low spirits, he will never make any progress. Mr. Baisha* said, "It is not a shame if one recognizes that he has made many mistakes. What worries me most is that one claims not to have made any mistakes in his life." How true the phrases are!

【English Annotation】

* Mr. Baisha: Chen Xianzhang (1428-1500), a man of letters in the Ming Dynasty (1368-1644). He lived as a hermit in his later years in Baishali, eastern Xinhui in Guangdong Province, hence styled. He had written many impressive poems and essays.

78. 一念贪私　坏了一生

78. A selfish desire will spoil the virtue one has accumulated over lifetime.

人只一念贪私，便销刚为柔，塞智为昏，变恩为惨，染洁为污，坏了一生人品。故古人以不贪为宝，所以度越[①]一世。

【中文注释】　① 度越：超越物质欲念。

【今文解译】　人只要一有贪私的欲念，他的刚正就会变成柔弱，他的智慧就会变成昏聩，他的仁慈就会变成冷酷，他的高洁就会变成污秽，甚而至于一世的人品就此被败坏殆尽。古人之所以以不贪为宝，进而一辈子活得潇洒超脱，道理就在于此。

【English Translation】

So long as a slight selfish desire emerges into a man's mind, his uprightness will become weakened and yielding, his intelligence dulled and invalid, his benevolent nature degenerated and cold, his pure aspiration sullied and unworthy. — And as a result, the virtue he has accumulated over lifetime will totally be spoiled. That is why the ancients took "Not be covetous" as the discipline to guide themselves aright in surmounting material desires all their lives.

79. 心不所动　焉受诱惑

79. An unswerving heart helps to guard against exterior temptations.

耳目见闻为外贼，情欲意识为内贼。只是主人翁惺惺不昧[①]，独坐中堂[②]，贼便化为家人矣！

【中文注释】 ① 惺惺不昧：保持清醒的头脑和纯净的心灵。惺惺，警惕，清醒。
② 独坐中堂：独自静坐在厅堂中央。此处喻保持定力或不受外界的诱惑和干扰。

【今文解译】 耳朵所听到的，眼睛所看到的，都好比是外贼；情思所向往的，意识所感悟的，都好比是内贼。只要一家之主能保持定力和清醒的头脑，排除诱惑的干扰，这些外贼和内贼就都可以被一个个育化为自己的家人。

【English Translation】

Sounds the ears hear and spots the eyes see may be likened to thieves from without. Emotions and desires may be compared to thieves from within. But so long as you can guard against all the temptations by keeping your heart unswerving, either of them, within or without, can be cultivated into your family members.

80. 保已成业　防将来非

80. Better keep the exploits already gained and prevent mistakes in the future.

图未就之功，不如保已成之业；悔既往之失，不如防将来之非。

【今文解译】 与其谋划未来的事业，不如尽力保持好已经完成的事业。与其追悔过去的失误，不如预防将来可能会发生的错误。

【English Translation】

It is better to preserve the exploits already in hand than to attempt the future ones. Likewise, it is better to prevent possible mistakes in the future than to regret the past ones.

81. 气象高旷　心思缜密

81. As a man’s makings must be dignified, so must his thoughts be deliberate.

气象要高旷，而不可疏狂；心思要缜密，而不可琐屑；趣味要冲淡，而不可偏枯；操守要严明，而不可激烈。

【今文解译】　做人气象要高远旷达，而不可疏狂放浪；思虑要缜密周到，而不可凌乱琐碎；趣味要清淡高雅，而不可偏废枯燥；操守要严明磊落，而不可偏执激烈。

【English Translation】

A man’s makings must be dignified rather than unbridled. His thoughts must be deliberate rather than trifling. His temperament must be mild rather than lopsided. His behavior must be impartial rather than extreme and untrammeled.

82. 风不留声　雁不留影

82. No sound will be heard when the wind is gone; no shadow will remain when a wild goose has passed.

风来疏竹，风过而竹不留声；雁渡寒潭，雁去而潭不留影。故君子事来而心始现，事去而心随空。

【今文解译】　风从稀疏的竹林吹过，风过去了而竹林却未留下风的声音；雁从寒冷的潭水上空飞过，雁飞走了而潭水却未留下雁的身影。因此我们看到：君子总是临事才动用心思，事毕心就又恢复到最初的平静。

【English Translation】

Scattered bamboos rustle in the wind, but there will be no sound left behind when the wind is gone. Wild geese are mirrored on the surface of a cold pond while they fly over, but there will be no shadows remaining when they have passed. Likewise, the accomplished man only activates his mind when something comes up, but as soon as the thing is disposed of his mind will return to stillness again.

83. 君子懿德　中庸之道

83. It is an admirable virtue for an accomplished man to adopt the doctrine of the mean.

清能有容，仁能善断，明不伤察，直不过矫，是谓蜜饯不甜，海味不咸，才是懿德①。

【中文注释】　① 懿德：高贵的品德，即美德。

【今文解译】　清廉但却有包容心，仁慈但却能明断是非，有洞察力但不咄咄逼人，性格直率但不矫情，——这些都是高贵的中庸品质，就像蜜饯虽甜但却不腻味，海鲜虽咸但却不苦涩。

【English Translation】

To be pure and upright in morality, and yet magnanimous in bearing; to be softhearted in handling affairs, and yet acute in decision; to be clear-sighted in observation, and yet not excessive in judgment; to be forthright in character, and yet not aggressive in action; — all these are excellent qualities that are esteemed as the doctrine of the Mean, saying that the candied fruit should not taste too sweet and seafood not too salty.

84. 穷当益工　不失风雅

84. It is a grace not to give up but to try harder in face of destitution.

贫家勤扫地，贫女净梳头，景色虽不艳丽，气度自是风雅。士君子一当穷愁寥落①，奈何辄自废弛②哉?

【中文注释】　① 穷愁寥落：因贫困而忧愁，因失意而潦倒。
② 辄自废弛：动不动就自暴自弃。

【今文解译】　穷人家的地经常打扫得干干净净，穷人家的姑娘天天把头梳得整整齐齐。虽然这并不能给家室增添靓丽，但却能给人以一种自然纯朴的清新感。读书人又怎能一遇到穷愁不解、仕途受阻的逆境就自暴自弃呢?！

【English Translation】

The housewife of a poor family sweeps the floor frequently and its daughter combs her hair neatly and cleanly. Either has nothing to do with luxury, but their doings are still full of natural grace and simple elegance. How can a man of learning be lightly self-abandoned the very moment he encounters destitution and desolation!

85. 未雨绸缪　有备无患

85. Repair the house before it rains and get prepared against want.

闲中不放过，忙处有受用；静中不落空，动处有受用；暗中不欺隐，明处有受用。

【今文解译】 空闲时抓紧时间多学点知识，这样才能在需要时派上用场。

没事时加强自己的真才实干，这样才能在遇事时应对自如。

独处时不做见不得人的事，这样才能在众人面前受到尊重。

【English Translation】

Make good use of time and endeavor to learn something while not busy; thus one will benefit from doing so when needed.

Get well cultivated in talent and intelligence while at ease; thus one will be master of the situation in case of action.

Be not involved in wicked events upon the sly; thus one will be respected on public occasions.

86. 念头起处　切莫放过

86. Never let off a vicious thought the moment it evolves.

念头起处，才觉向欲路上去，便挽从理路上来。一起便觉，一觉便转，此是转祸为福、起死回生的关头，切莫轻易放过。

【今文解译】 发觉贪婪的欲望刚冒头，就要将它拉回到理性的轨道上来。一冒头就发觉，一发觉就使其转换方向，——这是转祸为福、起死回生的紧要关头。切不可轻易放过！

【English Translation】

As soon as a covetous thought comes into being and is sensed approaching the path of material desire, bring it back immediately to the rational path. Sense the covetous thought the moment it arises, and reverse it the moment it is sensed. This is a critical moment to turn bad fortune into good and bring the dying back to life. Never let off such moment.

87. 静闲淡泊　观心证道

87. Only by preserving tranquility, leisure and simplicity can one properly examine man's nature and comprehend the Way of the world.

静中念虑澄澈，见心之真体；闲中气象从容，识心之真机；淡中意趣冲夷①，得心之真味。观心证道②，无如此三者。

【中文注释】 ① 冲夷：冲和平易，谦虚平和。
② 观心证道：佛家用语。观心，反省自悟；证道，修行得道。佛教主张的修为之法。

【今文解译】 平静中产生的念想和思虑最为清澄，因而也最能体现人的品格；悠闲时表现出的气质和形象最为从容，因而也最能反映人的品性；淡泊中拥有的意趣和兴致最为纯粹，因而也最能说明人的品位。所谓反省自悟、修行得道，皆不出以上三个方面。

【English Translation】

The true characters of man's heart can mostly be seen when one bears a clear and pure mind in stillness. The true disposition of man's heart can mostly be perceived when one keeps calm and unhurried at leisure. The true interest of man's heart can mostly be found when one makes oneself courteous and moderate in a simple life. There is no way more desirable than the above three respects to examine man's heart and comprehend the Way of the world.

88. 动中真静　苦中真乐

88. That attained amid noise is tranquility indeed and so is delight that gained in adversity.

静中静非真静，动处静得来，才是性天①之真境②；乐处乐非真乐，苦中乐得来，才是心体③之真机④。

【中文注释】 ① 性天：天性，即人的自然本性。
② 真境：真正的境界。
③ 心体：心里的感受。
④ 真机：真正的自然乐趣。机，机趣，天然的乐趣。

【今文解译】 在安静的环境中保持平静，这不是真正的平静；能在躁动的环境中保持平静，才是由内而外的平静。
在欢快的气氛中保持乐观，这不是真正的乐观；能在艰苦的环境中保持乐观，才是发自内心的乐观。

【English Translation】

The genuine tranquility is not that attained amidst quietude but that attained amidst noisy conditions, which counts as the realm of man's natural characters. The real delight is not that sought on joyous occasions but that sought under adverse circumstances, which counts as the true subtlety of man's hearted feelings.

89. 舍己勿疑　施恩勿报

89. Do not hesitate when you are to sacrifice your own interests and to bestow favors, do not anticipate return.

舍己毋处其疑，处其疑，即所舍之志多愧矣；施人毋责其报，责其报，并所施之心俱非矣。

【今文解译】 既已决心牺牲自己的利益去帮助别人，就不要再犹豫不决；犹豫不决就辱没了慷慨助人的初衷，只会使自己蒙羞。
既已自愿施惠于人，就不能要求别人回报；要求别人回报，施惠的初衷就不再是善愿，施惠的行为也不再是善举。

【English Translation】

The one who is determined to sacrifice his own interests should not hesitate about doing so, for hesitation of this kind would bring shame on his original intent of self-sacrifice.

The one who is going to bestow favors onto others should not anticipate return, for anticipation for return would distort both charity and benefaction.

90. 厚德载福　逸心补劳

90. Great virtue carries fortune with it, while a leisurely mind remedies weariness in body.

天薄我以福，吾厚吾德以迓①之；天劳我以形，吾逸吾心以补之；天厄②我以遇，吾亨吾道以通③之。天且奈我何哉?

【中文注释】 ① 迓：迎接。

② 厄：使受困，使遭受。

③ 通：使通顺。

【今文解译】 上天赐我的福祉不多，我就行善积德以求福报；上天要劳我的筋骨，我就自己给自己减负以补充体能；上天要让我的前行之路充满坎坷，我就增强自己的修为以求通达。做到了这些，上天还能拿我怎样呢?!

【English Translation】

Should the fate make my fortune inadequate, I would increase the store of my virtue to replenish it. Should the fate make my body exhausted in labor, I would relax my mind to reinforce it. Should the fate make my road ahead obstructed, I would enhance my moral principles to smooth it. That way, what, then, can the fate do to me?

91. 天机最神　智巧何益

91. The magic power of Providence is so supernatural that the resources of human beings can do nothing to it.

贞士无心徼福，天即就无心处牖①其衷；憸人②着意避祸，天即就着意中夺其魄。可见天之机权③最神，人之智巧④何益?

【中文注释】 ① 牖：穿壁而成的木窗，通“诱”。此处喻成全。
② 憸人：小人，奸佞之人。
③ 机权：机智权谋。此处喻神力或法力。
④ 智巧：智谋与技巧。

【今文解译】 贞节之士无意为自己祈福，可上天却趁他不注意的时候将福赐予了他，圆了他的心愿；奸佞之人刻意躲避灾祸，可上天却在他拼命躲避灾祸的时候将他的魂魄夺走。由此可见，上天的法力是无边的，而人的智巧在上天面前又有何作为?！

【English Translation】

A faithful man has no intent to pray for happiness, but Providence, without his notice, favors him with it and thus helps him fulfill his wishes. A sinister-minded man does his utmost to shun calamities, but just when he is bent on it, Providence deprives him of his soul and snaps his vitality. It is obvious that the magic power of Providence is supernatural. How can the resources of human beings prevail against it?

92. 人生态度　晚节更重

92. To judge a man's life attitude, it is best to look at his moral integrity in his later years.

声妓①晚景从良②，一世之烟花③无碍；贞妇白头失守，半生之清苦俱非。语云：“看人只看后半截。”真良言也。

【中文注释】 ① 声妓：通常所说的歌舞妓。
② 晚景从良：晚年放弃卖娼生涯，赎身嫁于好人家。

③ 烟花：即妓女。此处指妓女在风月场上的营生。

【今文解译】 风尘女子卖唱一辈子，但是如果晚年的时候能结束这种营生而成为良家妇女，那么风月场上的经历对她今后的生活就不会有什么妨碍；贞节妇人守节一辈子，但是到了晚年若失却了自己的贞节，那么前半生她为守节而吃的苦也就前功尽弃了。俗话说："一个人的节操如何，关键要看他的后半生。"这话说得很有道理！

【English Translation】

Once a courtesan puts an ending to her trade and gets married into a good family in her later years, all she has done before will not hinder her life any more. Once a chaste woman loses her chastity in her later years, all the hardships she has gone through to keep chastity for first half of her life will be in vain. There is a saying like this, "To judge a person, it is better to observe his moral integrity in his later years." Quite a sophisticated remark!

93. 种德施惠　无位公相

93. Cultivating morality and bestowing favors make an ordinary person a duke without rank.

平民肯种德施惠，便是无位的公相；士夫[①]徒贪权市宠[②]，竟成有爵的乞人。

【中文注释】 ① 士夫：即士大夫。此处泛指达官贵人。
② 市宠：争宠。

【今文解译】 普通百姓若肯尽其所能地积德行善，就能成为无爵无位的公卿相国。
达官贵人若一味贪恋权势，倾慕恩宠，最终就会变成有爵有位的乞丐。

【English Translation】

An ordinary person who is willing to cultivate his morality and bestow benevolence on others will be esteemed as a duke though without rank.
A noble official who is only interested in seeking higher rank and more favors

will be looked down upon as a beggar though with title.

94. 积累念难　倾覆思易

94. Keep in mind both the hardships to accumulate wealth and the aptness to ruin it.

问祖宗之德泽，吾身所享者是，当念其积累之难；问子孙之福祉，吾身所贻者是，要思其倾覆之易。

【今文解译】　我们现在所享有的美满幸福生活都是祖辈留给我们的德泽，我们千万要时刻牢记：这一切来之不易。
子孙后代所享的福都是我们这辈子辛苦攒下来的财富，我们可要提醒他们：失去这一切也十分容易。

【English Translation】
The life we are living today is just the bounties our forefathers left over to us. Therefore, we should remember well all the time the hardships they had undergone to accumulate them.
The fortune our descendants are to inherit from us lies in the wealth we have been creating. Therefore, we should constantly remind them of the aptness there might be to squander it.

95. 君子诈善　无异小人

95. An accomplished man pretending to be virtuous is no more than a villain.

君子而诈善，无异小人之肆恶；君子而改节，不及小人之自新。

【今文解译】　君子为欺世盗名而施惠行善，无异于小人为争利益而肆意妄为。
君子为一己私欲而放弃志节，不及小人为重新做人而痛改前非。

【English Translation】

If an accomplished man feigns charity, he is no different from a villain who has done all manners of evil.

If an accomplished man changes his aspiration, he is no better than a scoundrel that has corrected his errors for a fresh start.

96. 家人有过　春风解冻

96. In dealing with the faults of family members, one should act like the spring breeze thawing the frozen land.

家人有过，不宜暴怒，不宜轻弃。此事难言，借他事隐讽之；今日不语，俟来日再警之。如春风解冻，如和气消冰，才是家庭的型范。

【今文解译】　家人有过错，不宜暴跳如雷，怒不可遏，也不要视而不见，置之不理。如果觉得这事不太好开口，那就借其他的事隐晦地予以贬斥和理喻；如果觉得今天不好提这事，那就等来日合适时再规劝和警示。像春风化解冻土，暖湿气候融化冰雪，这才是治家理家应当借鉴的模式。

【English Translation】

In case any of the family members happen to have done something faulty, we should not stamp with fury, nor should we easily let them off as if nothing had happened. If we feel unsuitable to blame them directly, we may draw lessons from others to satirize them metaphorically; and if we cannot find an opportunity to expostulate with them about the faults today, we might as well leave it over until the day available. Just like the vernal breeze thawing the frozen land and the warm climate melting the ice, this is the right way to deal with domestic affairs and a model for household management.

97. 看得圆满　放得宽平

97. Regard the world as perfect, and the world in the heart will be open and fair.

此心常看得圆满，天下自无缺陷之世界；此心常放得宽平，天下自无险侧[①]之人情。

【中文注释】 ① 险侧：险恶邪僻，奸诈。古人常以此形容小人。

【今文解译】 如果自己心里没有什么不满，眼睛所看到的世界自然也就完美无缺了。

如果自己心里能够坦荡泰然，眼睛所看到的世界自然也就没有奸诈了。

【English Translation】

Make a habit of regarding the world as perfect, and then the world in your eyes will naturally become flawless.

Make a habit of regarding the world as open and fair, and then the world in your eyes will naturally become free of evil and craft.

98. 坚守操履　不露锋芒

98. Seek no limelight while persevering in moral cultivation.

澹泊之士，必为浓艳者所疑；检饬[①]之人，多为放肆者所忌。君子处此，固不可少变其操履[②]，亦不可太露其锋芒。

【中文注释】 ① 检饬：做事检点，为人谨慎。

② 操履：操守。指人平时的行为和品德。

【今文解译】 淡泊名利的人必然会被热衷名利的人所猜疑；为人谨慎的人往往会被肆无忌惮的人所忌恨。面对这种情况，君子绝对不可改变自己的操守，也不可过于锋芒毕露。

【English Translation】

It always follows that a man despising fame and wealth should arouse the suspicion of those who are crazy for the same. It is more than common that a man discreet in word and deed should incur the jealousy of those who are reckless and unbridled. In the face of such situations, the worthy man must not change his aspirations, nor must he seek the limelight.

99. 逆境砺志　顺境杀人

99. Adverse circumstances whet aspirations, while favorable ones snap willpower.

居逆境中，周身皆针砭①药石②，砥节砺行而不觉；处顺境内，眼前尽兵刃戈矛，销膏靡骨③而不知。

【中文注释】 ① 针砭：古代治病用的金属针谓“针”，石针谓“砭”。
② 药石：用植物配成的中药谓“药”，用矿物配成的中药谓“石”。
③ 销膏靡骨：销膏，油脂耗尽；靡骨，粉身碎骨。此处均表示危险之意。

【今文解译】 人处于逆境时，就像全身布满了针灸药石，浑然不知自己的操守会因此而得到升华。
人处于顺境时，即使眼前布满了兵刃戈矛，也全然意识不到自己已经陷入危险境地。

【English Translation】

When put into adversity, one would feel as if his whole body were placed in medications and stone needles for acupuncture, definitely not knowing that the refinement of his virtue and conduct is under going.

When riding on the crest of success, even if the path ahead is supposed to be fully covered with swords and dagger-axes, one would not be aware that the mortal danger is approaching.

100. 富贵如火　必将自焚

100. Lust for riches and honor is like raging flames; whoever has it will get burned in the end.

生长富贵丛中的，嗜欲如猛火，权势似烈焰。若不带些清冷气味，其火焰不至焚人，必将自烁矣。

【今文解译】 生养在富贵人家的人，他们的欲望会像火一样猛烈，权势会像烈焰一样灼人。如果他们不能以清醒的态度约束自己，那么，即使猛火烈焰焚烧不到别人，也必将伤及他们自身。

【English Translation】

Those who were born and have grown up in a clan of riches and honor are mostly like this: their desires for material gains seem as fierce as prairie fire and their lust for power and influence as scorching as raging flames. If they do not harmonize their hearts with coolness, the fire and flames may unlikely burn others, but would burn themselves for sure.

101. 精诚所至　金石为开

101. Complete sincerity of a man can affect metal and stone.

人心一真，便霜可飞，城可陨，金石可镂。若伪妄[1]之人，形骸徒具，真宰[2]已亡，对人则面目可憎，独居则形影自愧。

【中文注释】 ① 伪妄：伪，虚伪；妄，胡作非为。
② 真宰：上天的主宰。此处喻人的灵魂。

【今文解译】 一颗赤诚的心能使六月天里降霜飞雪，使城墙因有人哭泣而倾覆，使金属和石头都变成刻刀下的雕琢物。虚伪而胡作非为的人，忝有一副人的皮囊，而灵魂却早已不在。大庭广众之下，他们的面目令人厌恶；一个人独处时，他们又不免为自己的形影感到羞愧。

【English Translation】

Complete sincerity of a man could let frostworks fall in June, make city walls collapse by wail and get metal and stone affected. But for a treacherous, hypocritical man, it seems that his soul has already departed and only his body remains. Such a man will disgust people with his repulsive looks while walking in the street and will feel ashamed of himself for his own body and shadow when alone.

102. 文章恰好　人品本然

102. A piece of writing which attains the right extent is the best, and so is the moral character which reflects a man's inborn nature.

文章做到极处，无有他奇，只是恰好；人品做到极处，无有他异，只是本然。

【今文解译】　作文的最高境界没什么奇妙的，就是恰到好处。
做人的最高境界没什么特别的，就是保持本色。

【English Translation】

When a piece of writing is made to have reached the acme of perfection, what counts is not how peculiar its style appears but the right way in which it is expressed and the right extent it has attained.

When a man has refined his moral standing to the loftiest realm, what deserves to be admired is not how outstandingly he behaves but how exactly he acts in accord with his pure and honest inborn nature.

103. 能看得破　才认得真

103. Only by seeing through the world of illusions can one understand the world of realities clearly.

以幻境[①]言，无论功名富贵，即肢体亦属委形[②]；以真境[③]言，无论父母兄弟，即万物皆吾一体。人能看得破，认得真，才可以任天下之负担，亦可脱世间之缰锁[④]。

【中文注释】　① 幻境：虚幻的世界。
② 委形：《列子·天瑞》："吾身非吾有，孰有之哉？曰：是天地之委也。"意思是说我的形体是上天赋予的，并非是我自己的。
③ 真境：真实的世界。
④ 缰锁：缰绳与枷锁。

【今文解译】　从虚幻的角度看，所有的功名富贵都只是假象，就连上天赋予我的躯体也是假象；从真实的角度看，家里的父母兄弟与我是一体的，就连世界上其他的一切与我也是一体的。一个人只有看得透彻，认得真切，才可担负起天下的重任，才有能力摆脱世俗的束缚与羁绊。

【English Translation】

From the point of view of the world of illusions, not only riches and honor are false appearances but also our bodies are merely the shapes given by the heaven. And from the point of view of the world of realities, not only the parents and brothers but also all things on earth are one with me. Therefore, in dealing with the world, only by penetrating the illusions and understanding clearly the realities can one take on social responsibilities and shake off the worldly bindings.

104. 美味快意　享用五分

104. Foods agreeable to the taste and things pleasant to the mind are all desirable if only half assumed.

爽口之味，皆烂肠腐骨之药，五分便无殃；快心之事，悉败身丧德之媒，五分便无悔。

【今文解译】 可口的美味跟药一样，吃多了会损伤人的肠胃，如果只是吃个半分饱就不会有伤害之虞了。

可心的事情像一种媒介，受用多了会败身丧德，如果受用一半放弃一半就不会有此遗憾了。

【English Translation】

Foods agreeable to the taste are all like drugs which are liable to hurt intestines and stomach; but if you assume only half of them they will do you no harm.

Amusements pleasant to the mind are all like medium which easily bring forth disgrace and ruin; but if you go only half way in the enjoyment they will invite no regret.

105. 忠恕待人　养德远害

105. Whoever is faithful and tolerant in getting along with others can refine his morality and keep clear of calamities.

不责人小过，不发①人阴私②，不念人旧恶。三者可以养德，亦可以远害。

【中文注释】　① 发：揭发，泄露。
② 阴私：不愿公开的个人秘密，亦可作“隐私”解。

【今文解译】　不责备别人的小过小错，不泄露别人的个人隐私，不记恨别人的旧日恶行。做到以上这三点，不仅可以提高自己的道德修养，而且还可以远离祸害。

【English Translation】

Do not censure others with their minor faults. Do not disclose others' privacy. Do not bear in mind old grievances. Whoever knows how to practice the above three taboos can nourish his moral standings and stay out of calamities as well.

106. 持身勿轻　用心勿重

106. Not be frivolous in personal behaviors nor be too rigid in attaining personal objectives.

士君子持身①不可轻，轻则物能挠我，而无悠闲镇定之趣；用意②不可重，重则我为物泥③，而无潇洒活泼之机。

【中文注释】　① 持身：立身处世之道。具体指言行举止。
② 用意：用心。此处指计较名利得失。
③ 物泥：受物质诱惑所累。

【今文解译】　读书人持身不可太随意，太随意就会因为外界的物质诱惑而失去悠闲淡定的趣味。
名利心不可太重，太重了就会因为受制于外界的物质诱惑而失去潇洒活泼的生气。

【English Translation】

A man of learning should not behave himself with frivolousness; if he does, he will first be perplexed by material temptations from without and then lose the temperament of leisure and composure from within. Meanwhile, he should also not give too much thought to his own interest; if he does, he will first be fettered by material temptations and then be deprived of unrestrained vivacity.

107. 人生百年　不可虚度

107. A man's life-span is only a hundred years long, so one should not idle away his time.

天地有万古，此身[①]不再得；人生只百年，此日[②]最易过。幸生其间者，不可不知有生之乐，亦不可不怀虚生[③]之忧。

【中文注释】 ① 此身：人的肉身。此处喻人的生命。
② 此日：指前半句中提到的“百年”。
③ 虚生：虚度人生。

【今文解译】 天地亘古不变，而人的生命却只有一次；人生一世仅百年而已，而就是这百年也只不过是一眨眼的工夫。有幸来到这人世间，我们切不可不知道拥有生命的幸运，也不可不思虑自己的一生是否会因为碌碌无为而虚度。

【English Translation】

Heaven and earth are everlasting, but the flesh of human beings can never be regenerated. A man's life-span is only a hundred years long and will pass easily with the lapse of time. Those who are fortunate to have come to live in this world should not be unaware of the bliss for being given life, nor should they disregard the concern that idling away time is censurable.

108. 德怨两忘　恩仇俱泯

108. Better make others forget both gratitude and resentment and let both bounties and enmities fall into oblivion.

怨因德彰，故使人德我，不若德怨之两忘；仇因恩立，故使人知恩，不若恩仇之俱泯。

【今文解译】 行善不周会引起怨恨，所以，与其让人对我感恩戴德，不如让他们把感恩与怨恨一起忘掉。

施惠不匀会产生仇恨，所以，与其让人知道我的恩惠，不如把仇恨与恩惠一起都化为乌有。

【English Translation】

The rising of men's resentment is the result of partial benefaction. So when you show your benevolence it is better to let others forget both gratitude and resentment than to expect gratitude from them.

The being of men's enmity is the product of different bounties. So when you bestow bounties on others it is better to let both bounties and enmities be buried in oblivion than to make them aware of your bounties.

109. 持盈履满　君子兢兢

109. A worthy man should be circumspect in his heyday.

老来疾病，都是壮时招的；衰后罪孽，都是盛时造的。故持盈履满[①]，君子尤兢兢焉[②]。

【中文注释】 ① 持盈履满：指功成名就，事业圆满，生活幸福。此处指人生的鼎盛时期。

② 兢兢焉：小心翼翼的样子。

【今文解译】 老年时得的疾病，都是少壮时不注意而留下的病根；失意时所遭的罪，都是得势时造下的孽。所以说，事业有成、功德圆满时，君子尤其要谨慎行事，好自为之。

【English Translation】

Diseases in old age are the cause of carelessness in youth. Sufferings in decline are the aftermath of wickedness in prosperity. So, the worthy man should be especially circumspect in his heyday.

110. 扶公却私　种德修身

110. Be selfless by rendering assistance to the public and cultivate your moral integrity by accumulating benevolence.

市私恩[①]，不如扶公议[②]；结新知，不如敦旧好；立荣名，不如种隐德[③]；尚奇节，不如谨庸行[④]。

【中文注释】 ① 市私恩：出于私心而施恩行善。

② 扶公议：字面意思是“维护公众言论”。此处理解为“民心”“民意”或“公众利益”则更好，更贴近原文本意。

③ 隐德：暗地里所做的好事。也即“阴德”。

④ 庸行：平淡无奇的作为。

【今文解译】 与其出于私心而施恩与人，不如做些扶持公益的实事。与其泛泛地到处结交新朋友，不如与老朋友多叙叙旧。与其为自己扬名，不如暗地里帮助那些需要帮助的人。与其为猎奇而标新立异，不如就甘于平凡而谨言慎行。

【English Translation】

It is better to act in favor of the public interests than to bestow favors for selfish motives.

It is better to enhance the relationship with old friends than to make new acquaintances.

It is better to accumulate virtues without attracting others' attention than to seek personal reputation.

It is better to do something commonplace but good than to aspire after fantastic achievements.

111. 公论不犯　权门不沾

111. Never go against a popular verdict nor be associated with those from a circle of bigwigs.

公平正论，不可犯手，一犯，则贻羞万世；权门[①]私窦[②]，不可著脚，一著，则玷污终身。

【中文注释】 ① 权门：有权有势的人家。
② 私窦：玩弄权势，营私舞弊。

【今文解译】 公平公正是社会大众的共识，千万不要去触犯这个共识，一旦触犯，就会遗臭万年。
有权有势的人家好玩弄权势，千万不要涉足其中，一旦涉足，一世便与清白无缘。

【English Translation】
Never go against a popular verdict; to do so is to bring eternal blame and shame on yourself.
Never set foot in places where the bigwigs are playing with power and influence; to do so is to sully your own reputation for life.

112. 直躬不畏人忌　无恶不惧人毁

112. Fear no jealousy when keeping upright nor slander when having no vicious deeds.

曲意而使人喜，不若直躬而使人忌；无善而致人誉，不若无恶而致人毁。

【今文解译】 与其违背意愿去讨好别人，不如刚正不阿而使人忌恨。
与其未做善事而受人赞扬，不如未做恶事而招人诋毁。

【English Translation】
To ingratiate yourself with others by going against your own will is less desirable than to invite jealousy by preserving your uprightness.
To win praise by having no philanthropic acts is less desirable than to court slander by having no vicious deeds.

113. 从容处变　剀切规友

113. Be calm and unhurried while facing an unforeseen event and while admonishing a friend, be firm and pertinent.

处父兄骨肉之变，宜从容，不宜激烈；遇朋友交游[1]之失，宜剀切[2]，不宜优游[3]。

【中文注释】 ① 交游：结交朋友；人际往来。
② 剀切：切实。此处指恳切规劝。
③ 优游：悠闲游乐。此处指事不关己，听之任之。

【今文解译】 面对父兄骨肉之间的过节，我们应该从容应对，而不应该态度生硬激化矛盾。
遇到朋友交游方面的不慎，我们应该严肃规劝，而不应该置身事外听之任之。

【English Translation】

When something unexpected has happened among the family members, we should keep calm and unhurried in our dealings rather than act indignantly to intensify the situation.
When aware that a friend of ours errs in his daily association, we should give him firm, pertinent admonition rather than treat it with indifference.

114. 大处着眼　小处着手

114. Set your mind on the general goal but put your hand to minor details.

小处不渗漏[1]，暗处不欺隐[2]，末路[3]不怠荒[4]，才是个真正英雄。

【中文注释】 ① 渗漏：指纰漏或过失。
② 欺隐：做见不得人的事。
③ 末路：到了极其困难的境地。
④ 怠荒：松懈，泄气，消极。

【今文解译】 真正的英雄好汉是这样的：不忽略细枝末节的小事，不在人背后搞小动作，即使穷途末路也决不懈怠。

【English Translation】

A real hero is he who is neither the least negligent on minor details nor dishonest even if behind people's back, and never discouraged in an awkward predicament.

115. 爱重为仇　薄极成喜

115. Love taken to its maximum may convert to enmity, while a trivial kindness may result in heart-felt contentment.

千金难结一时之欢[1]，一饭竟致终身之感[2]。盖爱重反为仇，薄极反成喜也。

【中文注释】 ① 千金难结一时之欢：由“千金难买一笑”引申而来。
② 一饭竟致终身之感：韩信年轻时家境贫寒，经常饥一顿饱一顿。淮水边上有个为人家漂洗纱絮的老妇人，人称“漂母”，见韩信可怜，就把自己的饭菜分给他吃。天天如此，从不间断。韩信深受感动。韩信被封为淮阴侯后始终没忘漂母的一饭之恩，派人四处寻找，最后以千金相赠。这个感人的故事自古流传至今。

【今文解译】 有时候撒尽千金也换不来真心相许的一时之欢，有时候一碗饭竟能让人感念一辈子。由此可知，越是相爱的人就越是容易反目成仇，小小的一点恩惠却最终反而能变成让人惊喜的福报。

【English Translation】

Sometimes a thousand pieces of gold can scarcely get in return a momentary joy; sometimes a paltry kindness like offering a simple meal earns a lifelong appreciation.

It always follows that love taken to its maximum can convert to enmity, while a trivial bounty can result in heart-felt contentment.

116. 藏巧于拙　以屈为伸

116. Hide ingenuity in clumsiness and take recoil as extension.

藏巧于拙，用晦[1]而明[2]，寓清于浊，以屈为伸，真涉世之一壶[3]，藏身之三窟[4]也。

【中文注释】 ① 晦：隐藏。此处指隐藏才能，收敛锋芒。
② 明：聪明。
③ 壶：通"瓠"，意即"葫芦"。葫芦质轻浮于水。古时候，人们乘船渡河身上往往系个葫芦，这样，万一沉船，溺水者就可凭借它脱离危险。所以，葫芦素有"腰舟"之美称，也被视作救生法宝。
④ 三窟：由"狡兔三窟"而来，原意指逃生有方。

【今文解译】 宁可笨拙些，也不要显得聪明过人；宁可收敛些，也不要锋芒毕露；宁可随便些，也不要自命清高；宁可退缩些，也不要咄咄逼人。——这些都是为人处世、安身立命的法宝。

【English Translation】

Hide ingenuity in clumsiness, show light by appearing to be obscure, let clarity have its home in muddiness, and take recoil as extension. — These are the magic tactics for a person to get on with his pursuit and shelter himself from harm.

117. 居安虑患　处变当坚

117. Beware of danger at a time of peace and stick it out in face of disasters.

衰飒[1]的景象就在盛满[2]中，发生的机缄[3]即在零落[4]内。故君子居安宜操一心以虑患，处变当坚百忍以图成。

【中文注释】 ① 衰飒：枯萎，凋落。此处喻衰败之意。
② 盛满：巅峰，鼎盛。
③ 机缄：此处喻新的生机，也可理解成转机。
④ 零落：衰落，衰败。

【今文解译】 衰败之象往往出现在事业处于鼎盛的时候，蓬勃的生机常常孕育于万物凋零的景象之中。因此，作为一个君子：生活安逸时，一定要有忧患意识；事态有变时，一定要坚定自己的意志，以争取最后的成功。

【English Translation】

Every decline conceals itself in the great prosperity. Every vigorous lease of life breeds in withering seasons. So, it is imperative for a wise man to guard against possible danger at a time of peace, and go with presence of mind to win success in the face of disasters.

118. 奇人乏识　独行无恒

118. A man fascinated by novelties lacks profound knowledge and that inclined to isolation has no perseverance.

惊奇喜异者，无远大之识；苦节[1]独行[2]者，非恒久之操。

【中文注释】 ① 苦节：过于约束自己。
② 独行：离群索居。

【今文解译】 为了猎奇而标新立异的人，一定没有高深的学问和远大的见识。
为了修行养德而遁世苦绝的人，一定还不具备历久弥坚的操守。

【English Translation】

Those who are fascinated by wonders and novelties certainly have no profound learning and outstanding knowledge.
Those who are inclined to ascetic practices and complete isolation surely have no perseverance in moral cultivation.

119. 放下屠刀　立地成佛

119. A butcher becomes a Buddha the moment he drops his cleaver.

当怒火欲水正腾沸处，明明知得，又明明犯著。知的是谁？犯的又是谁？此处能猛然转念，邪魔便为真君[1]矣。

【中文注释】 ① 真君：真宰。

【今文解译】 当一个人的愤怒像火焰一样喷射、欲望像开水一样沸腾时，他往往克制不了自己，心里明知不可为但却偏要为之。明知不可为的是谁？而偏要为之的又是谁？此时若能猛然醒悟，恢复平静，纵然恶魔也会变成令人景仰的善主。

【English Translation】

When a man's rage blazes out like fire and his desires bubble up like boiling water, he would mostly act recklessly. He is clear about what he is doing but only unwilling to restrain himself. Who is it that knows the recklessness clearly? And who is it that would just persist in doing so? If, at this moment, he can resolutely calm down and stop the attempt to commit a folly, then the monster, however vicious, can be transformed into an amiable master.

120. 毋形人短 毋忌人能

120. Do not counter others' demerits with your own merits, nor make yourself jealous of others' talents for your own incompetence.

毋偏信而为奸所欺，毋自任[①]而为气所使，毋以己之长而形人之短[②]，毋因己之拙而忌人之能。

【中文注释】 ① 自任：自以为是，不把别人放在眼里。
② 形人之短：（用自己的长处）去对照别人的短处。

【今文解译】 不要因为偏听偏信而被奸诈的小人蒙骗，也不要总以为自己什么都正确而意气用事。
不要用自己的长处去和别人的短处比高低，也不要因为自己笨拙而妒忌别人的才华。

【English Translation】

Do not heed and trust only one side so as to avoid being cheated by trickeries.
Do not be self-opinionated so as to avoid abandoning yourself to emotions.
Do not counter others' shortcomings with your own strong points.
Do not be jealous of others' talents for your own incompetence.

121. 己所不欲　勿施于人

121. Do not impose on others what you yourself do not desire.

人之短处，要曲为弥缝①，如暴而扬之②，是以短攻短；人有顽固，要善为化诲，如忿而疾之③，是以顽济顽。

【中文注释】 ① 曲为弥缝：婉转地掩饰别人的缺点。
② 暴而扬之：揭露扩散别人的缺点。
③ 忿而疾之：痛斥别人的缺点。

【今文解译】 别人的短处我们要设法婉转地予以弥补；如果四处张扬他们的短处,这完全是在用自己的短处攻击别人的短处。别人的顽劣我们要循循善诱慢慢开导；如果因为怒其不争而怨恨他们，这完全是在用自己的顽劣对付别人的顽劣。

【English Translation】
When someone is found to have some shortcomings, it is better to help him cover them up in a roundabout way. If you expose them to the public, then you are simply using your own shortcomings to counter his.
When someone is found to be of stubbornness, it is better to help him dissolve it with the best of your intentions. If you accuse him with indignation, then you are simply using your own stubbornness to counter his.

122. 阴者勿交　傲者勿言

122. Never befriend an insidious fellow nor talk too much to an arrogant guy.

遇沉沉不语之士①，且莫输心②；见悻悻自好之人③，应须防口④。

【中文注释】 ① 沉沉不语之士：阴沉寡言的人。
② 输心：把心里话说出来。
③ 悻悻自好之人：愤愤不平、傲气十足的人。
④ 防口：说话谨慎。

【今文解译】 如遇性格阴沉而寡言少语的人，切莫说掏心窝子的话。

如遇性格自傲而满腹牢骚的人，切记说话要小心谨慎。

【English Translation】

In the event that you meet a sinister, evasive fellow, you should not open your mind to him.

In the event that you meet an indignant, arrogant guy, you should be careful about what you are going to say.

123. 调节情绪　一张一弛

123. A man's mood should be timely adjusted by alternating tension with relaxation.

念头昏散[①]处，要知提醒；念头吃紧时，要知放下。不然恐去昏昏之病[②]，又来憧憧之扰[③]矣。

【中文注释】　① 昏散：精神涣散，心不在焉。

② 昏昏之病：昏昏沉沉、萎靡不振的迷乱状态。

③ 憧憧之扰：憧憧，往来不定，摇曳不定。憧憧之扰，心神不定的困扰。

【今文解译】　当头脑昏昏沉沉、注意力集中不起来时，要知道及时使自己清醒；当心里烦躁、情绪紧张时，要知道及时让自己放下。不然的话，恐怕头脑不清醒的毛病刚好，心神不定的毛病就又找上门来。

【English Translation】

In the event that you feel dazed and absent-minded, you must know how to calm down and keep a level head. In the event that you feel plagued and strained, you must know how to put aside the work on hand for relaxation. Otherwise, you might be dazed one moment and become distracted the next.

124. 君子之心　毫无障塞

124. The heart of an accomplished man should go freely without a momentary blockade.

霁日晴天，倏变为迅雷震电；疾风怒雨，倏转为朗月晴空。气机何尝一毫凝滞？太虚何尝一毫障塞？人心之体，亦当如是。

【今文解译】 刚才还艳阳高照、碧空万里，转眼间就电闪雷鸣、乌云密布；刚才还疾风怒吼、暴雨连天，转眼间就明月当空、乾坤朗朗。大自然有规律的运动何曾有过片刻的停歇？无边无际的宇宙又何曾有过丝毫的阻塞？人的心性跟大自然和宇宙也是一样的。

【English Translation】

An azure sky may suddenly be messed up by swift thunderclap and flashing lightning. Likewise, a stormy night may suddenly turn into a scene brimming with bright moonlight. Has there ever been any suspension of Nature's vitality even for a short while? Or has there ever been a momentary blockade of the universe? The disposition of man's heart is more or less the same.

125. 智慧识魔　意志斩妖

125. To discern the inner demons depends on wit and to decapitate them, on willpower.

胜私制欲[1]之功，有曰识不早、力不易者，有曰识得破、忍不过者。盖识是一颗照魔的明珠，力是一把斩魔的慧剑[2]，两不可少也。

【中文注释】 ① 胜私制欲：战胜自我，抑制物欲。
② 慧剑：佛家将智慧比喻成能斩断一切世俗烦恼的利剑。

【今文解译】 战胜自己的私心和克服自己的欲念是一件需要下功夫的事情。有的人说：没有早早地认识到这个问题的严重性，所以未能克服；有的人说：已经认识到这个问题，但是自己还是拒绝不了诱惑。众所周知，人的洞察力好比一颗照鉴妖魔的明珠，而人的意志力犹若一柄斩妖除魔的智慧之剑。要想战胜私心、克服欲念，这两样东西缺一不可。

【English Translation】

When people fail to overcome their selfish motives and material desires, they always find excuses like: they failed only because they hadn't perceived the harm therein early enough; or they were unable to withstand the temptation thereof even though they had attained such perception. Thus we say that man's perception is like an illuminating pearl with which we discern the demons hidden in our hearts and man's willpower is like a sharp sword with which we decapitate the demons discerned. Neither can be dispensed with.

126. 宽而容人　不动声色

126. Be tolerant towards the folly of others and stay calm and collected when offended.

觉人之诈，不形于言；受人之侮，不动于色。此中有无穷意味，亦有无穷受用。

【今文解译】 见人行欺诈之事但不把自己心里的反感放在嘴上；受人欺侮但不把自己的愤怒情绪挂在脸上。——这样的处事方式，其中的意味无比深长，其中的受用无穷无尽。

【English Translation】

When you are aware that someone is cheating you, do not let your displeasure slip from the mouth. When someone is insulting you, do not have your indignation shown on the face. These are the ways by which you can attain profound implications and inexhaustible advantages over there.

127. 英雄豪杰　经受锤炼

127. Heroes must be tempered in hardships.

横逆困穷是锻炼豪杰的一副炉锤。能受其锻炼，则身心交益；不受其锻炼，则身心交损。

【今文解译】 突然降临的挫折和艰难是锻炼英雄豪杰的熔炉。经得住锻炼的，则身心俱益；经不住锻炼的，则身心俱损。

【English Translation】

Unforeseen misfortune, adversity, hardship and poverty are all a furnace in which heroes and eminent personages are steeled. If they can withstand these tribulations, it will be beneficial to their bodies and minds; if they cannot, it will get both of them injured.

128. 天地父母 万物敦睦

128. Heaven and earth, by acting like father and mother, can harmonize myriad things.

吾身一小天地也，使喜怒不愆①，好恶有则，便是燮理②的功夫；天地一大父母也，使民无怨咨③，物无氛疹④，亦是敦睦的气象。

【中文注释】 ① 不愆：愆，过失或失当。不愆即不失常。
② 燮理：调和治理。
③ 怨咨：怨恨；怨言。
④ 氛疹：因凶恶之气而发生的不祥或灾祸。

【今文解译】 人的身体就是个小天地，如能做到喜怒不失常，好恶有原则，这便是成就和谐人生的功夫了。
天地是人类的父母，如百姓没有怨言，万事万物皆和和美美，这便是天上人间的太平景象了。

【English Translation】

Man's self can be compared to a tiny world. One who knows well about ruling his passions of pleasure and anger and regulating his feelings of likes and dislikes will be master of his own behavior.

Heaven and earth can be compared to the father and mother of all people and all things. If they let all people free from resentment and all things free from disasters, the picture they present would undoubtedly be brimming with peace and harmony.

129. 戒疏于虑 警伤于察

129. Advisable are admonition to negligence and counsel to overcaution.

“害人之心不可有，防人之心不可无。”此戒疏于虑也。“宁受人之欺，勿逆人之诈[①]。”此警伤于察也。二语并存，精明而浑厚[②]矣。

【中文注释】 ① 逆人之诈: 预测别人的奸诈。

② 浑厚: 淳朴, 敦厚。

【今文解译】 “害人之心不可有, 防人之心不可无。”这条戒律是说给那些疏于防范的人听的。“宁受人之欺, 勿逆人之诈。”这句警言是说给那些过于谨慎的人听的。若能将这两句话都铭记于心, 人也就兼备了精明和敦厚两种品质。

【English Translation】

“One should never intend to do harm to others, but should have the heart to guard against the harm others might do to him.” This advice is taken as an admonition to those who neglect precautions. “It is better to risk being deceived than to predict the deceiving intentions of others.” This advice is taken as a counsel to those who are overcautious. By paying equal attention to the two pieces of advice one will surely be a man of smart sagacity and upright honesty.

130. 明辨是非 大局为重

130. Distinguish clearly between right and wrong, and take the interests of the whole into account.

毋因群疑[①]而阻独见[②]，毋任己意而废人言，毋私小惠而伤大体，毋借公论以快私情。

【中文注释】 ① 群疑: 众人的猜疑。

② 阻独见: 妨碍自己的见解。

【今文解译】 切不可因为质疑多了就不敢提出自己的见解。

切不可因为自己有主张就不准别人发表意见。

切不可为了谋取一己之私而损害大家的利益。
切不可为了达到个人目的而假借公众的舆论。

【English Translation】

Never let the masses' suspicious attitude interfere with your personal views.
Never forbid others to express themselves while sticking to your own ideas.
Never infringe on the common interests for the sake of your private gains.
Never try to achieve your own goals by making advantage of the public opinion.

131. 亲善杜谗　除恶防祸

131. Prevent slanders when befriending good men and avoid curse when getting rid of vicious men.

善人未能急亲，不宜预扬①，恐来谗谮之奸②；恶人未能轻去，不宜先发③，恐遭媒孽④之祸。

【中文注释】 ① 预扬：事先或过早予以宣扬。
② 谗谮之奸：说别人坏话的小人。
③ 先发：时机尚未成熟就揭露。
④ 媒孽：酒母。此处指酿成祸害。

【今文解译】 对好人不可急于亲近，也不宜在完全了解他之前表扬他，以防奸邪小人前来进献谗言。
对坏人不可轻易除去，也不宜在时机尚未成熟时将他发落，以防他寻衅滋事报复陷害。

【English Translation】

When associating with a good man, one should not be too anxious to show endearment to him, nor should he praise him for his virtue prematurely, for fear that it may stir up the slanders of evil men.
When getting rid of a vicious man, one should not dismiss him too willingly, nor should he reveal his offences before the time is ripe, for fear that it may give birth to the curse of revenge and frame-up.

132. 培养节操　磨炼本领

132. A man’s morality should be cultivated through hardships and his ability fostered in the process of surmounting difficulties.

青天白日的节义，自暗室屋漏中培来；旋乾转坤的经纶，自临深履薄[1]处缫[2]出。

【中文注释】　① 临深履薄：喻面临危情时的小心谨慎。
② 缫：把蚕茧浸泡在热水里，抽出蚕丝。

【今文解译】　像青天白日一样光明磊落的气节，是在艰苦条件和环境中培养出来的。
像扭转乾坤这样的经世才干，是靠险境中谨慎行事渐渐磨炼出来的。

【English Translation】

Man’s moral integrity, as bright as the sunshine in blue sky, is cultivated in places unknown to the public and full of hardships.

Man’s ability to reverse the course of events and take on important task is gradually steeled in the process of surmounting various difficulties and dangers, like reeling silk from cocoons.

133. 父慈子孝　伦常天性

133. Fathers’ kindness to their sons and sons’ filialness to their fathers are one of the natural bonds and ethical relationships between the members of a family.

父慈子孝，兄友弟恭，纵做到极处，俱是合当如此，着不得一丝感激的念头。如施者任德，受者怀恩，便是路人，便成市道矣。

【今文解译】　父母爱子女，子女孝顺父母，兄弟姐妹互敬互爱，这一切即使做到极致也都是理所当然的，不应该存有任何互相感激的念头。假如施惠者以恩人自居，而受惠者念念不忘感恩戴德，家人岂不成了路人，亲情岂不成了市井交易？！

【English Translation】

It goes naturally that fathers are kind to their sons and sons filial to their fathers, and that elder brothers care for younger brothers and younger brothers respect elder brothers. It is nothing but part of their duties. There is no need for them to express gratitude to each other even if they all conduct themselves so well or even to the utmost. If they fancy themselves as benefactors after bestowing favors or feel indebted for the benefits they have received, they would become strangers in the street or traders on the marketplace.

134. 不夸妍洁　谁能丑污

134. Boast of your beauty and cleanliness not, and nobody can call you ugly or dirty.

有妍必有丑为之对。我不夸妍，谁能丑我？有洁必有污为之仇[1]。我不好洁，谁能污我？

【中文注释】　① 为之仇：与之形成对照。前句的“为之对”也是同样意思。

【今文解译】　在这个世界上，有美丽就一定会有丑陋与之相对应。如果我自己不夸自己美丽，又有谁会嫌我丑陋呢？
在这个世界上，有洁净就一定会有污秽与之相对照。如果我自己不称自己洁净，又有谁会说我污秽呢？

【English Translation】

Where there is beauty there must be ugliness to contrast with. If I do not boast of my beauty, how can I be called ugly?
Where there is cleanliness there must be dirt on the opposite. If I do not boast of my cleanliness, how can I be called dirty?

135. 富多炎凉　亲多妒忌

135. Fickleness is common among the rich and so is jealousy between kinsfolk.

炎凉之态，富贵更甚于贫贱；妒忌之心，骨肉尤狠于外人。此处若不当以冷肠，御以平气，鲜不日坐烦恼障中矣。

【今文解译】 世态炎凉，富贵人家要比贫苦人家表现得尤为明显；攀比嫉恨，至亲骨肉之间要比陌生人之间做得更加无情。这种情况下，一个人如果不能以冷静和克制的态度加以应对，就免不了会被烦恼折腾得永无宁日。

【English Translation】

Inconstancy of human relationships is more common among the rich and noble than among the poor and humble. Psychology of jealousy is more biting between kinsfolk than between strangers. Under such circumstances, if people do not go with cool-headed approach nor restrain themselves with ease, few of them could be free from everyday vexation.

136. 功过要清　恩仇勿明

136. Merits and demerits should be distinctly demarcated, while bounties and enmities should not.

功过不容少混，混则人怀惰隳[①]之心；恩仇不可太明，明则人起携贰之志。

【中文注释】 ① 惰隳：慵懒堕落。

【今文解译】 功和过不容混淆，混淆了，那些原本勤勤恳恳的人就会变得懒惰起来且不思进取。

恩与仇不可太分明，太分明了，那些跟随你左右的属下就会心怀不满并萌生去意。

【English Translation】

Merits and demerits must not be slightly obscured; otherwise, people who work diligently will become sluggish and lose enterprising spirit. Whereas, bounties and enmities should not be too distinguished; otherwise, subjects who follow you around will become unfaithful and fall away.

137. 位盛危至　德高谤兴

137. Rank of nobility too elevated is easy to bring about dangers and so is virtue too outstanding to court slanders.

爵位不宜太盛，太盛则危；能事①不宜尽毕，尽毕则衰；行谊不宜过高，过高则谤兴而毁来。

【中文注释】　① 能事：能力和本事。

【今文解译】　官运不宜太亨通，太亨通了就会招来危险。
才华不宜太显露，太显露了就会导致衰退。
行事不宜太高调，太高调了就会遭人毁谤。

【English Translation】

The rank of nobility should not be too elevated; if too elevated there would be dangers.

Talent and energy should not be fully used; if fully used there would be exhaustion and decline.

Words and deeds should not stand too aloof; if too aloof it will easily court slanders.

138. 阴恶祸深　阳善功小

138. Evil deeply hidden produces more harm, while good widely advertised brings less benefit.

恶忌阴，善忌阳。故恶之显者祸浅，而隐者祸深；善之显者功小，而隐者功大。

【今文解译】　暗地里做坏事而不被人发现是最让人担心的，为了让人看到而做好事是最要不得的。因此有理由这么认为：坏事做在明里其祸害就会小些，做在暗里其祸害就会大些；好事做在明里其功德就会小些，做在暗里其功德就会大些。

【English Translation】

It is a fear that evil is done behind people's back and good done in the sight of all. That is why we say that it will bring in less harm when evil is done openly, but more harm when done on the sly; and that it will produce less benefit when good is done overtly, but more benefit when done in secret.

139. 以德御才　恃才败德

139. Rule your talent with virtue, knowing that unduly relying on talent spoils your virtue.

德者才之主，才者德之奴。有才无德，如家无主而奴用事矣，几何[1]不魍魉[2]猖狂？！

【中文注释】 ① 几何：用于反问句，表示“没有多少”或“有几个”。此处可理解为“哪能”或“哪有”。
② 魍魉：传说中的鬼怪。

【今文解译】 品德是才能的主人，才能是品德的奴仆。一个人光有才能而无品德，就好比一个家庭没有主心骨而尽由着奴仆自行其是，哪有不无法无天的？！

【English Translation】

Virtue is the master of talent. Talent is the servant of virtue. Talent without virtue is the same as a household without a master, where the servants will act willfully. If this be the case, how can the servants not run wild like demons and monsters?

140. 穷寇勿追　投鼠忌器

140. Not press the enemy at bay and in order to save the dishes, spare the rat.

锄奸杜幸[1]，要放他一条去路。若使之一无所容，譬如塞鼠穴者，一切去路都塞尽，则一切好物俱咬破矣。

【中文注释】 ① 杜幸：杜，杜绝；幸，古代皇帝身边专事谄媚的佞人。

【今文解译】 在铲除奸邪的小人、杜绝谄媚的佞人时，要给他们留条出路，以观后效。若是不留出路，就会像将所有洞穴通道都堵住而使老鼠无处遁逃那样，一切值钱的东西都会被它咬得稀巴烂。

【English Translation】

When wiping out malefactors or sycophants, you'd better leave them a way out. If you press them too tightly, making them find nowhere to hide, it is like driving away a rat, having all rat-holes blocked up. As a result, the cornered rat will bite up all your valuables.

141. 有过归己　有功让人

141. One should have the merit to put on himself the blame for faults and give others the credit for accomplishment.

当与人同过，不当与人同功，同功则相忌；可与人共患难，不可与人共安乐，安乐则相仇。

【今文解译】 别人有过要与其分担，别人有功不要与其同享，因为同享功劳会引起相互的猜忌。

可以与别人共患难，但切不可与别人共享安乐，因为共享安乐会导致彼此的不满。

【English Translation】

One should rather take the same blame with others for faults than share the credit with them for a joint accomplishment. For sharing the credit for a joint accomplishment with others would cause mutual suspicion and envy.

One should rather go through thick and thin together with others than share peace and happiness with them. For sharing peace and happiness with others would lead enmity between each other.

142. 警言救人　功德无量

142. To help others by submitting a sincere advice is also a sort of beneficence beyond measure.

士君子贫不能济物者，遇人痴迷处，出一言提醒之，遇人急难处，出一言解救之，亦是无量功德。

【今文解译】 一个因贫寒而不能提供物质帮助的读书人，若能在别人有错还执迷不悟时上前进言提醒一下，或能在别人有急难而一筹莫展时帮着出出主意使其解脱出来，同样也是功德无量的大善行。

【English Translation】

If a man of virtue and learning is in low water, he may not necessarily offer material assistance. But when he happens upon a man who is pertinaciously obsessed with wrong ideas, he ought to give an advice to remind him of the way right to follow. And when he happens upon a man who is in a hurry and at a loss, he ought to forward a suggestion to see him through his troubles. Such beneficence is also regarded as measureless.

143. 趋炎附热　人之通病

143. To fawn upon the rich and powerful is one of the common failings of human nature.

饥则附①，饱则翱②；燠③则趋④，寒则弃；人情通患⑤也。

【中文注释】 ① 附：依附，投靠。
② 翱：翱翔。此处指远走高飞。
③ 燠：温暖。此处喻富贵人家。
④ 趋：投奔，归附。
⑤ 通患：通病。

【今文解译】 饥肠辘辘时就去投靠人家，吃饱了就拍拍屁股走人；看到人家发达了就去巴结人家，发现人家败落了就掉头而去。——这些都是常见的人的劣根性。

【English Translation】

It always follows that when people are hungry and frustrated they tend to go and live as dependents on others, but as soon as having adequate food and clothing they will slip away from their benefactors to distant places. And also it follows that when people meet the rich and powerful they tend to fawn on them, but as soon as the latter become declining they will fling off at once. All these are the common failings in human nature.

144. 冷眼观物　轻动刚肠

144. Observe the world with cool detachment and show your uprightness with deliberation.

君子宜净拭冷眼[1]，慎勿轻动刚肠[2]。

【中文注释】　① 冷眼：冷静的眼光。
② 刚肠：刚正不阿的性格。此处可理解为“冲动”。

【今文解译】　遇到事情时，君子要擦亮眼睛，保持冷静，切不可冲动行事，不计后果。

【English Translation】

It is better for an accomplished man to observe the world with cool detachment and show his uprightness with deliberation.

145. 德量共进　识见更高

145. A man's knowledge increases along with the improving of his virtue and broadening of his mind.

德随量进，量由识长。故欲厚其德，不可不弘其量；欲弘其量，不可不大其识。

【今文解译】　一个人的道德水准总是随着气量的增大而提高，气量总是通过见识的增长而愈加宏大。因而：要想提高道德水准，首先就得从增大气量入手；要想增大气量，首先就得从增长见识做起。

【English Translation】

A man's virtue is improved with the broadening of his mind and his mind broadened with the enriching of his knowledge. Therefore, the person who wants to improve his virtue should do so by broadening his mind, and to broaden his mind should do so by enriching his knowledge.

146. 人心惟危　道心惟微

146. Human heart is unfathomable and power of virtue negligible.

一灯萤然，万籁无声，此吾人初入宴寂[1]时也；晓梦初醒，群动未起，此吾人初出混沌[2]处也。乘此而一念回光[3]，炯然返照，始知耳目口鼻皆桎梏[4]，而情欲嗜好悉机械[5]矣。

【中文注释】 ① 宴寂：佛教用语，意为“安然进入寂灭（死亡）状态”。此处仅指进入睡眠状态。
② 混沌：传说中宇宙形成以前模糊一团的景象。此处喻人刚从睡眠状态下醒来，神志尚处迷迷糊糊的时候。
③ 回光：语出“回光返照”，指太阳刚落到地平线下时，由于反射作用而发生的天空中短暂发亮的现象。生活中，常被用来比喻人临死前精神忽然兴奋的现象。佛教中用以表示反省。
④ 桎梏：枷锁。此处指束缚人或事的东西。
⑤ 机械：此处指迷惑人心或败坏德行的东西。

【今文解译】 夜幕降临，油灯忽闪，万籁俱寂，这正是人们准备睡觉的时候；东方泛白，晓之伊始，万物待苏，这正是人们出梦初醒的时候。此时若能静下心来反省一下自己就会幡然醒悟：耳目口鼻都只是束缚心智的桎梏，而情欲嗜好也都只是搅乱我们性灵的机关。

【English Translation】

When there twinkles the weak light of an oil lamp and all is hushed up, it is the moment we have just dropped asleep. When people awake from their dreams at daybreak and everything has not yet fully resuscitated, it is the moment we are still lingering abed. If we could avail ourselves of such moment to cleanse our hearts and reflect on ourselves, we would come to realize that the ears, eyes, mouths and noses are nothing but shackles to our intelligence, and that our lusts and addictions are the very stuff to disturb our spirits.

147. 反省从善　尤人成恶

147. Self-reflection guides one to good while blame shifted onto others breeds the root of evil.

反己者，触事皆成药石；尤人①者，动念即是戈矛。一以辟众善之路，一以浚诸恶之源，相去霄壤②矣。

【中文注释】 ① 尤人：埋怨、指责别人。
② 霄壤：一天一地，差别巨大。

【今文解译】 常常自我反省的人，每一件遇到的事都会成为警示自己的良药；动辄怨天尤人的人，每一个心里的动念都是充满杀气的戈矛。前者是通向各种善行的道路，而后者是滋生各种恶行的源头。二者相去甚远！

【English Translation】

One able to count everything he comes into contact with as a good reminder that keeps him alert does so by often reflecting on himself. And one liable to hurt others with his invasive thoughts which act like dagger-axes and spears does so by always laying blames upon others. Of the two fashions, one can be called a path leading to universal good and another a source breeding various evils. They are as different as heaven and earth.

148. 功名一时　气节万古

148. Honor and rank are only in fashion for a time, but the integrity of aspiration will ever be immortal.

事业文章随身销毁，而精神万古如新；功名富贵逐世转移，而气节千载一日。君子信[1]不当以彼易此也。

【中文注释】 ① 信：的确。

【今文解译】 所有的事业和文章都会随着个人的离世而消亡，唯独人的精神万世永存；所有的功名和富贵都会随着时代的变迁而改变，唯独人的气节千古不朽。君子绝不会用不朽的精神和气节去换取一时的事业文章和功名富贵。

【English Translation】

All personal achievements and literary fames vanish with their creators, but the spirit therein will last and remain as fresh as ever. Scholarly honor, official rank as well as riches alter along with the lapse of time, while moral integrity will live long. Hence, by no means should the accomplished man abandon the eternal spirit and moral integrity and get in return the short-lived personal achievements and literary fames, scholarly honor, official rank, and riches.

149. 机里藏机　变外生变

149. An unknown skilful contrivance always hides in another and a new event often crops up unexpectedly.

鱼网之设，鸿则罹[1]其中；螳螂之贪，雀又乘其后。机里藏机，变外生变，智巧何足恃[2]哉！

【中文注释】 ① 罹：遭遇，遭受。此处喻落入。
② 恃：依靠。

【今文解译】 渔民撒网是为了捕鱼，但却网住了会飞的鸿雁；螳螂潜行是为了捕蝉，哪想黄雀却悄悄跟在后面。事情往往如此：玄机里面还暗藏着玄机，变故之外还有新的变故。人的聪明才智何足为恃？！

【English Translation】

Fishnet is set to net fish, but eventually a swan goose is netted. A mantis is so anxious to stalk the cicada that it is unaware of the oriole behind. Actually, things are usually going like this: an unknown skilful contrivance always hides in another and a new event often unexpectedly ensues from the old one. How can man's wisdom and intelligence be counted upon?

150. 诚恳为人　灵活处世

150. Be sincere in conducting yourself and in dealing with the world, be flexible.

作人无点真恳念头，便成个花子[1]，事事皆虚；涉世无段圆活机趣，便是个木人[2]，处处有碍。

【中文注释】 ① 花子：古代妇女脸上的装饰。此处喻华而不实、徒有其表的人。
② 木人：即木头人，指呆板的人。

【今文解译】 做人要真诚恳切，不然就是个虚头花脑的人，做什么都没个准头。
涉世要圆滑灵活，不然就是个呆板迂腐的人，时时处处都吃不开。

【English Translation】

If a person has no sincerity in conducting himself, he will become like a flashy creature; whatever he does is simply for presentation.
If a person lacks flexibility and adroitness in social intercourse, he will become like a dull fellow; wherever he goes he runs his head against a wall.

151. 去混心清　去苦乐存

151. There emerges a tranquil mind the moment one discards his distracting thoughts and a joy the moment one is apart from pains.

水不波则自定，鉴[1]不翳[2]则自明。故心无可清，去其混之者而清自现；乐不必寻，去其苦之者而乐自存。

【中文注释】 ① 鉴：古人用的铜镜。
② 翳：遮蔽，遮掩。此处喻落满灰尘。

【今文解译】 水里没有波浪，水面自然也就平静；镜子没有灰尘，镜面自然也就明亮。同理：清静无须刻意去保持，只要摒弃了私欲杂念，人的心自然就会清静；快乐不必刻意去寻找，只要把哀苦烦愁抛诸脑后，人自然就会快乐。

【English Translation】
When there rolls no wave, the water of a pond will become still of itself. When covered with no dust, the mirror is naturally bright and clean. Therefore, one needn't look for mental tranquility purposely; so long as he quits himself of the distracting thoughts, he will certainly attain tranquility. Likewise, one needn't seek after pleasures deliberately; so long as he is apart from pains and vexation, he will certainly find pleasures.

152. 一言一行　切戒犯忌

152. When you speak or act, do your utmost to avoid violating taboos.

有一念而犯鬼神之禁、一言而伤天地之和、一事而酿子孙之祸者，最宜切戒。

【今文解译】 凡有念头触犯鬼神禁忌的，凡有言论伤害人伦和谐的，凡有事情殃及后辈子孙的，我们都应该毫不犹豫地尽全力去制止。

【English Translation】
Whenever there is a thought offending the taboos of the gods and ghosts, or a word bringing harm to the harmony of human relations, or an action entailing calamities on our descendants, we should do our best to prevent them from happening.

153. 宽之自明　纵之自化

153. As things might be clear of themselves if more time is spared, so people might be moved to action if less binding is laid.

事有急之不白者，宽之或自明，毋躁急以速其忿[1]；人有操之不从者，纵之或自化，毋操切以益其顽[2]。

【中文注释】 ① 忿：不满，怨恨。此处将其理解成“复杂化”则更为贴切。
② 以益其顽：加剧冥顽不化的程度。

【今文解译】 有些事情越是急于想搞清楚就越是搞不清楚，搁置几天或许会变得清楚起来，千万不要因为情绪急躁而使它们变得复杂化。
有些人你越是想点拨他们，他们就越是不开窍，索性随他们去，他们或许会有所领悟，切不可操之过急而加剧他们的愚顽。

【English Translation】
Sometimes it is difficult to make things clear in a hurry; but if more time is spared they might be clear of themselves. So we should not be so impetuous as to make them more complicated.
Sometimes it is hard to make people follow what is instructed; but if less binding is laid they might be moved to action in the end. So we should not be so impatient as to provoke their stubbornness.

154. 不能养德　终归末技

154. Without moral cultivation man’s skill can only be a small trick.

节义傲青云[1]，文章高白雪[2]，若不以德性陶镕之，终为血气之私[3]、技能之末。

【中文注释】 ① 青云：高的地位。此处指高官厚禄，飞黄腾达。
② 白雪：此处指阳春白雪，战国时代楚国的一种高雅歌曲。
③ 血气之私：因一时冲动而做出的行为。

【今文解译】 忠肝义胆胜过官场得意，文章高论胜过阳春白雪。但若不能用道德去加以陶冶规范，这些看似傲人的质素最终都不免会沦为头脑发热的一时冲动和摆弄文字的雕虫小技。

【English Translation】

Loyalty and uprightness are superior to high position and handsome salary. Vivid literary writings are more striking than the famous composition of the Spring Snow*. Nevertheless, if one does not cast them with moral principles, the above-mentioned good qualities can only degenerate into a momentary impulse or vulgar means of insect-carving tricks.

【English Annotation】

* The Spring Snow: A kind of melody that belonged to the elite in the State of Chu during the Warring States Period (475BC-221BC); (in broad sense) highbrow literature and art, as opposed to the "Songs of the Rustic Poor", meaning popular literature and art.

155. 急流勇退　与世无争

155. Retire at the height of your official career and hold yourself aloof from the world.

谢事，当谢于正盛之时；居身，宜居于独后①之地。

【中文注释】　① 独后：与世无争，独善其身。

【今文解译】　辞官隐退，应选在自己职业生涯尚处鼎盛的时候。
安身落户，要选择既无争斗又没纷扰的清静之地。

【English Translation】

A person who intends to retire from office should do so at the height of his career.

A person who wants to lead a peaceful life should do so in place where there is no conflict.

156. 细处着眼　施不求报

156. Adhere to morality by starting with trivialities and bestow favors without expecting for return.

谨德，须谨于至微之事；施恩，务施于不报之人。

【今文解译】 谨守道德，必须从最不起眼的细碎事情着手。
施惠布恩，务必施予那些没有能力回报的人。

【English Translation】

A person who makes his mind bent on moral cultivation should do so by starting with the most trivial matters.

A person who wishes to bestow favors should do so upon those who are unable to requite.

157. 清心去俗　趣味高雅

157. Clear your heart by banishing vulgarity and hold your interest by acting with elegance.

交市人[①]，不如友山翁；谒朱门[②]，不如亲白屋[③]；听街谈巷语，不如闻樵歌牧咏；谈今人失德过举，不如述古人嘉言懿行[④]。

【中文注释】 ① 市人：市井之人。
② 朱门：有钱人家。可用以泛指富贵人家或有权有势的人家。
③ 白屋：古代不施油彩、露出材料本色的房屋，比喻出身卑微的平民或者寒士。
④ 嘉言懿行：富有教益的言论和令人感佩的行为。

【今文解译】 与市井中人你来我往，不如跟山里的人交交朋友。
出没于富贵人家，不如常去贫苦百姓的茅庐走走。
听闻街谈巷议，不如倾听打柴人和放牧人的歌谣。
议论今人的失德过举，不如聊聊古人的嘉言懿行。

【English Translation】

To associate with a mean fellow in the marketplace is not as good as to befriend people amidst the mountains.

To frequent the mansions of the mighty is not as good as to pay a visit to a thatched hut.

To give a hearing to street corner gossip is not as good as to lend an ear to the songs of a woodcutter or buffalo boy.

To relate the moral forfeiture and misconducts of the contemporary people is not as good as to narrate the fine words and exemplary deeds of the ancients.

158. 修身种德　事业之基

158. Virtue is the foundation of a career.

德者事业之基，未有基不固而栋宇①坚久者。

【中文注释】　① 栋宇：栋，房子的正梁；宇，四周的垂檐。泛指房屋。

【今文解译】　品德是事业的基础，这就好比盖房子，没有牢固的地基就盖不成经久耐用的房子。

【English Translation】

Virtue is the foundation of a career. It is like building a house, if not solid-founded, the ridgepoles and eaves will impossibly be sturdy and durable.

159. 心善子盛　根固叶荣

159. Mercy gives birth to the prosperity of our descendants and sturdy root brings about luxuriant foliage.

心者后裔之根，未有根不植而枝叶荣茂者。

【今文解译】　仁慈之心是子孙繁衍的根本，这就好比栽花种树，没有茁壮的根基，就没有繁茂如盖的枝叶。

【English Translation】

Mercy is the root of the prosperity of our descendants. It is like planting trees and flowers, if not sturdy-rooted, the branches and leaves will impossibly be flourishing and luxuriant.

160. 勿昧所有　勿夸所得

160. Not belittle what we have possessed nor boast of what we have gained.

前人云："抛却自家无尽藏[1]，沿门持钵效贫儿。"又云："暴富贫儿休说梦，谁家灶里火无烟？"一箴[2]自昧所有，一箴自夸所有，可为学问切戒。

【中文注释】 ① 无尽藏：数不尽的家藏财富。
② 箴：箴言，具有劝诫、告诫、规劝等意。

【今文解译】 古人说过："抛却自家无尽藏，沿门持钵效贫儿。"古人还说过："暴富贫儿休说梦，谁家灶里火无烟？"前一句话是告诫人们不要妄自菲薄，后一句话是告诫人们不要妄自尊大。这两句话都可以用在勉励我们的学习上。

【English Translation】

There is an old saying which goes, "Casting away the boundless wealth of one's family, one imitates a poor man to beg in the streets with a bowl." And another which goes, "A poor man of sudden wealth ought not to think himself terrific. Is there any fire in kitchen range without smoke?" The first saying is to exhort us not to belittle what we have possessed, and the second is to exhort us not to boast of what we have gained. Both of them can be taken as exhortations in our learning.

161. 真理学问　人皆可求

160. Everyone is entitled to seek truth and engage in learning.

道[1]是一重[2]公众物事，当随人而接引[3]；学是一个寻常家饭，当随事而警惕[4]。

【中文注释】 ① 道："道"是一种非常抽象的古代哲学概念，且出现在不同的地方就有不同的解释和理解。此处不妨将其理解为"追求真理"，以和下文中的"学（探索学问）"相对应。

② 一重：一种。
③ 接引：佛家用语。即引导众生进入西天净土。此处仅指引导，指导。
④ 随事而警惕：意即随时随地关注发生身边的事，有所警惕。

【今文解译】 追求真理这件事，凡有志者皆可为之，关键的是如何引导追求者根据自己的情况去实现目标。
探索学问这件事，一如家常便饭那样平淡无奇，但是真要把学问做好还得随时关注身边的事。

【English Translation】
Truth-seeking is a thing everyone can do; but still the way to guide them to it should be in accordance with the different dispositions of each individual.
Learning is as common as preparing everyday homely fare; but still it should be done by paying close attention to the things happening around.

162. 信人己诚　疑人己诈

162. He who has trust in others is sincere and deceitful is he who has a distrust of others.

信人者，人未必尽诚，己则独诚[①]矣；疑人者，人未必皆诈，己则先诈矣。

【中文注释】 ① 独诚：自己做到诚实。

【今文解译】 一个信任别人的人，尽管别人未必都是诚实的，他自己就已经是个诚实可信的人了。
一个怀疑别人有诈的人，不管别人是否真的有诈，他自己就已经先于别人而有诈了。

【English Translation】
He who has trust in others should be sincere himself, even though others may not all be sincere and trustworthy.
He who has a distrust of others must be deceitful himself, even though others may not all be deceitful and untrustworthy.

163. 春风催生　寒风残杀

163. Spring breeze hastens the growth of life, while piercing cold wind brings life to ruin.

念头宽厚[①]的，如春风煦育[②]，万物遭之而生；念头忌刻[③]的，如朔雪[④]阴凝，万物遭之而死。

【中文注释】 ① 宽厚：宽仁厚道。
② 煦育：温暖地养育。
③ 忌刻：尖刻。
④ 朔雪：北方的大雪。

【今文解译】 宅心仁厚的人让世界充满生机，一如温暖的春风催生万物。
为人刻薄的人让世界充满冷漠，一如北国的风雪逢物必毁。

【English Translation】
A man of generosity is like the vernal breeze which brings about a warm and hastens the growth of all things on earth.
A caustic man is like the north snow which brings about chill and ruins everything it comes into contact with.

164. 善根暗长　恶损潜消

164. The benefit of good deeds grows without being noticed and the harm of evil ones vanishes from sight secretly.

为善不见其益，如草里冬瓜，自应暗长；为恶不见其损，如庭前春雪，当必潜消。

【今文解译】 做好事未必能立即看到什么益处，好事的益处就像草丛里的冬瓜，是在不知不觉中悄悄长大的。
做坏事未必能马上看到什么害处，坏事的害处就像庭院里的春雪，必然会渐渐露出自己的原形。

【English Translation】

Probably no instant benefit can be perceived the very minute one does good. The benefit of good deeds is like a wax gourd hidden in the grass; it grows without being noticed.

Perhaps no immediate harm can be discerned the very minute one does evil. The harm of an evil deed is like spring snow in the courtyard; it is bound to show itself gradually.

165. 愈隐愈显　愈淡愈浓

165. The more esoteric the thing, the more we should be open-minded; the less associated the one, the more we should be warm-hearted.

遇故旧之交，意气[①]要愈新；处隐微[②]之事，心迹宜愈显；待衰朽[③]之人，恩礼当愈隆。

【中文注释】 ① 意气：情意。
② 隐微：隐秘，微妙。
③ 衰朽：年老体弱。

【今文解译】 遇到过去的老朋友，意气和情感要比以前更加投入才是。面对隐晦微妙的事情，自己的心底要更加光明磊落才是。对待年老体衰的人，礼节礼貌要做得更加周到体贴才是。

【English Translation】

When meeting an old friend of ours long apart, we should be more warm-hearted than ever before.

When engaged in something esoteric and subtle, we should be as open-minded as we may.

When dealing with the old and frail, we should show courtesy more thoughtfully and considerately.

166. 君子立德　小人图利

166. Accomplished men pay attention to moral cultivation, while petty ones are only keen on seeking material gains.

勤者敏于德义，而世人借勤以济其贫；俭者淡于货利，而世人假俭以饰其吝。君子持身之符，反为小人营私之具矣。惜哉！

【今文解译】 勤奋的人重视道德义理方面的修养，而绝大多数人都只是想通过勤奋改变自己的贫穷现状；节俭的人对金银钱财看得很淡，而绝大多数人都只是想用节俭来掩饰自己的吝啬。本来是堂堂君子立身处世的准则，而今竟成了小人蝇营狗苟的工具。可惜喽！

【English Translation】

Men of diligence pay great attention to moral cultivation and character building, but still there are many people who only take diligence as a means to shake off poverty. Men of thrift are less interested in seeking for riches and wealth, but still there are many people who narrowly take thrift as an excuse to gloss over their niggardliness. How regrettable it is that the conduct criteria of accomplished men are usurped by petty ones to feather their own nests!

167. 意气用事　难有作为

167. Men of easy temperament can scarcely make great achievements.

凭意兴作为者，随作则随止，岂是不退之轮①？从情识解悟者，有悟则有迷，终非常明之灯。

【中文注释】 ① 不退之轮：不向后退的车轮。佛家认为，佛法犹如到处碾转的车轮，所到之处，众生的罪恶和邪恶魔鬼就像山岳岩石一样被碾得粉碎。

【今文解译】 凭意气或兴致做事的人，随时会因情绪的起伏而做做停停，这样的人岂能指望他像不退之轮那样百折不挠永远向前？

惯用感情去解悟事物的人，常会因为感情出现问题而一阵清楚一阵糊涂，这样的人终不能像长明灯那样给人以指引。

【English Translation】

A man of easy temperament is likely to act on impulse one moment and stop immediately the next. How can such a man be a wheel not rolling backwards? A person who simply bases his comprehension upon personal emotions will sometimes be sober-minded and sometimes puzzled. Such a person can never be an eternally lit lamp.

168. 律己宜严　待人宜宽

168. Better be strict with ourselves and lenient to others.

人之过误宜恕，而在己则不可恕；己之困辱[1]宜忍，而在人则不可忍。

【中文注释】　① 困辱：困难和屈辱。

【今文解译】　对别人的过失应当宽恕，而对自己的过失则不能宽恕。自己的困辱应当忍受，而别人的困辱则不能置之不理。

【English Translation】

We should forgive the faults and mistakes of others, but should not excuse those of our own.

We should do our utmost to endure the sufferings and humiliations of our own, but should not ignore those of others.

169. 为奇不异　求清不激

169. To be outstanding is not the result of a queer deed, nor is that of an extreme one to be noble and unsullied.

能脱俗便是奇，作意[1]尚奇者，不为奇而为异；不合污便是清，绝俗求清者，不为清而为激。

【中文注释】 ① 作意：刻意。

【今文解译】 能够超凡脱俗的人是奇人，但是一味地为了做个奇人而标新立异，就不再是奇人而是怪人了。

不同流合污的人是高洁的人，但是为了标榜自己高洁而与世隔绝，就不再是高洁而是偏激了。

【English Translation】

One who can rise above vulgarities is outstanding; but if he makes every attempt to be so, he is no more than a queer fellow.

One who scorns to associate himself with the vicious is unsullied; but if he tries to be so by isolating himself from the society, he is simply going to extremes.

170. 恩宜后浓　威宜先严

170. Favors should be bestowed from small to great while authority go first with severity and then with tolerance.

恩宜自淡而浓，先浓后淡者，人忘其惠；威宜自严而宽，先宽后严者，人怨其酷。

【今文解译】 施恩应该由淡而浓，如果由浓而淡，受惠的人就会忘记施惠的人。

立威应该先严后宽，如果先宽后严，受制的人就会说你冷酷无情。

【English Translation】

When bestowing favors on others, you should start it from small to great; if you do the contrary, the beneficiaries will forget the favors they have received.

When exerting yourself on authority among people, you should first go with severity and then with tolerance; if you do the opposite, you will be blamed for your callousness.

171. 心虚性现　意净心清

171. The true nature emerges when internal distracting thoughts are banished; the heart becomes clear when the mind is purified.

心虚则性现[1]，不息心而求见性，如拨波觅月；意净则心清，不了意而求明心，如索镜增尘。

【中文注释】　① 性现：本性显露。佛家认为，人的本性是纯朴无瑕的。

【今文解译】　心无杂念的时候，人的本性就会显露出来；心沉静不下来但却想看到自己的本性，这就好比拨开波浪在水中捞月，到了一场空。

意念澄净的时候，人的内心就会亮堂起来；意念不澄净但却想求得亮堂的内心，这就好比在已经模糊不清的镜子上再增添灰尘。

【English Translation】

When the distracting thoughts are banished, the true nature will emerge of itself. If one tries to seek the true nature by not banishing the distracting thoughts, it is like seeking the moon in a pool.

When the mind is purified, the heart will then become clear. If one tries to keep a clear heart by not purifying his mind, it is like strewing more dust onto a misty mirror.

172. 我自为我　物自为物

172. I am but my self; all the things I have are only my possessions.

我贵而人奉之，奉此峨冠大带[1]也；我贱而人侮之，侮此布衣草履也。然则原非奉我，我胡为喜？原非侮我，我胡为怒？

【中文注释】　① 峨冠大带：高高的帽子和宽大的衣带，古代为官者的装束行头。此处喻富贵。

【今文解译】　我富贵了就有人来奉承我，其实他们奉承的是我的峨冠大带；我贫贱了就有人瞧不起我，其实他们瞧不起的是我的布衣草履。事情就是这样：他们奉承的不是我而是我的峨冠大带，我有什么可高兴的？他们瞧不起的不是我而是我的布衣草履，我又有什么好不高兴的？

【English Translation】

Given that I am rich and powerful, people would respect me; actually, what they respect is not me but the wealth and title I have. Given that I am poor and lowly, people would despise me; actually, what they despise is not me but the coarse clothes and straw sandals I wear. Should I be glad if it is not me but my wealth and title that are respected? And should I be annoyed if it is not me but my coarse clothes and straw sandals that are despised?

173. 慈悲心肠　繁衍生机

173. Kind-heartedness ensures endless procreation.

为鼠常留饭，怜蛾不点灯。古人此等念头，是吾人一点生生之机[①]。无此，便所谓土木形骸而已。

【中文注释】 ① 生生之机：繁衍不息的生机。此处指人类和其他万物和谐相处之意。

【今文解译】 吃饭的时候常想着给老鼠留些米粒，到了晚上因为怜惜飞蛾而不点油灯。古人的悲悯之心由此可见一斑，人类正是因为这种悲悯之心才得以生生不息。如果没了这种悲悯之心，我们人类也就只剩下泥塑木雕一般的躯壳了。

【English Translation】

Ancient people were used to sparing several grains of cooked rice after meals lest the rat might suffer hunger, and to not lighting the oil lamp at night lest the moth might dart into the flame. Such kind-heartedness is mercy with which we human beings have been surviving all the ages. Without it, we would be no more than the wood and soil at all.

174. 心体天体 人心天心

174. Man's heart and the cosmos resemble each other in essence.

心体便是天体[①]。一念之喜，景星庆云；一念之怒，震雷暴雨；一念之慈，和风甘露；一念之严，烈日秋霜。何者少得？只要随起随灭，廓然无碍，便与太虚[②]同体。

【中文注释】 ① 天体：各种星体和星际物质的统称。联系下文中的各种自然现象，此处应指大自然。
② 太虚：天；天空。此处亦指大自然。

【今文解译】 就本质而言，人的心和大自然是一样的。当人的心里有了喜悦的念头，就像大自然里出现景星庆云；当人的心里有了愤恨的念头，就像大自然里出现震雷暴雨；当人的心里有了仁慈的念头，就像大自然里出现和风甘露；当人的心里有了严酷的念头，就像大自然里出现烈日秋霜。对于人来说，这些形形色色的念头哪个少得了？只要很好地控制它们，让它们产生之后又能很快平复下去，不形成对人的气息的阻塞，这样就能与大自然合而为一了。

【English Translation】

Man's heart and Nature resemble each other in essence. When there emerges a joy in the heart of a man, it is like Nature when it is draped with auspicious stars and propitious clouds. When there appears indignation in the heart of a man, it is like Nature when it is dominated by deafening thunder and torrential rain. When there engenders mercy in the heart of a man, it is like Nature when it is permeated with warm breeze and sweet dew. When there arises a severe thought from the heart of a man, it is like Nature when it suffers from the scorching sun and autumnal frost. Can any of the above phenomena be dispensed with? As long as we keep good control over the rising and falling of our changeable moods and remove the spiritual obstacles from within, our hearts would naturally merge into one organic whole with Nature.

175. 无事寂寂　有事惺惺

175. Preserve tranquility while unoccupied and keep a clear head while occupied.

无事时心易昏冥[①]，宜寂寂[②]而照以惺惺[③]；有事时心易奔逸[④]，宜惺惺而主以寂寂。

【中文注释】 ① 昏冥：昏沉迷乱。
② 寂寂：沉静。
③ 惺惺：清醒。
④ 奔逸：飞快地逃跑。此处喻躁动不安。

【今文解译】 没事可做的时候，人往往会胡思乱想，此时最要紧的是让自己静下心来，以保持清醒的头脑。
有事在做的时候，人往往会心浮气躁，此时最要紧的是保持清醒的头脑，以让自己静下心来。

【English Translation】

When occupied with nothing, one easily becomes perplexed. At this moment one should keep a clear head by preserving composure.

When occupied with something, one lightly gives way to rashness. At this moment one should preserve composure by keeping a clear head.

176. 议事任事　明晓利害

176. Before making comments on a matter he has nothing to do with, one should first endeavor to find out all the right and wrong causes in it.

议事者身在事外，宜悉利害之情；任事者身居事中，当忘利害之虑。

【今文解译】 谈论事情的人，由于是置身事外，所以开口前最好先弄清楚是非曲直。
在做事情的人，由于是身在其中，所以最好不要患得患失、斤斤计较。

【English Translation】

Before a man comments on a matter he has nothing to do with, he should first endeavor to find out all the right and wrong causes in it.

When a man deals with a matter he is personally involved in, he should cast off all the considerations of the gains and losses of his own.

177. 操履严明　但毋偏激

177. In preserving moral principles one should be strict rather than drastic.

士君子处权门要路，操履要严明，心气要和易①，毋少随而近腥膻之党②，亦毋过激而犯蜂虿之毒③。

【中文注释】 ① 和易：和气、平易。

② 腥膻之党：鱼虾的气味叫腥，牛羊的气味叫膻。腥膻之党即指臭味相投、结党营私之徒。

③ 蜂虿之毒：蜂，黄蜂；虿，蝎子；毒，陷害。“蜂虿”常被用来比喻阴险使坏的小人。蜂虿之毒即指小人陷害。

【今文解译】 为学之士身居要职，操守要清廉严明，心气要平易随和，既不要放弃原则与结党营私之徒为伍，也不要言行过激而招致宵小之徒的陷害。

【English Translation】

When a man of learning is in an important position of power, his moral principles should be fortified and his temperament moderated. In the meantime, he should not slacken his moral fortitude, nor should he hobnob with the crafty coterie. Moreover, he should also not be too drastic in his uprightness, nor should he too severe with the vicious so as to avoid being framed up by them.

178. 浑然和气　居身之珍

178. To preserve an easy-going manner is the golden rule of getting on in the world.

标节义者，必以节义受谤；榜道学[①]者，常因道学招尤。故君子不近恶事，亦不立善名，只浑然和气[②]，才是居身之珍[③]。

【中文注释】 ① 道学：道家的学问。
② 浑然和气：浑然，全然，完全地。浑然和气就是一团和气。
③ 居身之珍：为人处事的法宝。

【今文解译】 标榜节义的必因节义而受人诽谤；标榜道学的常因道学而招人怨恨。所以，君子既不要染指丑事、恶事，也不要因为贪图名声而美化自己。要知道，只有为人一团和气，才是处世最可珍贵的法宝。

【English Translation】
The one who flaunts his moral rectitude will surely be slandered by others in the name of the same. The one who flaunts his virtue and learning will normally be censured by others for the sake of the same. Therefore, the accomplished man should keep clear of wrongdoings and avoid prettifying himself, merely by maintaining an easy-going manner all round. This is the golden rule of conduct in the world.

179. 诚心和气　激励陶冶

179. Nobody cannot be roused and molded with sincerity and gentleness.

遇欺诈之人，以诚心感动之；遇暴戾[①]之人，以和气熏蒸[②]之；遇倾邪私曲之人，以名义气节激励之。天下无不入我陶冶[③]中矣。

【中文注释】 ① 暴戾：残暴凶狠。
② 熏蒸：影响、感化之意。
③ 陶冶：改造、熏陶之意。

【今文解译】 遇到行为狡诈的人，我就以真诚的心去感动他；遇到性格暴戾的人，我就以平和的态度去感染他；遇到品行不端且自私自利的人，我就以道德气节去激励他。这样，天下就没有我感化不了的人了。

【English Translation】

When you encounter a deceitful man, move him with sincerity. When you encounter a ruthless, tyrannical man, affect him with gentleness. When you encounter a conspiratorial, selfish man, rouse him with morality and justice. With these influences in effect, nobody under heaven cannot but be molded.

180. 一念慈祥　寸心洁白

180. A thought of kind-mindedness makes the heart pure and clean.

一念慈祥，可以酝酿①两间和气；寸心洁白，可以昭垂②百代清芬。

【中文注释】 ① 酝酿：喻营造。

② 昭垂：昭示流传。

【今文解译】 一个慈祥的念头可以酝酿出天地间的一派谐和。

一颗纯洁的心灵可以使一个人的清名流芳百世。

【English Translation】

A thought of kind-mindedness can create a peaceful atmosphere between the heaven and earth.

A feeling of pure-heartedness can leave behind a good reputation for posterity.

181. 异行奇能　涉世祸胎

181. Unusual behaviors and queer talents are the sources of disasters in social relations.

阴谋怪习，异行奇能，俱是涉世的祸胎。只一个庸德庸行①，便可以完混沌②而召和平。

【中文注释】 ① 庸德庸行：平庸无奇的品德和言行。

② 完混沌：此处喻合乎自然的本性。

【今文解译】 阴险的算计、古怪的陋习、诡秘的行为，以及奇异的能力，这些都是为人处世的祸根。其实，只有那些最为平常的品德和行为才是最贴近自然的，也是最能带来和平的。

【English Translation】

Sinister craft, eccentric habit, extraordinary behavior and queer talent are all the curses in human relations. Only by abiding by ordinary moral principles and general code of conduct can one create peaceful atmosphere in accord with the essence of Nature.

182. 忍得耐得 自在之境

182. Endurance is the gateway to the realm of freedom.

语云："登山耐侧路①，踏雪耐危桥②。"一"耐"字极有意味。如倾险③之人情，坎坷之世道，若不得一"耐"字撑持过去，几何不堕入榛莽坑堑哉?

【中文注释】 ① 侧路：指险峻难行的小路。
② 危桥：高耸的桥梁。
③ 倾险：险恶。

【今文解译】 俗话有云："登山耐侧路，踏雪耐危桥。"这里的"耐"字意味十分深长。居心叵测的人情和坎坷不平的世道，若不用一个"耐"字应对过去，又有几人不掉入布满荆棘的深涧中去?！

【English Translation】

As a saying goes, "When climbing a mountain, be ready to endure the risk of taking rugged paths; and when treading the snows, be ready to endure that of crossing towering bridges." How meaningful the word "endure"! In regard to the uncertainty of human relationships or the corrupted manners and morals of the time, if people cannot go through them with endurance, few of them will be able to escape falling into a chasm full of thistles and thorns.

183. 心体莹然　本来不失

183. A pure heart enables one to retain his true characters.

夸逞[1]功业，炫耀文章，皆是靠外物作人。不知心体[2]莹然[3]，本来不失[4]，即无寸功只字，亦自有堂堂正正作人处。

【中文注释】 ① 夸逞：夸耀；炫耀。
② 心体：心；心地。
③ 莹然：纯洁。
④ 本来不失：保持本性。

【今文解译】 夸赞自己的功业，炫耀自己的文章，这些都是在用身外之物证明自己的能耐。殊不知只要做到心地纯净、本性不失，即使没有半点功业或片纸文章，也一样可以堂堂正正地做人。

【English Translation】

Those who boast of their exploits and flaunt their literary writings are merely showing themselves by relying on external possessions. They don't understand that as long as a person can preserve himself a pure heart and true character, he can be addressed as an open, aboveboard man even if he fails to have made the slightest accomplishment or written a single word.

184. 一张一弛　事先安排

184. Alteration of work and relaxation should be arranged beforehand.

忙里要偷闲，须先向闲时讨个把柄[1]；闹中要取静，须先从静处立个主宰[2]。不然，未有不因境而迁[3]、随事而靡[4]者。

【中文注释】 ① 把柄：喻把握、安排。
② 主宰：保持、控制。
③ 因境而迁：因情况变化变得无所适从。
④ 随事而靡：遇事就不知所措。

【今文解译】 要在忙忙碌碌中偷得一点闲工夫，必须首先要在空闲的时候做出适当的安排；要在喧闹的环境中拥有一份清静，必须首先要在清静的时候养成守静的习惯。不然，一遇到忙碌或喧闹就会手忙脚乱，无所适从。

【English Translation】

If you wish to enable yourself to enjoy relaxation when occupied, you must first make proper arrangement beforehand. If you wish to enable yourself to enjoy quietude in times of noise and clamor, you must first develop the habit of keeping quiet while at tranquility. Otherwise, you can only be confused and disoriented in case of being occupied or in times of noise and clamor.

185. 为民固本　造福子孙

185. Ensure the lifeblood of the people so as to benefit the coming generations.

不昧己心，不尽人情①，不竭物力。三者可以为天地立心，为生民立命，为子孙造福。

【中文注释】 ① 不尽人情：不违背人之常情。尽，灭绝，丧失。

【今文解译】 不违背自己的良心，不逆拂人之常情，不涂炭物资财力。做到这三点就可以在天地间树立公心，为百姓关切奔走，为子孙后代造福。

【English Translation】

Not to go against your conscience, nor to run counter to the way of the world, nor to waste the resources of Nature and society are the three exhortations, abiding by which we are able to set up the world's public spirit, ensure the interests of the people and benefit the coming generations.

186. 为官公廉　居家恕俭

186. Be impartial and white-handed when holding office and when managing a household, be lenient and frugal.

居官有二语，曰：唯公则生明，唯廉则生威。居家有二语，曰：唯恕则情平，唯俭则用足。

【今文解译】　有两句话是说居官的：一句是公正无私方能明鉴是非，一句是为官清廉方能树立威信。还有两句话是说居家的：一句是彼此包容方能和睦相处，一句是勤俭节约方能用度有余。

【English Translation】

There are two maxims for office-holding. One is that it is only by being impartial in public service that one will have fair judgment on right and wrong. Another is that it is only by being white-handed in administration that one will upgrade his prestige among the people. Equally, there are also two maxims for managing a household. One is that it is only by mutual inclusion that the family members will be pleasant and composed. Another is that it is only by living a frugal life that a family will have adequate domestic expenses.

187. 富贵知贫　少壮念老

187. Be aware of poverty when rich and wealthy and think of being old when young and strong.

处富贵之地，要知贫贱的痛痒；当少壮之时，须念衰老的辛酸。

【今文解译】　生活在富贵人家的人，应当知道贫贱人家的疾苦。年轻力壮的时候，不可不虑及年老体衰时的悲哀。

【English Translation】

When living in a family of riches and wealth, we must be aware of the weal and woe of the poor and lowly.

When still young and strong, we must think of the sadness of being old and decrepit.

188. 气量宽厚　兼容并包

188. Be large-minded so as to tolerate people of different qualities.

持身不可太皎洁[①]，一切污辱垢秽[②]要茹纳[③]得；与人不可太分明，一切善恶贤愚要包容得。

【中文注释】 ① 皎洁：纯净洁白。此处喻清高。
② 污辱垢秽：泛指一切邪恶肮脏的东西。
③ 茹纳：接受并宽容。

【今文解译】 立身处世不可太清高，而应该对所有诸如污浊、侮辱、丑陋和低俗之类的情事，都要能够接受。
与人打交道不要太挑剔，而应该对一切人，善良的或邪恶的、聪明的或愚昧的，都要能够包容。

【English Translation】

In dealing with the world one should not be too self-contained, but should, on the contrary, learn how to endure and tolerate all forms of iniquity.
In associating with others one should not be too distinctive, but should, on the contrary, learn how to condone and accept different persons, good or bad, capable or incapable.

189. 勿仇小人　勿媚君子

189. Never be the enemy of mean fellows nor curry favor with gentlemen.

休与小人仇雠[①]，小人自有对头；休向君子谄媚，君子原无私惠[②]。

【中文注释】 ① 仇雠：作对，为敌。
② 私惠：因私情而给予恩惠。

【今文解译】 不要与小人斗气结仇，小人自有冤家对头。
不要在君子面前献媚，君子不屑因私开恩。

【English Translation】

Never be the enemy of mean fellows, for they have their opponents and foes in kind.

Never curry favor with gentlemen, for they would not bend the laws or principles for showing their charity.

190. 疾病易医　魔障难除

190. Physical diseases are easy to cure, while mental barriers set up by a demon are hard to remove.

纵欲之病可医，而势理①之病难医；事物之障可除，而义理②之障难除。

【中文注释】 ① 势理：此处指对形势的判断。

② 义理：此处指对事物的认识。

【今文解译】 因纵欲而得的病好治，而因不明事理而导致的病难治。有形的障碍容易排除，而义理层面的障碍则很难排除。

【English Translation】

Diseases resulted from indulgence in sensual pleasures are curable, but disorders from misconception of situations are difficult to rectify.

Physical obstacles and material things are removable, but barriers to argumentation are difficult to dismantle.

191. 百炼成金　轻发无功

191. Gold can only be made with great effort.

磨砺当如百炼之金，急就①者，非邃养②；施为宜似千钧之弩③，轻发者，无宏功。

【中文注释】 ① 急就：急于求成。

② 邃养：高深的修养。“非邃养”指修炼不到家。

③ 千钧之弩：需花大力气才能拉开的弓弩。

【今文解译】 磨炼意志品质一定要像炼金一样，非得千锤百炼不可，如果急于求成，结果一定修炼不到家。
做事要像拉强弓劲弩一样，非得用尽全力不可，如果只是软绵绵地轻拉轻射，就击不中目标。

【English Translation】

Tempering will and virtue resembles making gold; it needs to be done in repeated efforts. Any attempt to have it done at one stroke will end in failure to gain ideal result.

Embarking upon an undertaking resembles bending a mighty crossbow; it requires one to exert his full strength. Those who intend to do it with ease will fail to score well.

192. 戒小人媚　愿君子责

192. Better be blamed by a worthy man than be flattered by a mean fellow.

宁为小人所忌毁，毋为小人所媚悦；宁为君子所责备，毋为君子所包容。

【今文解译】 宁可被小人嫉妒诋毁，也不要被小人奉承谄媚。
宁可被君子批评指摘，也不要被君子包容迁就。

【English Translation】

Rather be envied and slandered than be flattered by men of low characters.

Rather be reproached than be forgiven by men of moral integrity.

193. 好利害浅　好名害深

193. He who is greedy for wealth brings less harm but more does he who is eager for fame.

好利者，逸出[①]于道义之外，其害显而浅；好名者，窜入[②]于道义之中，其害隐而深。

【中文注释】 ① 逸出：超出。
② 窜入：此处喻藏匿或伪装。

【今文解译】 贪图利益的人，即使干出些突破道德底线的事情来，所造成的危害虽然明显但危害却也不大。
贪图名声的人，所作所为皆以道德信义为幌子，所造成的危害虽然很隐蔽但影响却十分恶劣。

【English Translation】

One that is greedy for wealth is liable to go off the track of morality and justice; nevertheless, the harm he brings about is not serious though obviously known to all.
One that is eager for fame and name tends to behave himself sanctimoniously in the garb of morality and justice; therefore, the harm he brings about is serious though deeply concealed.

194. 忘恩报怨　刻薄之极

194. To forget others' kindness and requite it with ingratitude is a thing most contemptible in the world.

受人之恩，虽深不报，怨则浅亦报之；闻人之恶，虽隐不疑，善则显亦疑之。此刻之极，薄之尤也，宜切忌之。

【今文解译】 接受别人很大的恩典但却不思回报，而对别人稍有点怨恨就试图报复；听闻别人做了坏事便不分青红皂白地深信不疑，而明明知道别人做了好事却始终不肯相信。——此等极端的刻薄行为，务必坚决戒除！

【English Translation】

There are persons who do not think of paying back after having received bountiful kindness, but are swift to make reprisals when suffering trivial wrong; and persons who do not make any doubt when told of someone else's secret wrongdoings, but become skeptical when clearly aware of another's philanthropic act. No deeds in the world are as contemptible as this! We must spurn them resolutely.

195. 不畏谗言　却惧蜜语

195. Fear no slanders, but beware of flattery.

谗夫毁士[1]，如寸云蔽日，不久自明；媚子阿人[2]，似隙风[3]侵肌，不觉其损。

【中文注释】 ① 谗夫毁士：谗夫，说别人坏话的人；毁士，诋毁正人君子。
② 媚子阿人：媚子，讨好别人的人；阿人，对人阿谀奉承。
③ 隙风：从缝隙中穿出来的风。

【今文解译】 搬弄是非的人针对正人君子的诽谤，就像一小片乌云遮住太阳，片刻之后太阳便又会大放光明。
阿谀奉承的人为讨好别人所说的话，就像隙风侵袭人的身体，所造成的伤害是一时无法察觉的。

【English Translation】

Calumny against the upright persons is like a wisp of cloud blotting out the sun; but away with the cloud the sun will soon shine forth bright and clear again.

Flattery is like the wind through a crack infiltrating our body and causing harm to us without our prompt notice.

196. 清高褊急　君子重戒

196. An accomplished man should attentively guard against being too stiff and narrow-minded.

山之高峻处无木，而溪谷回环则草木丛生；水之湍急处无鱼，而渊潭停蓄[1]则鱼鳖聚集。此高绝之行，褊急之衷[2]，君子重有戒焉。

【中文注释】 ① 渊潭停蓄：渊潭，平静的深水潭。停蓄，水流平静之意。
② 褊急之衷：气量狭小，容易冲动。

【今文解译】 山势高拔险峻的地方不容易生长树木，而蜿蜒曲折的溪谷中却草木森森；水流湍急的地方没有鱼在游动，而在平静的深水潭里却聚集着各种鱼虾蟹鳖。由此可见，为人过于清高，遇事容易冲动，这些都是一个君子绝对需要鉴戒的。

【English Translation】

At the high, steep places of a mountain there grow no trees, but along a winding valley there vegetate thick plants. In the rapids of a river there linger no fish, but in deep, still pools there gather shoals of aquatic animals. It is thus enlightened that the accomplished man should do his utmost to avoid being too stiff and unbending in action, and prevent himself from becoming narrow-minded and short-tempered when pondering issues.

197. 虚圆建功　执拗偾事

197. Modesty and flexibility lead to success, while stubbornness avails nothing.

建功立业者，多虚圆之士；偾事①失机者，必执拗之人。

【中文注释】 ① 偾事：把事情搞坏。

【今文解译】 能建功立业的人，大多是一群处世方面既谦虚又圆通的人。

成事不足败事有余的人，必是一帮固执己见不知变通的人。

【English Translation】

Those able to make achievements are mostly the ones who are modest and flexible in dealing with the world.

Those unable to seize the chances to succeed are surely the ones who are pigheaded and inflexible in tact.

198. 处世之道　不同不异

198. In dealing with the world, do not totally act in accord with the social mores, nor totally go against them.

处世不宜与俗同，亦不宜与俗异；作事不宜令人厌，亦不宜令人喜。

【今文解译】　处世不一定要随俗，也没有必要与风俗对着干。
做事不宜让别人讨厌，也不宜刻意去讨好别人。

【English Translation】
In dealing with the world, one should not totally accord with the customs nor totally be against them.
When handling affairs, one should not disgust others nor ingratiate himself with them.

199. 烈士暮年　壮心不已

199. The heart of a hero in his old age is as stout as ever.

日既暮而犹烟霞绚烂，岁将晚而更橙桔芳馨。故末路晚年，君子更宜精神百倍。

【今文解译】　太阳落山时，升腾在空中的烟雾云霞会显得格外绚烂迷人；深秋初冬时节，满树金黄色的橙橘会变得更加芳香诱人。所以，越是到了晚年，君子就越是应该精神百倍地面对人生。

【English Translation】
When the sun is setting, the mist and clouds in the twilight become more splendid. When late autumn is approaching, the fruits on orange trees grow to be more fragrant. Hence we know that the accomplished man in his old age should live on a hundred times more spirited than ever before.

200. 聪明不露　才华不逞

200. A wise man should never show off his intelligence nor parade his talent.

鹰立如睡，虎行似病，正是它攫人噬人[①]手段处。故君子要聪明不露，才华不逞，才有肩鸿任钜[②]的力量。

【中文注释】　① 攫人噬人：此处喻向猎物发起进攻。
② 肩鸿任钜：喻担当重任。钜，通“巨”。

【今文解译】　老鹰站立的姿势像是在睡觉，老虎走起路来像是有病在身，然而这正是它们攻击和攫取猎物的招数。所以，君子若想有力量担当起重任，平日里就不要炫耀自己的聪明，也不要显摆自己的才华。

【English Translation】

Perching at the edge of a cliff the eagle looks as if falling asleep. Prowling in a sluggish way the tiger looks as if afflicted with illness. Nevertheless, these are the very artifices with which they launch attack and seize their prey. From this we realize that a wise man should not show off his intelligence nor parade his talent, so that he will be in a power to be entrusted with important task when time comes.

201. 过俭者吝　过谦者卑

201. Undue thrift is regarded as miserliness and over-modesty as lowliness.

俭，美德也，过则为悭吝[①]，为鄙啬[②]，反伤雅道[③]；让，懿行也，过则为足恭[④]，为曲谨[⑤]，多出机心。

【中文注释】　① 悭吝：吝啬，小气。
② 鄙啬：小家子气。
③ 雅道：此处指前面所说的美德。
④ 足恭：过度谦恭。
⑤ 曲谨：过分谨慎。

【今文解译】 生活俭朴是一种美德，然而过分俭朴则有吝啬和小家子气之嫌，反而辱没了俭朴这种美德。
为人谦卑是一种懿行，然而过分谦卑则会显得卑躬屈膝谨小慎微，反而让人觉得心机太重。

【English Translation】
To be thrifty in daily life is a good virtue; but if taken unduly it might become stingy and miserly, and will hurt the virtue itself.
To be modest is an exemplary conduct; but if taken out of sense it might become lowly and overcautious, and will be regarded as scheming.

202. 喜忧安危　勿介于心

202. Not turn a hair in the face of joy and worry, safety and danger.

毋忧拂意①，毋喜快心，毋恃久安，毋惮初难②。

【中文注释】 ① 拂意：此处指不合心意的事。
② 初难：事情开始时遇到的困难。

【今文解译】 不要因为事有不顺就忧心忡忡。
不要因为事情称心就得意忘形。
不要因为太平日久就高枕无忧。
不要因为始遇困难就缩手缩脚。

【English Translation】
Do not worry about the things that go against your will.
Do not fall into raptures over the matters that please you.
Do not rest easy because the world remains peaceful for long.
Do not be afraid when difficulties crop up at the beginning of your ventures.

203. 声华名利　非君子行

203. An accomplished man should not sink himself in sensual pleasures nor seek fame and wealth.

饮宴之乐多，不是个好人家；声华[①]之习胜[②]，不是个好士子[③]；名位之念重，不是个好臣士。

【中文注释】 ① 声华：歌舞声色。
② 胜：多。此处喻沉溺，奢靡。
③ 士子：读书人。与本书中其他篇章里出现的“士君子”同义。

【今文解译】 经常设宴摆席、饮酒作乐的人家，不是好人家。
整天耽于声色、生活奢靡的士子，不是好士子。
一心只想着名誉和地位的臣子，不是好臣子。

【English Translation】
It is not a good family that takes overmuch enjoyment in carouses and banquets.
He is not a good scholar who deeply indulges himself in sensual pleasures.
He is not a good official who thinks only of seeking fame and rank.

204. 乐极生悲　苦尽甜来

204. Extreme pleasure ends in sorrow, and after suffering comes happiness.

世人以心肯[①]处为乐，却被乐心引在苦处；达士[②]以心拂[③]处为乐，终为苦心换得乐来。

【中文注释】 ① 心肯：可心，称心如意。
② 达士：通情达理的人。
③ 心拂：不称心。

【今文解译】 普通的人一般都把自己称心如意的事情视为乐趣，但最后却偏偏被这种所谓的乐趣引到了痛苦中。
通达的人都习惯把经历不尽如人意的事情当作快乐，且最终凭着坚忍不拔的吃苦精神换来了快乐。

【English Translation】

Ordinary people regard the things satisfying their minds as pleasures; but finally the indulgence in such pleasures lures them into misery.
The enlightened man regards the things dissatisfying his mind as pleasures; eventually he acquires the real pleasure with pains.

205. 过满则溢　过刚即折

205. Overfullness begets spillage and overrigidness induces fracture.

居盈满者①，如水之将溢未溢，切忌再加一滴；处危急者，如木之将折未折，切忌再加一搦②。

【中文注释】 ① 居盈满者：泛指各方面都圆满称心的人。
② 搦：原意为持（拿着）或挑（挑逗；招惹）。此处可指按、压、拽等动作。

【今文解译】 当一个人得到了他想要的一切，就像水缸装满水且快要溢出来的样子，切忌再往里加入一滴。
当一个人处在危急关头时，就像树木将要折断但还没有折断的样子，切忌再往下拖拽一下。

【English Translation】

A man fully satisfied or contented is like a vat fully filled with water which is about to spill. Do not add another drop in it.
A man in a desperate situation is like a piece of weighted wood which is about to snap. Do not press it any more.

206. 冷眼观人　冷心思理

206. Be sober-eyed when observing the people around you and when pondering the reasons in things, be sober-minded.

冷眼观人，冷耳听语，冷情当感，冷心思理。

【今文解译】 观察旁人要冷静，听人说话要冷静，处理事情要冷静，思考问题要冷静。

【English Translation】

Be sober-eyed when observing the people around you; be sober-eared when listening to their words; be sober-hearted when conducting your affairs; be sober-minded when seeking the reasons in things.

207. 心宽福厚　量小福薄

207. Open-mindedness brings in profound happiness, while narrow-mindedness only slight one.

仁人心地宽舒，便福厚而庆长①，事事成个宽舒气象；鄙夫念头迫促，便禄薄而泽短②，事事得个迫促规模③。

【中文注释】 ① 福厚而庆长：福星高照，吉祥长久。
② 禄薄而泽短：福禄微薄，恩泽短暂。
③ 规模：此处喻局面、境地，或者格局。

【今文解译】 仁慈的人胸襟宽阔、心态舒展，所以福星总能为其高照，吉祥总能长久伴其左右，做什么都有个宽阔舒展的气象。鄙俗的人心胸狭隘、见识浅薄，所以能够受享的福禄和恩泽都十分有限，做什么都透着一股狭隘浅薄的小家子气。

【English Translation】

A kind man is open-minded and full of generosity; so he always has the luck to enjoy profound happiness and eternal blessings, and whatever he does is tinged with open-mindedness and generosity.

A mean fellow is narrow-minded and full of stinginess; so he only has the chance to receive slight fortune and transient favors, and whatever he does is signed with narrow-mindedness and stinginess.

208. 闻恶防谗 闻善防奸

208. Guard against the slanderous when hearing someone has done evil and when hearing someone has done good, watch out for the treacherous.

闻恶不可就恶，恐为谗夫泄怒；闻善不可即亲，恐引奸人进身。

【今文解译】 听说有人作恶，不可马上就产生反感，要防止谗佞之人为发泄私愤而诬陷好人。
听说有人行善，不可立即就表示亲近，要防止奸邪之人为升官进爵而阴险使诈。

【English Translation】

When you hear that someone has done evil, do not detest him in a hurry, lest that an enemy of his should frame a case against him. Likewise, when you hear that someone has done good, do not take a liking to him immediately, lest that it might be a trick used by the treacherous to promote himself.

209 躁急无成 平和得福

209. Rash-temperedness ends in failure, while calm-heartedness brings about good fortune.

性躁心粗者一事无成，心和气平者百福自集。

【今文解译】 性情粗暴的人，终将一事无成。
心平气和的人，必定百福自集。

【English Translation】

Nothing can be accomplished by the one who is rash-tempered and rude-minded.

All blessings will smile upon the one who is calm-hearted and good-humored.

210. 用人不刻　交友不滥

210. Not be too fastidious in choosing a person for a job and in making friends, not be too indiscriminate.

用人不宜刻，刻则思效者去；交友不宜滥，滥则贡谀者来。

【今文解译】 用人不宜苛求，苛求则会让本想实心效力的人离去。
交友不宜过滥，过滥则献媚取宠的人就会纷至沓来。

【English Translation】

One should not be too fastidious in choosing a person for a post; if too fastidious those who intend to render a service will quit.
One should not be too indiscriminate in making friends; if too indiscriminate those who are good at flattering will pour in.

211. 立得脚定　著得眼高

211. Get your foothold firm and let your gaze roam afar.

风斜雨急处，要立得脚定；花浓柳艳处，要著得眼高；路危径险处，要回得头早。

【今文解译】 形势吃紧的时候，要站稳脚跟，以免失去自己的立场。
眼花缭乱的时候，要高瞻远瞩，以免迷失自己的方向。
遇到危险的时候，要早做应变，以免受不必要的损失。

【English Translation】

In times of confusion and emergency one should get a firm foothold.
When in dazzling conditions one should stand high and be far-sighted.
In times of crisis and danger one should turn round before it is too late.

212. 和衷少争　谦德少妒

212. Amiability evokes no dispute and modesty arouses no jealousy.

节义之人济以和衷，才不启忿争之路；功名之士承以谦德，方不开嫉妒之门。

【今文解译】 崇尚节义的人要注意加强自己和善的气质，这样才不至于因刚直而与人格格不入。
功名在身的人要注意培养谦虚谨慎的美德，这样才不至于因自己成功而遭人羡妒。

【English Translation】

A man of rectitude and moral integrity should temper himself with amiability, and thus he will evoke no dispute with others.
A man of scholarly honor and rank should cultivate himself with modesty, and thus he will arouse no jealousy from others.

213. 居官有节　居乡有情

213. Be moderate when on an official position and when in retirement, be amiable and easy of approach.

士大夫居官，不可竿牍[①]无节，要使人难见，以杜幸端；居乡，不可崖岸太高[②]，要使人易见，以敦旧好[③]。

【中文注释】 ① 竿牍：书信。此处喻求职索官的信函。
② 崖岸太高：架子太大。
③ 以敦旧好：敦，加深。旧好，过去的情谊。

【今文解译】 身居高位的人，不可无节制地接受求职索官的信函，而要少接待那些怀有此意前来觐见的人，以不使其侥幸得逞；辞官回乡后，不可对乡里乡亲摆架子，而要平易近人，加深与他们的情谊。

【English Translation】

When assuming office, a high-ranking official should not lose moderation in receiving letters of seeking position, but rather should decline to give interviews to those who have such intentions, in this way he will prevent petty men from taking advantage of the moment. And when he retires to live in his native land, he should not appear arrogant nor stand aloof from his fellow countrymen, but should instead make himself amiable and easy of approach, in this way he will enhance the old friendships with them.

214. 事上警谨　待下宽仁

214. Be careful when attending upon your superiors and in dealings with your inferiors, be generous.

大人不可不畏，畏大人则无放逸之心；小民亦不可不畏，畏小民则无豪横[1]之名。

【中文注释】 ① 豪横：蛮横。

【今文解译】 对尊贵者不可没有敬畏之心，敬畏尊贵者可以收敛自己放纵轻浮的心性；对普通百姓也不可没有敬畏之心，敬畏普通百姓可以使自己远离霸道的恶名。

【English Translation】

It is imperative to regard dignitaries with reverence, so that one would restrain the heart of indulgence and frivolousness. It is also imperative to treat commoners with reverence, so that one would stay clear of ill repute of peremptoriness.

215. 逆境消怨　怠荒思奋

215. When in adversity, try to dispel the grievances from your heart; and when becoming indolent, think about how to rouse yourself.

事稍拂逆，便思不如我的人，则怨尤[1]自消；心稍怠荒[2]，便思胜似我的人，则精神自奋。

【中文注释】 ① 怨尤：怨气，不满。
② 怠荒：懒惰，松懈。

【今文解译】 遇事稍有不顺的时候，就想想那些境遇不如自己的人，这样心头的怨尤就会自然消失。

心劲稍有堕怠的时候，就想想那些能力比自己强的人，这样精神就会立即振作起来。

【English Translation】

When you suffer setbacks in running your ventures, you'd better think of those whose conditions are worse than yours; thus the grievances in your heart will disappear of themselves.

As soon as you have an indolent thought in mind, you'd better think of those who are more capable and industrious than you are; thus it will rouse you to high spirits.

216. 轻诺惹祸　倦怠无成

216. Promise lightly made courts disasters and indolence makes previous work undone.

不可乘喜而轻诺，不可因醉而生嗔①；不可乘快而多事，不可因倦而鲜终②。

【中文注释】　① 生嗔：发泄怒气。

② 鲜终：中途放弃，有始无终。

【今文解译】　不可在自己得意忘形的时候轻易承诺，也不可因醉意阑珊而泄愤撒泼。

不可在兴头正浓的时候惹是生非，也不可因自己身心疲倦而有始无终。

【English Translation】

We should not make rash promises at a time when we are pleased, nor should we lose our tempers under the pretext of our drunkenness.

We should not be meddlesome and cause troubles at a time when we are elated, nor should we give up halfway on the pretence of our weariness.

217. 读书得其要领　观物达其实质

217. When reading a book, try to understand its essence; when observing an object, try to reach its substance.

善读书者，要读到手舞足蹈处，方不落筌蹄[①]；善观物者，要观到心融神洽[②]时，方不泥迹象[③]。

【中文注释】 ① 不落筌蹄：筌，捕鱼的竹器；蹄，捕兔的工具。此处指不为文字所囿。
② 心融神洽：心神贯注于事物的内在并与之融为一体。
③ 不泥迹象：不拘泥于表面现象。

【今文解译】 善于读书的人，要读到不知不觉地手舞足蹈的时候，才算领悟到了隐含在字里行间的真义。
善于观察事物的人，要观察到心神皆融于被观察事物中去的时候，才不致被表面现象迷惑。

【English Translation】
The one good at reading should enjoy his reading to such an extent that he could not help dancing with excitement; only then can he be thought to have comprehended the true meaning of the given words.
The one adept in observation should, through an attentive study of the object, try to merge his heart and spirit into the core of it; only then can he surmount superficial phenomena and reach the substance.

218. 勿以长欺短　勿以富凌贫

218. Do not humiliate others with your strong points, nor bully the poor with your wealth.

天贤[①]一人，以诲众人之愚，而世反逞所长，以形人之短；天富[②]一人，以济众人之困，而世反挟所有，以凌人之贫。真天之戮民哉！

【中文注释】 ① 贤：贤达。
② 富：财富。

【今文解译】 上天授一人以贤达，为的是让他育化大众的愚昧，但是世间还是有人卖弄自己的才能，并以自己所长羞辱别人所短。

上天授一人以财富，为的是让他接济大众的贫困，但是世间还是有人利用手中的财富去欺凌贫穷困苦中的平民百姓。

如此大逆不道的罪人上天岂能容之！

【English Translation】

Heaven bestows wisdom on one man so that he can influence the multitude to relieve their ignorance. But there are men who apply themselves to publicizing the shortcomings of others by displaying their own strong points.

Heaven grants wealth to one man so that he can help the masses with their sufferings and difficulties. But there are men who use their riches to bully the poor.

Such men are really the vessels of the wrath of Heaven.

219. 中才之人　高低难成

219. A medium-gifted man is fit for neither a higher post nor a lower one.

至人[①]何思何虑，愚人不识不知，可与论学，亦可与建功。唯中才之人，多一番思虑知识，便多一番臆度[②]猜疑，事事难与下手[③]。

【中文注释】 ① 至人：品行和智慧完美无缺的人。

② 臆度：主观推断。

③ 难与下手：难以合作共事。

【今文解译】 修为至深的人不喜欢为思虑所困，而秉性愚钝的人做什么想法都很简单，与这两种人探讨学问，甚至与他们一起建功立业——都行。倒是那些有点才能但才能平平的人，他们遇事往往思来想去，臆想和猜疑不断，与这种人合作共事——难。

【English Translation】

Men of supreme virtue and talent prefer to be untroubled, and men of ignorance unconcerned. None the less it is still possible for one to do something together with either of them in making academic researches and contributions to the society. While the medium-gifted men, who only have a smattering of knowledge, always act in a shilly-shally way on assumptions and suspicions; it is hard to collaborate with them in anything.

220. 守口应密　防意应严

220. The mouth should be closely guarded and the minds well controlled.

口乃心之门，守口不密，泄尽真机；意乃心之足，防意不严，走尽邪蹊。

【今文解译】　嘴巴是心的门户，门户把守不严，你的秘密就会泄露无遗。

意念是心的双足，双足看管不紧，它们就会把你带入歧途。

【English Translation】

The mouth is the doorway of the heart; if you cannot have it closely guarded, your true intentions and motives will be divulged.

Thoughts are the feet of the heart; if you cannot have them well controlled, they will lead you astray for good and all.

221. 责人宜宽　责己宜严

221. Better be lenient when censuring another for a fault but strict when making self-reproaches.

责人者，原无过于有过之中，则情平；责己者，求有过于无过之内，则德进。

【今文解译】 责备别人时，我们如果能从其错误中找出并无过错的地方加以肯定和原谅，那么犯错者就会心服口服地接受批评。

自我检讨时，我们如果能从并无过错的地方找出自己的过错并承担一些责任，那么我们的修为会因此而得以提高。

【English Translation】

When taking another to task, one should somehow affirm something impeachable in his fault. Thus the mood of the faulty will smooth down.

When making self-accusation, one should somehow bear some blame for the fault he is innocent of. So he will be able to make progress in moral cultivation.

222. 幼时定基　少时勤学

222. Characters should be tempered from childhood and diligent study begins in youth.

子弟者，大人之胚胎；秀才者，士大夫之胚胎。此时若火力[①]不到，陶铸不纯，他日涉世立朝，终难成个令器[②]。

【中文注释】 ① 火力：修炼的力度。

② 令器：优秀的人才。

【今文解译】 儿童是成人的雏形，秀才是朝臣的雏形。如果这个阶段对他们管教不到位，要求不严格，日后等到他们走进社会或踏上仕途，终将难以成为出类拔萃的人才。

【English Translation】

Children are the embryonic forms of adults and scholars are those of court ministers. But if not well-tempered and fine-molded at this stage, someday when they are engaged in the life of a community or enlisted as court officials, neither of them will become leading characters.

223. 君子忧乐　亦怜茕独

223. A man of virtue will be consumed with circumspection in a time of joy and with pity when together with the abandoned and helpless.

君子处患难而不忧，当宴游而惕虑[1]，遇权豪而不惧，对茕独[2]而惊心。

【中文注释】　① 惕虑：谨慎小心，有所顾忌。
② 茕独：无兄弟曰茕，无子曰独。

【今文解译】　君子的本色应该是：身处困境时不焦虑，宴饮游乐时能保持警醒，遇到权门豪强时面无惧色，面对无依无靠的人时有恻隐之心。

【English Translation】

A man of virtue will not be depressed when confronted with difficulties, but will be circumspect and scrupulous while at a feast or on a sightseeing tour. He will be undaunted when encountering the powerful and peremptory, but will be moved with compassion when together with the abandoned and helpless.

224. 浓夭淡久　大器晚成

224. Gaudy colors and rich flavors are inferior to light but constant ones and early flourish is not as good as late maturity.

桃李虽艳，何如松苍柏翠之坚贞？梨杏虽甘，何如橙黄桔绿之馨冽[1]？信乎！浓夭[2]不及淡久，早秀[3]不如晚成也。

【中文注释】　① 馨冽：清香。
② 浓夭：浓艳的东西消失得快。
③ 早秀：早早地开花结果。

【今文解译】　桃花和李花虽然艳丽，但怎比得上苍松翠柏的坚贞无畏?！梨子和杏子虽然甘甜，但怎比得上黄橙绿橘的爽口润齿?！的确如此：但凡浓烈的都不及清淡的那么持久，早熟的都不如晚熟的那么杰出。

【English Translation】

Gorgeous are the blossoms of peaches and plums; but how can they match the constancy of dark green pines and cypresses? Sweet are the fruits of pears and apricots; but how can they match the fragrance of golden oranges and green tangerines? It is true that gaudy colors and rich flavors are often inferior to light but constant ones, and that early flourish is not as good as late maturity.

225. 静中真境　淡现本然

225. The true realm of a man's life exists amid tranquility and his natural characters emerge from simplicity.

风恬浪静中，见人生之真境；味淡声稀①处，识心体之本然。

【中文注释】　① 味淡声稀：饭菜清淡，音乐稀少。此处喻淡泊之意。

【今文解译】　在风平浪静的环境里，人生的真实境界才得以显见。
在无名利之争的地方，人性的本来面目才得以鉴识。

【English Translation】

Only in the midst of peace and quiet can the true realm of man's life be perceived.

Only in places where the folks are of few desires can the disposition of human nature be recognized.

226. 乐者不言　言者不乐

226. Those who understand happiness may not talk about it; those who talk about happiness may not understand it.

谈山林之乐者，未必真得山林之趣；厌名利之谈者，未必尽忘名利之情。

【今文解译】　动辄谈论山林之乐的人，未必真的知道山林之乐的妙趣何在。
口口声声说厌恶名利的人，未必都真的已经抛却了名利之心。

【English Translation】

It does not necessarily follow that those who are fond of talking about the delights in living amid the mountains and forests really understand the bliss of such a life. Neither does it so that those who declare themselves to be disgusted at the talk about fame and wealth have completely banished from their minds the desires for fame and wealth.

227. 省事为适 无能全真

227. Less engagement leads to leisureliness; incompetence keeps man’s nature intact.

钓水，逸事也，尚持生杀之柄；弈棋，清戏也，且动战争之心。可见喜事①不如省事之为适，多能不若无能之全真。

【中文注释】 ① 喜事：相对于后面的“省事”，此处的“喜事”意为好找事情做，闲不住。

【今文解译】 临水垂钓是身心惬意的消遣，然而鱼儿的生死予夺之权却掌握在垂钓者的手里；棋局对弈是清静悠闲的游戏，但是弈棋的双方心里却都怀着你死我活的杀伐动机。由此可见，多一事不如少一事更让人闲适，能干的不如无能的更能保全人的本性。

【English Translation】

Fishing by the waterside is a pleasant, elegant recreation, yet the fisher wields the power of life and death. Playing chess is a gentle, quiet game, yet the players harbor in their minds the desire to contend. Thus we get to know that in living a leisurely life, to be engaged in something is not as good as not to be engaged; and in maintaining the intactness of man’s nature, competence is inferior to incompetence.

228. 艳为虚幻　枯为胜境

228. The reality of Nature is revealed by decay instead of brilliance which is nothing but an illusion.

莺花茂[1]而山浓谷艳，总是乾坤之幻境；水木落而石瘦崖枯，才见天地之真吾[2]。

【中文注释】 ① 莺花茂：百鸟齐鸣，百花盛开。莺，黄莺。此处泛指各种鸟类。
② 真吾：真正的我。此处指事物的原形。

【今文解译】 山浓谷艳的风光全赖鸟语花香来点缀，但这一切都只是天地间的幻境罢了；石瘦崖枯皆因河流干涸、树木凋零，此时的衰败景象才是大自然的真实写照。

【English Translation】

Birds' twitter, fragrance of flowers, luxuriant mountains and gorgeous valleys are all nothing but the illusive scenery arranged by Nature. Quite the contrast, dried-up riverbeds, withered trees, barren cliffs and naked rocks are all the real features Nature has designed for us human beings.

229. 天地之闲　因人而异

229. The realization of whether the world is of leisure or not varies from man to man.

岁月本长，而忙者自促；天地本宽，而卑者自隘；风花雪月[1]本闲，而劳攘者自冗。

【中文注释】 ① 风花雪月：此处指大自然的美景。

【今文解译】 岁月本就悠长，而忙忙碌碌的人却觉得时间短暂。
天地本就宽广，而心胸狭窄的人却觉得空间局促。
风花雪月本就悠闲，而疲于奔波的人却无暇欣赏。

【English Translation】

Time is, in fact, endless; while those who are on the go feel it short and pressing.
The world is wide and broad; while those who are narrow-minded think it small and cramped.
The wind, the flowers, the snow and the moon are all romantic factors acquirable for a leisurely life; while those who are fluttering have no time to stop and enjoy them.

230. 盆池竹屋　意境高远

230. Even a basin-sized pool or a bamboo house can bring in profound subtleties.

得趣不在多，盆池拳石间，烟霞俱足；会景不在远，蓬窗竹屋下，风月自赊[①]。

【中文注释】　① 赊：多。

【今文解译】　生活的情趣不在多，即便是盆景大小的人工山水，也足够具备自然山川的烟霞浩渺。
领略自然美景不必远足，即便在蓬窗竹屋下，也可将魅力无限的秀丽风光尽收眼底。

【English Translation】

To appreciate the joys of life, it is not up to how many of them you have experienced; even in sight of a basin-sized pool of clean water or a pile of fist-shaped stones, you may not miss the magic of the lakes veiled in the mist and the mountains surrounded by the floating clouds.
To grasp the subtlety of Nature, it is not necessary to have a long journey to the scenic spots afar; even out of the windows of a thatched cottage or under the eaves of a bamboo house, you may have sufficient pleasure to enjoy the mild breeze and bright moonlight.

231. 静夜梦醒　月现本性

231. The sound of a temple bell on a still night wakens the dream of life; the moon reflection in the pool reveals the origin of man's nature.

听静夜之钟声，唤醒梦中之梦[1]；观澄潭之月影，窥见身外之身[2]。

【中文注释】 ① 梦中之梦：中国人自古将人生比作梦。在这里，前一个"梦"指人生，后一个"梦"指幻觉中的梦，即梦幻。
② 身外之身：第二个"身"是佛家所谓的肉身之外的灵魂，也即人性中的真我。

【今文解译】 夜深人静时聆听寺庙的钟声，可以把我们从梦幻中唤醒。凝望清澈池塘里的月影，可以使我们洞见人性中的真我。

【English Translation】

Listen to the ringing of a temple bell afar on a still midnight, and so you will wake up from a fancy and stay sober.
Gaze upon the moon reflection on the surface of a limpid pool, and so you will perceive the true characters of your nature.

232. 天地万物　皆是实相

232. Everything in the world has its own way to express itself.

鸟语虫声，总是传心之诀；花英草色，无非见[1]道之文。学者要天机清澈[2]，胸次玲珑[3]，触物皆有会心处。

【中文注释】 ① 见：古文中通"现"，即显现，表现。
② 天机清澈：神智清明透澈。此处喻敏锐的洞察力。
③ 胸次玲珑：心思灵巧敏捷。此处喻灵巧的想象力。

【今文解译】 鸟的啼鸣和虫的呻吟，都是表达心声的方法；花的美艳和草的青葱，都是大自然展现的风采。为学者要具备敏锐的洞察力和灵动的想象力，这样，接触到任何事物才会有别样的领悟。

【English Translation】

The twitter of birds and the chirping of insects are the expressions they use to transmit their innermost feelings. The splendor of flowers and the hues of grasses are the elegance shown by Nature. As a man of learning, he should entertain a penetrating insight and rich imagination so that he will be in a power to grasp the extraordinary meaning of the things encountered.

233. 知无形物　悟无尽趣

233. To apprehend a thing by its essence instead of its form leads to boundless subtlety.

人解读有字书，不解读无字书；知弹有弦琴，不知弹无弦琴。以迹用，不以神用[①]，何以得琴书之趣?

【中文注释】 ① 以迹用，不以神用：只看重事物的外表，不看重事物的内在或本质。

【今文解译】 只会读有字之书，不会读大自然这本无字之书；只知道弹有弦之琴，不知道弹大自然这架无弦之琴。——一味地执着于事物的外在，不理解事物的内涵，这样的人又岂能明白弹琴读书的真趣?!

【English Translation】

People can only read the books written in words, but cannot read the book of Nature, which has no written words. They only know how to play the lute with strings, but do not know how to play the lute without. If they merely gaze on the outer forms of a thing and do not gain an insight into its essence, how can they apprehend the subtlety of playing the lute and reading books?

234. 淡欲有书　神仙之境

234. Books help to weaken men's material desires and guide them into the fairyland.

心无物欲，即是秋空霁海[①]；坐有琴书，便成石室丹丘[②]。

【中文注释】 ① 秋空霁海：秋高气爽的天空和雾霭散尽后的大海。
② 石室丹丘：古时候专指隐士或神仙的居所。

【今文解译】 一个人的内心如不被物欲所蒙蔽，就会像秋天的碧空和一望无际的大海那样豁达开朗。
一个人如果有怡情悦心的琴韵和书香做伴，就会像远离尘嚣的隐士一样活得逍遥自在。

【English Translation】

If a man has no desire for material gains, his heart would become as clear as the cloudless autumnal sky and as vast as the boundless sea under the sunshine.
If a man sits himself in company with a lute and books, his life would become as free and unfettered as that of the supernatural beings in a fairyland.

235. 盛宴散后　兴味索然

235. When a grand feast comes to an end, flatness appears.

宾朋云集，剧饮淋漓[①]，乐矣！俄而[②]漏尽烛残，香销茗冷，不觉反成呕咽[③]，令人索然无味。天下事，率类此[④]，奈何不早回头也？

【中文注释】 ① 剧饮淋漓：开怀畅饮。
② 俄而：少顷，不久。
③ 呕咽：本指“倒胃口”，此处喻兴致全无，与后句中的“索然无味”意思相近。
④ 率类此：大概都是如此吧。

【今文解译】 宾朋云聚一堂，推杯换盏，畅饮狂欢，好不快活！然而转眼之间，夜至深更，烛光萎靡，炉香燃尽，茶水冰凉，方觉刚才还浓浓的快意竟已烟消云散，顿时兴味全无。世间万事万物无不如此，人又怎能不知见好就收，早早回头？！

【English Translation】

When guests and friends are gathered, they enjoy good wines and happy greetings heartily. What a cheerful occasion! But shortly when deep into the night, there are only left empty hourglasses, burned-out candles, ashes of joss sticks and cold tea. At such a moment, all the joys have vanished like mist and smoke and the participants feel flat and insipid. Things are always going like this: grievance treads on the heels of pleasure. Why not stop and reflect in good time?

236. 得个中趣　破眼前机

236. Ascertain the subtlety of Nature and perceive the deceptions and trickeries before your eyes.

会得个中①趣，五湖之烟月②尽入寸里③；破得眼前机，千古之英雄尽归掌握。

【中文注释】 ① 个中：其中。
② 五湖之烟月：泛指世界各地的风景。
③ 寸里：心里。

【今文解译】 如能将大自然的妙趣窥得一二，那么就等于把五湖四海的壮丽美景都装进了你心里。
如能及时识破出现在眼前的机缘，那么所有古往今来的英雄豪杰就都可以为你所用。

【English Translation】

If you could ascertain the subtlety contained in Nature, you would be able to have in your mind a panoramic view of the scenery of the whole world.
If you could promptly perceive every chance arising right before your eyes, you would be able to hold in your hands all the worthies through the ages.

237. 非上上智　无了了心

237. Only with supreme wisdom can one make a thorough comprehension of Nature and human life.

山河大地已属微尘，而况尘中之尘；血肉之躯且归泡影，而况影外之影。非上上智[①]，无了了心[②]。

【中文注释】 ① 上上智：绝顶的智慧。
② 了了心：洞彻一切的心。

【今文解译】 山川大地只是细小的尘粒，而况尘中之尘的人类；人的血肉之躯只是脆弱的泡影，而况影外之影的名利。没有超凡的智慧，人是无法彻悟其中道理的。

【English Translation】

The mountains, the rivers and the land are merely tiny specks of dust, and much more so are human beings. The blood and flesh of a man's body are simply bubbles, and much more so are fame and wealth. That is why people say that only those who have thoroughly comprehended the essence of Nature and human life are most intelligent.

238. 人生苦短　宇宙无限

238. Man's life is transient while the cosmos is boundless.

石火光[①]中争长竞短，几何光阴？蜗牛角[②]上较雌论雄，许大世界？

【中文注释】 ① 石火光：石头相互击打时迸发出的火星。比喻短暂。
② 蜗牛角：蜗牛的触角。比喻空间狭小。

【今文解译】 在短暂的石火光中争长竞短，即使争得了又能值几寸光阴？
在狭小的蜗牛角里对决雌雄，即使称雄了又能有多大地盘？

【English Translation】

Man's life is as transient as the spark struck from flint; how many inches of time can a man contend for?
The world is as tiny as a snail's horn; how much territory can a man seize by struggle?

239. 极端空寂　断不可取

239. Extreme void is absolutely undesirable.

寒灯无焰，敝裘[①]无温，总是播弄光景；身如槁木，心似死灰，不免堕在顽空[②]。

【中文注释】 ① 敝裘：破旧的毛皮衣服。
② 顽空：冥顽空虚。

【今文解译】 微弱的孤灯已经油尽焰冷，破旧的裘衣已经不堪御寒，这样的尴尬着实是造化弄人。
骨瘦如干枯的树木，心死如燃灭的灰烬，这样的境地无异于堕在万劫不复的冥空中。

【English Translation】

When the oil gives out and the lamp becomes cold, no more flame can be produced. When a fur coat becomes tattered, no more warmth can be retained. This is the time the god of destiny makes fools of the multitude. Those who let their bodies look like rotten woods and their souls dead ashes will unavoidably fall into a void plight.

240. 休无休时　了无了时

240. Take a rest when time allows; if you wish to do so till all the works in hand are completed, then you will never meet your wishes.

人肯当下休，便当下了。若要寻个歇处，则：婚嫁虽完，事亦不少；僧道虽好，心亦不了。前人云："如今休去便休去，若觅了时无了时。"见之卓矣。

【今文解译】 什么时候想停下来歇歇脚就该马上停下来，如果还要等等看找个合适的时机再停，这就好比：婚姻大事办妥了，而婚后的事还有一大堆；出家的和尚和道士虽然清静了，可他们的俗愿未必能全了。还是古人说得好："如今休去便休去，若觅了时无了时。"真是一语中的啊！

【English Translation】

People should stop for a rest so long as they will and do not have to wait till everything is fixed. If they persist in finding out a proper time to do so, it will be like marriage — although the wedding ceremony is over, there are still a lot of things to do afterwards; or like Buddhist monks or Taoist priests — although they have already denounced their homes for practicing religion, they still have worldly wishes unfulfilled. There is an ancient saying that goes, "Take a rest when time allows. If you wish to do so till all the works in hand are completed, then you will never meet your wishes." What a high perspicacity!

241. 从冷视热　从冗入闲

241. In times of calm, reflect on the boisterousness; while being busy, try to take a moment's respite.

从冷视热，然后知热处之奔驰①无益；从冗入闲，然后觉闲中之滋味最长。

【中文注释】　① 奔驰：此处指对名利的追逐。

【今文解译】　从名利场退出来再审视名利场，你会发现名利场中的你争我夺其实毫无意义。

从忙碌中解脱出来过上悠闲的生活，你会觉得安逸悠闲的生活其实滋味最长。

【English Translation】

When those who have abandoned Vanity Fair reflect on the boisterousness, they will understand how meaningless it is to bustle with ostentation.

When those who have been running about all the time return to a leisurely life, they will realize that the taste of leisure is most meaningful.

242. 轻视富贵　不溺酒中

242. Wealth and rank are what men should despise and wine is what they should not wallow in.

有浮云富贵[1]之风，而不必岩栖穴处[2]；无膏肓泉石之癖[3]，而常自醉酒耽诗[4]。

【中文注释】 ① 浮云富贵：如同浮云一般的富贵。形容对富贵的轻蔑。

② 岩栖穴处：以深山洞穴为家。比喻隐居生活。

③ 膏肓泉石之痴：意为“喜欢山水风景到了如痴如醉的程度，就像病入膏肓的病人一样不可救药”。膏肓，古代称心尖脂肪为膏，心脏与隔膜之间为肓，这两处皆为药力所不能达到的地方。泉石，此处指山水风景。

④ 醉酒耽诗：沉溺于饮酒作诗之中。

【今文解译】 一个人若能视富贵荣华如浮云，就没有必要再去深山幽谷修养身心了。

一个对山水风景不是太痴迷的人，即使常自饮酒吟诗也不失风雅如许。

【English Translation】

A man who has a bearing to regard wealth and rank as floating clouds does not have to go and dwell in the secluded cave to temper his virtue.

A man who has no ardent love of the scenery of mountains and fountains may still wallow in wines, recite poems and pose as a lover of culture.

243. 不嫌人醉　不夸己醒

243. Not cold-shoulder others if they are infatuated with fame and wealth, nor brag that you are the only one who is above the worldly considerations.

竞逐听人，而不嫌尽醉；恬淡适己，而不夸独醒。此释氏[1]所谓“不为法缠[2]，不为空缠[3]，身心两自在”者。

【中文注释】 ① 释氏：佛教的鼻祖释迦牟尼。此处指佛教。

② 不为法缠：不为外界事物所束缚。

③ 不为空缠：不为虚幻所羁绊。

【今文解译】 别人争名夺利由他们去，不必因为别人醉心于名利而故意疏远他们；恬静淡泊是自身修养的需要，所以没必要向世人夸耀唯我独醒。这就是佛家所说的“不为法缠，不为空缠，身心两自在”。

【English Translation】

When you see others chasing after fame and wealth, just let them; it's unnecessary to cold-shoulder them even if they are infatuated with such things. If you yourself seek no fame and wealth, just keep it; there is no need to brag that you are the only one who is above the worldly considerations. This is what Buddhism called "Not be fettered by mundane affairs nor be snared by illusions, thereby keeping both body and mind free and unrestrained".

244. 心闲日长　意广天宽

244. To a leisurely-minded person, a single day is longer than enough; to a broad-minded person, a tiny hovel seems as a large space.

延促由于一念，宽窄系之寸心。故机闲者，一日遥于千古；意广者，斗室宽若两间。

【今文解译】　时间的长短往往取决于人的心理感受，空间的宽窄常常取决于人的心理体验。所以：只要能把握时机、忙里偷闲，即使一天的时间也比千年还要绵长；只要意境高远、心胸旷达，即使小小的一间屋子也比天地还要宽敞。

【English Translation】

Whether time is long or short hinges on man's psychological feelings; likewise, whether space is broad or narrow rests with man's mental perception. Therefore, if you are a leisurely-minded person, even a single day could be as long as eternity; if you are a broad-minded person, even a small room could be as spacious as the universe itself.

245. 栽花种竹　去欲忘忧

245. Raising flowers and planting bamboos are conducive to removal of material desires and mundane worries.

损①之又损，栽花种竹，尽交还乌有先生②；忘③无可忘，焚香煮茗，总不问白衣童子④。

【中文注释】 ① 损：减少。此处指减少物欲。

② 乌有先生：中国古代文学中虚拟的人物，即本无其人的意思。延引自“子虚乌有”。

③ 忘，忘却。此处指忘却生活中的琐碎之事。

④ 白衣童子：身着白衣的侍童。常用以烘托悠闲的环境和气氛。

【今文解译】 对物质的追求要少之又少，通过栽花种竹来培养自己的生活情趣，让烦恼都见鬼去吧。

忘却生活中的琐碎之事，有空就焚几炷香、煮一壶茶，甚至不必劳烦问身边侍童是谁。

【English Translation】

Reduce, and reduce again, your lust for material gains, cultivate your temperament and interest only by raising flowers and planting bamboos, and then you will cast to the winds all the vexations and depressions you have.

Forget all the trifles of your life until nothing is left to be forgotten, enjoy yourself only by burning sandal incense and brewing aromatic tea, and then you will enter the realm of carefreeness.

246. 知足则仙　善用则生

246. Those content with their lot are happy; those good at making use of opportunities are prosperous.

都来眼前事①，知足者仙境，不知足者凡境；总出世上因，善用者生机②，不善用者杀机③。

【中文注释】 ① 都来眼前事：眼前的一切。

② 生机：此处喻事事顺遂。

③ 杀机：此处喻处处被动以致陷入危机。

【今文解译】 每天都有很多事情要面对，知足的人觉得自己仿佛生活在仙境里，而不知足的人则摆脱不了俗世的纷扰和困惑。纵观大千世界的成败因果，善于利用机会的人做起事来常常得心应手，而不善于利用机会的人却往往举步维艰。

【English Translation】

In dealing with everyday affairs, those who are content with their lot will feel as if they were living a happy life in a fairyland; but those who are discontent with their lot will fail to extricate themselves from the disturbance of vulgarity. Taking all the reasons of success and failure into consideration, those good at making use of opportunities will be in luck's way everywhere and accomplish whatever they wish to; but those not good at making use of opportunities will land themselves in a passive position and get bogged down in crises wherever they go.

247. 附势遭祸　守逸味长

247. Fawning upon the influential and powerful brings disaster, while preserving ease of mind produces durable taste.

趋炎附势之祸，甚惨亦甚速；栖恬守逸之味，最淡亦最长。

【今文解译】 依附权势的人固然能图得一时之利，但是因此而招引的祸害将会很惨且猝不及防。

恬淡守静的人免不了要受些寂寞的煎熬，但是从中所得到的淡然趣味却最为长久。

【English Translation】

Just as the disaster derived from fawning upon the influential and powerful is most horrible and swiftest, so the taste derived from preserving tranquility of life and ease of mind is mildest and most durable.

248. 松涧望闲云　竹夜见风月

248. At day, watch the floating clouds along the side of a pine-covered rivulet and at night, view the scene of the wind and moon in a bamboo shed.

松涧边，携杖独行，立处云生破衲①；竹窗下，枕书高卧，觉时②月侵寒毡③。

【中文注释】 ① 破衲：破旧的僧衣。
② 觉时：醒来时。
③ 寒毡：御寒的薄毛毡。

【今文解译】 在长满松树的山涧旁，我手拄拐杖独自散步，停立处，只见山雾弥漫升腾在我的破衲周围。
在简陋的竹窗下读书，读累了我就枕书而卧，一觉醒来竟然发现薄毡上已洒满清冷的月光。

【English Translation】
Alone with a walking stick, I took a stroll along the side of a pine-covered rivulet; and at a standstill, I found my ragged vestment enveloped in the thick fog.
After reading a lot, I slept beneath the bamboo window, with my head pillowed on books; and when awaking, I saw the limpid moon shining on my flimsy felt.

249. 欲时思病　利来思死

249. When lust rages in your mind, think of the trouble; and when benefit comes to you, think of the calamity.

色欲火炽，而一念及病时，便兴似寒灰；名利饴甘，而一想到死地，便味如嚼蜡。故人常忧死虑病，亦可消幻业①而长道心②。

【中文注释】 ① 幻业：佛家用语。此处指对功名利禄的贪欲。
② 道心：佛家用语。此处指自己的道德品行。

【今文解译】 当性的渴望像烈火一样燃烧时，只要稍微想一想染病的痛苦，欲火就立即会变成冰冷的灰烬；当追逐名利渐变成饴甘之乐时，只要稍微想一想死亡将意味着什么，所谓的饴甘之乐也就如同嚼蜡一般。所以，一个人要经常想想疾病和死亡，这有助于打消对身外之物的贪念，培养合乎道行的德性。

【English Translation】

Lust is as fierce as a blazing fire; but when one thinks of the suffering likely resulted from excessive sexuality, one's passionate desire will immediately become like a heap of cold ashes. Fame and wealth are as sweet as malt sugar; but when one thinks of the death possibly ensuing therefrom, one's avarice will at once become as tasteless as chewing wax. Therefore, constantly thinking about suffering and death would help one sever oneself from lust and avarice, and upgrade one's moral integrities as well.

250. 退后一步 清淡一分

250. A pace back makes a road more spacious，lightly seasoned food gives more taste.

争先的径路窄，退后一步，自宽平一步；浓艳的滋味短，清淡一分，自悠长一分。

【今文解译】 人人都争先恐后，道路就显得狭窄。此时若有人退后一步让别人先行，道路自会变得宽敞畅通。
食物味道太浓烈，滋味反会因为腻口而短暂。如果做得稍微清淡些，食物自然就会变得回味无穷。

【English Translation】

Rushing on like a swarm of hornets makes a road narrow. But if someone could at this moment step back a pace, the road would undoubtedly become spacious.

Food prepared to be extraordinarily rich and pungent damps the taste itself. But if it could be lightly seasoned, its flavors would naturally become lasting.

251. 忙不乱性　死不动心

251. Be steadfast and composed when occupied and fearless when facing death.

忙处不乱性，须闲处心神养得清；死时不动心，须生时事物看得破。

【今文解译】　要想在忙碌的时候做到心性不乱，必须在闲时就养成保持头脑清醒的习惯。

要想在死亡面前做到从容淡定，必须在平日里就把人之生死这个问题悟透。

【English Translation】

If a man wishes to be steadfast and well composed when occupied, he must have his mind cleansed and spirit purified when at leisure.

If a man intends to behave himself fearlessly in front of death, he must attain a thorough understanding of the issue of life and death at ordinary times.

252. 隐无荣辱　道无炎凉

252. To live as a hermit, give no thought to personal honor and disgrace; to seek morality, pay no heed to the fickleness of human nature.

隐逸林中无荣辱，道义路上无炎凉。

【今文解译】　对于隐逸山林的居士来说，个人的荣耀与耻辱已不值得计较。

对于崇尚道义的志士而言，世态的炎凉无常已无须再予关注。

【English Translation】

Those who have retired from office and now live in obscurity give no thought to personal honor and disgrace.

Those who have devoted themselves to the attainment of morality and justice disregard the fickleness of the world.

253. 心静自然凉　乐观无穷愁

253. Free from vexation, and one will feel cool of oneself; be optimistic, and one will have no distress about poverty.

热不必除，而除此热恼，身常在清凉台上；穷不可遣，而遣此穷愁，心常居安乐窝[1]中。

【中文注释】　① 安乐窝：北宋时期邵雍（字尧夫）一生远离官场，隐居山林，自称安乐先生，并将自己的住处称作“安乐窝”。此后，“安乐窝”一词常用来表示可以安享快乐和舒适的居所。

【今文解译】　暑热不必非要消除，只要能消除暑热带来的烦躁，人便会有置身凉台的感觉。
贫穷一时难以摆脱，只要能克服贫穷带来的忧愁，人照样可以有快乐的心境。

【English Translation】

It is unnecessary to make special efforts to banish heat; so long as you can banish from your mind the vexing thoughts about heat, you will feel as if you were on a cool and refreshing terrace.
It is impossible to relieve poverty in a short time; so long as you can relieve from your mind the distressing thoughts about poverty, you will feel as if you were living in a cosy nest.

254. 进时思退　得手思放

254. Think out a way to retreat when progress has been made, and consider how to let go when you set about a task.

进步处便思退步，庶免[1]触藩之祸[2]；著手时先图放手，才脱骑虎之危。

【中文注释】　① 庶免：以免。
② 触藩之祸：此处喻进退两难的危险境地。与下面的“骑虎之危”近义。

【今文解译】 平步青云的时候要有随时退下来的思想准备，免得像公羊触藩那样进不成退不得。
着手做一件事的时候先要有适时罢手的预案，这样才不至于遇到骑虎难下的尴尬。

【English Translation】

When you have made progress in your career, you'd better be ready to step back at any time when you would have to. Thus, you will be able to avoid being caught in a dilemma.
When you are to put your hand to a task, you'd better consider how to let go sometime in the future when necessary. Thus, you will be able to avoid landing yourself in an awkward position.

255. 贪者常贫　知足常富

255. Avarice of wealth begets poverty in morality; contentment leads to spiritual enrichment.

贪得者，分金恨不得玉，封公怨不授侯，权豪自甘乞丐；知足者，藜羹旨于膏粱，布袍暖于狐貉，编民不让王公。

【今文解译】 一个贪得无厌的人，得到了金银还埋怨没得到珠玉，得到了公爵的封号还埋怨没得到侯爵的封号，这样的权贵简直跟乞丐无异。
一个知道满足的人，即使咽野菜汤也觉得比山珍海味好吃，穿粗布衣衫也觉得比裘皮大氅暖和，这样的平头百姓远比王公快活。

【English Translation】

Those who are full of insatiable desires covet jade after given gold, and complain about not being granted the title of marquis after conferred a duke. They are all noblemen and high officials, but spiritually they are no more than beggars in the street.
Those who are content with their lot find humble fare more delicious than sumptuous food, coarse clothes warmer than fur coats. Although they are only ordinary people of the lowest class, they are actually happier than the princes and dukes.

256. 隐者多趣　省事心闲

256. To be obscure is to invite more pleasures, and to save trouble is to breed leisure in mind.

矜名不若逃名趣，练事何如省事闲。

【今文解译】　与其夸耀自己的名声，不如回避它更加明智。
与其事事逞能，不如少做些事情而图个清闲。

【English Translation】
It is more fascinating to elude fame and name than to flaunt them all about.
It is more comfortable to do less and stay in leisure than to be capable and busy in everything.

257. 自得之士　逍遥自适

257. Self-composed persons are always leisurely and carefree.

嗜寂者，观白云幽石而通玄；趋荣者，见清歌妙舞而忘倦。唯自得之士，无喧寂，无荣枯，无往非自适之天。

【今文解译】　喜欢安静的人，即使只看到天上的白云和幽谷里的石头，也能领悟到其中的玄妙；爱慕荣华的人，只要看到有人在放喉歌唱或者翩翩起舞，就会忘却身心的疲倦。唯有那些了悟人生的豁达之士，才不在乎喧嚣和寂寥、荣华和枯涩，走到哪里都无拘无束，自适其性。

【English Translation】
A person who is fond of tranquility can, just by gazing at the fleecy clouds in the sky and the secluded rocks amid the mountains, comprehend the profoundness of the arcane truth thereof.
A person who is keen on glory and splendor will, merely by enjoying elegant songs and refined dancing, forget weariness of the body and heart.
Only those who fully understand what life is can be neither vexed by clamor and tranquility nor afflicted with the shifts of success and dejection; wherever they go, they find a land suitable to their innate dispositions.

258. 孤云出岫　朗镜悬空

258. Be as free as the solitary cloud floating from the valley and as elegant as the bright moon hanging in the night sky.

孤云出岫，去留一无所系；朗镜①悬空，静躁两不相干。

【中文注释】 ① 朗镜：明亮的镜子。此处指月亮。

【今文解译】 一片白云从山峦中飘将出来，毫无牵挂地游荡在天际。一轮明月高悬空中，全然不理会人间是安静还是喧闹。

【English Translation】

Floating out of the valley, a patch of solitary cloud wanders with the wind, not caring where to go and stop.

Hanging in the night sky, the moon emits its bright beams, taking no heed of the earthly quietude or clamor.

259. 浓处味短　淡中趣真

259. Rich and pungent dishes only create a transient taste, while simplicity and plainness make a true delight.

悠长之趣，不得于醲酽①，而得于啜菽饮水②；惆恨之怀，不生于枯寂，而生于品竹调丝③。故知浓处味常短，淡中趣独真也。

【中文注释】 ① 醲酽：通常形容酒或茶的味道浓烈。此处喻奢华的生活。

② 啜菽饮水：吃豆子喝清水。此处喻清淡的生活。

③ 品竹调丝：欣赏音乐。此处喻声色之乐。

【今文解译】 悠远绵长的趣味，得之不在生活的奢华而在生活的简朴；惆怅悲哀的情绪，不会产生于枯寂平淡而会产生于声色犬马。由此可知，穷奢极欲是长久不了的，只有简朴平淡中获得的乐趣才是最为真实的。

【English Translation】

The profound and lasting taste can be attained not in rich and pungent dishes, but in plain food and drink. The feelings of melancholy and sorrow are derived not from desolation and hardships, but from excessive sensual pleasures. It can therefore be inferred that the taste attained in rich and pungent dishes is transient, while the delight derived from plain living is truest.

260. 高寓于平　难出于易

260. Just as the loftiest and most profound truth dwells in the most inconspicuous place, so the most difficult things originate from the easiest.

禅宗[①]曰："饥来吃饭倦来眠。"诗旨曰："眼前景致口头语。"盖极高寓于极平，至难出于至易；有意者反远，无心者自近也。

【中文注释】　① 禅宗：佛教的一派，以静坐默念为修行方法。相传南朝宋末（约5世纪）由印度和尚菩提达摩传入中国，唐宋时极盛。

【今文解译】　有一句禅宗偈语是这么说的："饥来吃饭倦来眠。" 有一句古诗是这么说的："眼前景致口头语。"由此可知，最深奥的哲理常常就蕴含在最平常的表达中，而最难表达的意思往往只是最为平常的一句话；刻意表达有时反而词不达意，而无意中脱口而出的一句话有时更加贴近原意。

【English Translation】

There is a chant of Chan Buddhism* which goes, "Eat when you are hungry; sleep when you are tired." And there is a verse that suggests, "Take the scene in front of our eyes, and just put it in pet phrases." From here we learn that the most profound philosophy mostly hides in the most common expression, and the most difficult expression is often just the most common utterance; sometimes a deliberate expression fails to convey meanings, and sometimes an inadvertent blurt is closer to the original meaning.

【English Annotation】

* Chan Buddhism: One of the Buddhist sects in China that advocates achieving enlightenment through meditation and silent reciting of Buddhist scriptures. According to Buddhist literature, it was introduced to China by the Indian monk Budhidharma towards the end of the Song Dynasty (420-479) of the Southern Dynasties (420-589), and reached its heyday during the Tang (618-907) and Song (960-1279) dynasties.

261. 处喧见寂　出有入无

261. Tranquility is attainable in a noisy environment and from Existence there emerges Nothingness.

水流而境无声，得处喧见寂①之趣；山高而云不碍，悟出有入无②之机。

【中文注释】 ① 处喧见寂：在喧闹声中感受静谧。
② 出有入无：道教理念。本意为“出于实有入于虚无”。

【今文解译】 水在静静的河谷里哗哗流淌，人们由此明白：喧闹的环境中仍有寂静的乐趣可以享受。
山再高也挡不住云的飘浮，人们由此悟得：生活在现实世界里的人可以达到无我的境界。

【English Translation】

The water is gurgling by day and night, and yet the valley remains quiet all the time. From this we perceive the subtlety that the joy of tranquility is attainable in a noisy environment.
High mountains are skyscraping, and yet they do not hinder the clouds from floating by. From this we see that human beings living in the real world can enter the realm of egolessness.

262. 心无系恋　乐境仙都

262. Not set your mind on the worldly gains, and so the place you live in will then become a land of immortals.

山林是胜地，一营恋[1]便成市朝；书画是雅事，一贪痴便成商贾[2]。盖心无染著[3]，欲境[4]是仙都；心有系恋，乐境成苦海矣。

【中文注释】 ① 营恋：沉迷留恋。
② 商贾：通指商人。中国自古就有行商坐贾之说。
③ 心无染著：保持心底纯净不被污染。
④ 欲境：充满物欲的环境。

【今文解译】 山川林泉是旅游胜地，倘若过于痴迷留恋，胜地也就成市井集市了；赏鉴书画是兴味雅事，倘若一味地沉溺其中而不能自拔，雅事也就成商人的买卖了。所以：倘能保持心地的纯净，即使身在物欲横流的滚滚红尘之中，也如同逍遥于仙境一般；倘若心为外物所累，即使身在其乐融融的仙境，也如同挣扎于苦海一般。

【English Translation】

Mountains and forests are the beautiful resorts for sightseeing; but if someone is too enchanted with them, they will turn into marketplaces. Collection and enjoyment of celebrities' calligraphy and painting are matters of elegance; but if someone is too crazy about them, he will then resemble a merchant or a businessman. So, whoever might be, if he can keep his heart unsullied, even though living in the mundane world, will feel as if he were in a land of immortals. But if he is reluctant to part with the longings for worldly gains, then the felt fairyland will soon become a sea of bitterness.

263. 静躁稍分　昏明顿异

263. A slight distinction made between clamor and tranquility brings different consequence of either muddle-headedness or clear-headedness.

时当喧杂，则平日所记忆者，皆漫然[1]忘去；境在清宁，则夙昔[2]所遗忘者，又恍尔现前[3]。可见静躁稍分，昏明顿异也。

【中文注释】 ① 漫然：全然，全部。
② 夙昔：以往，过去。
③ 恍尔现前：忽然出现在眼前。恍尔，恍然，忽然。现前，

出现在眼前。

【今文解译】 人在嘈杂的环境里，容易把平时记着的事情忘得一干二净；而人在清静的环境里，平素里被遗忘掉的东西又会忽然浮现在眼前。只要嘈杂和清静稍有区别，昏聩和清醒（的状态）顿时就会截然不同。可见此言不虚。

【English Translation】

When we are amidst clamor and disturbance, the things we thought about in times of tranquility will all slip our memories. Whereas, when we are in a state of repose, the things that slipped from our minds in the past will suddenly reemerge before our eyes. Thus it can be seen that so long as a slight distinction is made between clamor and tranquility, the consequence of either muddle-headedness or clear-headedness will be immediately different.

264. 卧雪眠云　绝俗超凡

264. Keep away from the vanity of the world by preserving a cool and quiet mind.

芦花被①下，卧雪眠云，保全得一窝夜气；竹叶杯中，吟风弄月②，躲离了万丈红尘③。

【中文注释】 ① 芦花被：以芦花用作填充料做成的被子。
② 吟风弄月：又作“吟风咏月”。古时有些诗人的诗常以风花雪月为题材，后来就把这种题材的诗词作品称为吟风弄月。
③ 红尘：佛家对人世的称呼。

【今文解译】 躺在芦花被里，犹如卧在雪做的床榻上和云做的帐篷里，照样能安稳地一觉睡到大天亮。
用竹叶做的杯子喝酒，就着清风明月作诗吟唱，全然一派远离万丈红尘的世外桃源景象。

【English Translation】

By sleeping in a quilt of reed catkins, feeling as if lying on a bed of snow or in a tent of fleecy clouds, one preserves a quiet breath congenial with the night.

By taking the bamboo leaf as a wine cup, enjoying the soft breeze and the limpid moon, one rejoices to find himself distanced from the vanity of the world.

265. 浓不胜淡　俗不如雅

265. Richness and gaudiness are not as good as plainness and lightness, nor is vulgarity a match for refinement.

衮冕[1]行中，著一藜杖[2]的山人，便增一段高风；渔樵[3]路上，著一衮衣的朝士[4]，转添许多俗气。故知浓不胜淡，俗不如雅也。

【中文注释】 ① 衮冕：古代帝王将相穿戴的礼服和礼帽。此处指达官贵人。

② 藜杖：用藜的老茎做成的拐杖。

③ 渔樵：渔夫和樵夫的合称，也即打鱼人和打柴人。

④ 朝士：朝官，在朝为官之人。

【今文解译】 在达官贵人聚集的场合，如果出现一位拄着藜杖的山野居士，场面立即就会变得高雅起来；在渔人樵夫往来的路上，如果出现一位穿着朝服的高官，反而会平添不少俗气。由此可知，华贵不及淡泊，庸俗不及高雅。

【English Translation】

Allow a recluse with a rude crutch to appear among the ranks of high officials and noble lords, and you will find that he would bring forth the refined charm toning up the group. Let a high official in court dress join the fishermen and woodcutters on the same road, and you will find that he would only beget lots of vulgarity. It is thus obvious that richness and gaudiness are not as good as plainness and lightness, nor is vulgarity a match for refinement.

266. 出世涉世　了心尽心

266. To transcend the mean world, go through it first; to comprehend the essence of man's inherent quality, put your whole brains onto it.

出世[1]之道，即在涉世中，不必绝人以逃世；了心[2]之功，即在尽心内，不必绝欲以灰心。

【中文注释】 ① 出世：佛教用语。摆脱尘世的束缚。
② 了心：佛教用语。领悟内心。

【今文解译】 要想摆脱尘世的束缚，只需待在尘世里不断地磨炼就能如愿以偿，没必要远遁山林与世隔绝。
要想彻悟自己，只需在内心下足功夫就行，没必要把自己弄得不食人间烟火灰心丧气的样子。

【English Translation】

To get rid of the shackles of the mean world, one should only stay in it and temper oneself constantly; there is no need to keep away from the multitude and live as a recluse.

To comprehend the essence of one's own inherent quality, one should only put one's whole brains onto it; there is no need to cast off all the worldly intentions and desires and leave the heart to look like dead ashes.

267. 身放闲处　心安静中

267. Stand aloof from the place of conflict and preserve your mind in a state of stillness.

此身常放在闲处，荣辱得失谁能差遣[1]我？此心常安在静中，是非利害谁能瞒昧[2]我？

【中文注释】 ① 差遣：此处作左右或奈何解。
② 瞒昧：欺瞒，蒙昧。

【今文解译】 常将自己置于清闲中，世间的荣辱得失又怎能奈何我？！
常使心情处在平静中，世间的是非利害又怎能欺蒙我？！

【English Translation】

So long as you constantly stand aloof from the place of conflict, how can the worldly honor and disgrace or gains and losses sway you?

So long as you constantly preserve your mind in a state of stillness, how can right and wrong or advantages and disadvantages deceive you?

268. 云中世界　静里乾坤

268. From clouds there emerges the wonderland of leisure; in silence there is a different world.

竹篱下，忽闻犬吠鸡鸣，恍似云中世界；芸窗[1]中，谛听蝉吟鸦噪，方知静里乾坤。

【中文注释】 ① 芸窗：书房。芸，古人常用来驱除书房蠹虫的一种香草，亦可入药。

【今文解译】 信步竹篱下，忽然听到几声鸡鸣狗叫，恍如自己就徜徉在虚无缥缈的神仙世界里。
静坐书房里，不时有蝉吟鸦噪之声传来，这才明白安静的环境里蕴藏着无限生机。

【English Translation】

Strolling by the bamboo fence, I hear a few dogs barking and some cocks crowing. All at once I feel as if I were roaming in a cloudy wonderland, leisurely and freely.

From outside the window of my study, the chirping of cicadas and the crying of crows are softly wafted into my ears. Just then I realize that in silence there is a world of eternal charm.

269. 不忧利禄　不畏仕祸

269. Disregard wealth and rank, and you will be free from the fear for the vicissitudes in officialdom.

我不希荣[1]，何忧乎利禄之香饵？我不竞进[2]，何畏乎仕宦[3]之危机？

【中文注释】 ① 希荣：追求荣华富贵。
② 竞进：与人竞争升官的机会。
③ 仕宦：指官场，仕途。

【今文解译】 我不稀罕荣华富贵，又怎会担心功名利禄诱惑于我？！
我不屑与人比高低，又怎会在乎仕途中的沉沉浮浮？！

【English Translation】

If I do not covet riches and glory, for what should I care about the enticement of wealth and rank?

If I do not vie with others for higher position, for what should I fear the vicissitudes in officialdom?

270. 山泉去凡心　书画消俗气

270. Cast aside mundane thoughts by roaming among mountains and springs; dispel vulgar interest by reposing feelings in calligraphy and painting.

徜徉于山林泉石之间，而尘心①渐息；夷犹②于诗书图画之内，而俗气潜消。故君子虽不玩物丧志，亦常借境调心③。

【中文注释】 ① 尘心：佛教用语。指世俗之心。
② 夷犹：流连之意。
③ 调心：道教用语。调理心性。

【今文解译】 漫步于山林中的清泉岩石间，凡尘之心就会渐渐平息；寄情于充满雅趣的诗书图画，低俗之气就会悄然消退。君子虽不屑玩物丧志，但有益情操的外物还是常可用来调节心境的。

【English Translation】

When we roam among hills and woods, springs and rocks, the mundane thoughts tossing in our minds will subside of themselves. When we repose our feelings in poetry, calligraphy and painting, the vulgar interest hidden in our hearts will vanish without being noticed. From here we see that although the accomplished man would not like to sap his spirit by seeking pleasures from external materials, he can still often harmonize his mood with the aid of them.

271. 秋日清爽　神骨俱清

271. The clarity and brightness of autumn brings freshness to man's body and spirit.

春日气象繁华，令人心神骀荡，不若秋日云白风清，兰芳桂馥，水天一色，上下空明，使人神骨俱清也。

【今文解译】　春天百花齐放，百鸟争鸣，气象万千，令人心旷神怡，然而总还是不如秋日里云白风清、兰芳桂馥、水天一色、上下空明那样，令人神形俱感无比爽朗畅快。

【English Translation】

When spring comes, there can be seen the scene of prosperity which makes people relaxed and joyful. But anyhow, spring is not on equal terms with autumn, in which the clouds are white, the breeze limpid, the air consumed with the fragrance of orchids and osmanthus, the sky and water of one color, and the heaven and earth crystal-clear and bright. The freshness brought by such a season to the body and spirit is peerless.

272. 得诗真趣　悟禅玄机

272. To write a poem, it is best to seek the subtlety to do so; to meditate on Zen Buddhism, it is best to perceive the mystery of it.

一字不识而有诗意者，得诗家真趣；一偈[①]不参[②]而有禅味者，悟禅教[③]玄机。

【中文注释】　① 偈：佛经中的唱词，四句为一偈。

② 参：探究，琢磨。

③ 禅教：佛教中的禅宗一派，以静坐默念为修行方式。

【今文解译】　一个字不识但说起话来却充满诗意，这样的人才真正具备了做一个诗人的趣味。

一句偈语都不参但开口却富有禅机，这样的人才真正领悟到了禅宗佛理的玄妙。

【English Translation】

One who can't read a word and yet can give utterances full of poetic sentiment has actually grasped the true subtlety of being a poet.

One who never meditates on the librettos in Buddhist scripture and yet can penetrate the allegorical words and gestures used by Chan monks has perceived the mystery of Buddhist principles.

273. 好用心机　杯弓蛇影

273. A person of sensitive imagination mistakes the shadow of a bow in his wine cup as a snake.

机动的[1]，弓影疑为蛇蝎，寝石视为伏虎，此中浑是杀气；念息的，石虎[2]可作海鸥，蛙声可当鼓吹，触处俱见真机[3]。

【中文注释】 ① 机动的：有臆想倾向、动辄惊慌的人。

② 石虎：又称豹猫，产于亚洲的猫科动物。俗称山猫或者钱猫。

③ 真机：此处喻祥和之气。

【今文解译】 好动心机的人，看到杯中的弓影就怀疑是蛇蝎在爬，看到草丛里有石头就以为老虎在那儿蹲伏，目光所及之处无不充满杀气。

意气平和的人，看到跳跃的豹猫就把它当作翔天的海鸥，听到青蛙的叫声就把它当成是美妙的音乐，所见所闻无不祥和宜人。

【English Translation】

One who is of sensitive imagination suspects the reflection of a bow in his wine cup as a snake or a scorpion, the rock sleeping amidst growth of grass as a crouching tiger in ambush; whatever he catches in sight is imagined to be sinister. Whereas, another who is peaceful-minded considers the leopard cat as a meek seagull, the croaks of frogs as sweet music; whatever he gets in touch with is replete with auspiciousness.

274. 身心自如　融通自在

274. Let the body and heart be as free and unrestrained as the air.

身如不系之舟，一任流行坎止；心似既炭之木，何妨刀割香涂。

【今文解译】　身体就像未系缆绳的小舟，尽可由着它顺流而行遇坎而止。
心就像烧成炭的树木，不惧利刃的劈砍也不怕香料的涂抹。

【English Translation】
The body is like an unanchored small boat, so just let it drift with the current and bump against banks.
The heart is like a piece of charred wood, so it fears neither sharp blade nor scent liniment.

275. 皆鸣天机　皆畅生意

275. The crying of animals and the vitality of vegetation are all the expressions of natural instincts.

人情听莺啼则喜，闻蛙鸣则厌，见花则思培之，遇草则欲去之，俱是以形气用事[①]。若以性天[②]视之，何者非自鸣其天机，非自畅其生意[③]也?

【中文注释】　① 形气用事：意气用事，凭好恶行事。
② 性天：自然本性。
③ 生意：生机，生气。

【今文解译】　人们总是听到黄莺啼就高兴，听到青蛙叫就厌烦，看到鲜花就想栽培，看到杂草就想铲除，凡此种种皆是凭好恶行事的表现。就自然禀赋而言，世上哪种动物不是随其天性而鸣叫，哪种植物不是在畅显其勃勃生机？！

【English Translation】
People would feel happy when hearing the chirping of orioles, and would feel sick when the croaks of frogs meet the ears. They would wish to cultivate the

lovely flowers when beholding them, and would intend to hoe the weeds up when seeing them. All these responses are stimulated by the external features of the objects, and by personal likes and dislikes as well. Take the nature of the objects into consideration, and we will see that there is no animal not displaying its instincts by crying with outstretched neck, and no vegetation not diffusing vitality by freely showing its congenital manners.

276. 盛衰始终　自然之理

276. The vicissitudes of life are the course destined by Nature.

发落齿疏，任幻形①之凋谢；鸟吟花开，识自性②之真如③。

【中文注释】 ① 幻形：佛教用语。指肉身，形体。
② 自性：本性。
③ 真如：佛教用语。喻人或物常恒不变之意。

【今文解译】 人老了就会头发脱落、牙齿稀疏，这是身体衰退的症状，就随它去吧。
鸟鸣花开是常恒不变的大自然现象，由此可知，万物的本性都是如此。

【English Translation】

When a man lives to an old age, his hair and teeth will become sparse and scattered. What he can do is to let them go in accordance with the decrepitude of the flesh. But, from the singing of birds and the blooming of flowers, we realize that the true nature of myriad things will never change and will remain to be what it is for ever.

277. 无欲则寂　虚心则凉

277. One can find both tranquility and cool when he is free from worldly desires.

欲其中者，波沸寒潭，山林不见其寂；虚其中者，凉生酷暑，朝市不知其喧。

【今文解译】 内心充满欲望的人，能使冰冷的潭水沸腾扬波，即使躲进深山老林也不见得会变得心平气和。

内心毫无物欲的人，三伏天里也不会感到炎热，就是在嘈杂的早市上也感觉不到那里的喧嚣。

【English Translation】

Those full of desires could bring the waves of a cold pond to the boil, but would not find tranquility even amidst the quiet mountains and forests. Whereas, those free from desires could find cool in the dog days of summer, and would not notice the clamor even in a crowded morning market.

278. 贫则无虑　贱则常安

278. Poverty gives no rise to fear, while humbleness brings more safety.

多藏者厚亡，故知富不如贫之无虑；高步者疾颠，故知贵不如贱之常安。

【今文解译】 敛财越多的人，一旦遭受损失，损失也就越大，可见有钱人不及没钱人过得轻松。

地位越高的人，一旦摔下来，摔得也就越重，可见高贵者还不如卑贱者过得安稳。

【English Translation】

The more the wealth one amasses, the greater his loss will be. This is the reason why the rich have more worries than the poor.

The higher one climbs, the harder he falls. This is the reason why the noble are not always as safe as the humble.

279. 晓窗读易　午案谈经

279. Read *The Book of Changes* against the window at dawn and at noon, expound Buddhist Scripture by the desk.

读易晓窗，丹砂①研松间之露；谈经午案，宝磬②宣竹下之风。

【中文注释】 ① 丹砂：一种矿物。古人用作写毛笔字的红色墨汁。亦称“朱砂”。
② 宝磬：古代用玉或石制作的打击乐器，多用于佛殿。此处系指“敲木鱼的声音”。

【今文解译】 清晨在窗下诵读《周易》，用松枝上滴下的露珠研磨朱砂圈点书中精要。
中午时分与人伏案谈论佛经，只听见木鱼声和着竹林间的清风传向远方。

【English Translation】

Reading *The Book of Changes* against the window at dawn, one is available to use the dewdrops from the pine trees to grind and moisten cinnabar into ink with which to mark the outstanding expositions.
Discussing Buddhist Scripture with others by the desk at noon, one is available to hear the sound of temple percussion instrument wafting afar off with the gentle breeze from the bamboo groves.

280. 花失生机　鸟减天趣

280. A pot-planted flower is bereft of vitality and a caged bird lacks natural amusement.

花居盆内终乏生机，鸟入笼中便减天趣[1]。不若山间花鸟错集成文，翱翔自若，自是悠然会心[2]。

【中文注释】 ① 天趣：自然的情趣。
② 会心：领会别人没有明白表示的意思。

【今文解译】 鲜花被移栽到盆里就失去了勃勃的生机，飞鸟被关进笼里就减少了盎然的天趣。它们已不再能像山间生长错落的花儿和自由翱翔的鸟儿那样悠然自若地将美景呈现给人们，也不能使人们对大自然产生美丽的联想。

【English Translation】

Once a flower is transplanted into a pot, its vitality will be deprived. Once a bird is caged, its natural exuberance will be decreased. The tableau created by the pot-planted flower and the caged bird can never match that in the depth of the mountains freely dotted with blooming flowers and soaring birds, which enables man to perceive the magic of Nature.

281. 诸多烦恼　因我而起

281. Many of the vexations are incurred by the sense of self-centeredness.

世人只缘认得“我”字太真，故多种种嗜好，种种烦恼。前人云：“不复知有我，安知物为贵？”又云：“知身不是我，烦恼更何侵？”真破的之言[1]也。

【中文注释】　① 破的之言：切中要害或讲到点子上的话，也即一语中的之意。破，射中；的，射箭的靶子。

【今文解译】　世人只因把“我”字看得太重，所以才会有这样那样的喜好和烦恼。古人说：“既然已不再知道自己的存在，你又怎么知晓何为重要？”又说：“既然知道此身不再是你，烦恼又如何能将你打搅？”真是一语中的啊！

【English Translation】

The reason why people have various addictions and vexations lies in the fact that they hold “I” too much in account. There is an ancient saying which runs, “If you are no longer aware of the existence of yourself, how can you tell the importance of external things?” And another, “If you are aware that the fleshly body is no longer yours, how can vexations disturb you?” What a remark that blurts out the truth!

282. 少时思老　荣时思枯

282. When you are young, think about the time of old age; when you go prosperous, ponder on the declining days.

自老视少，可以消奔驰角逐[1]之心；自瘁[2]视荣，可以绝纷华靡丽[3]之念。

【中文注释】 ① 奔驰角逐：此处意为“追逐名利”。
② 瘁：过度疲劳。此处喻衰败，没落。
③ 纷华靡丽：奢华，奢靡。

【今文解译】 以老年时的眼光看待年少时的行为和事情，可以摒弃许多追逐名利的想法。
从衰败的角度审视繁盛时的荣耀和奢侈，可以打消不少追求纷华靡丽的欲念。

【English Translation】

Think about youth from the view of old age, and you will be able to do away with many of your thoughts for fame and gain.
Look at prosperity from the angle of declining situations, and you will be able to cast aside many of your desires for brilliance and gorgeousness.

283. 人情世态　倏忽万端

283. The ways of the world are changing all the time.

人情世态，倏忽万端，不宜认得太真。尧夫[①]云：“昔日所云我，而今却是伊。不知今日我，又属后来谁？”人常作如是观，便可解却胸中罥矣。

【中文注释】 ① 尧夫：邵雍，北宋时期的哲学家和诗人。

【今文解译】 人情冷暖、世态炎凉，瞬间就会千变万化，所以凡事不必太过认真。尧夫先生曾经说过：“昨天所说的我，而今已变成了他。且不知今天的我，明天又将变成谁？”如果一个人常能这么看待人情世态，心里的纠结也就不解自化了。

【English Translation】

The ways of the world are changing all the time; it is no good being too serious about them. Yaofu* said, “It is me that was talked about yesterday, but today somebody else has taken my place. No one can tell who would be the next that will be replaced tomorrow.” If a man would take such occurrences as usual and common, he could get rid of the entanglements from his heart.

【English Annotation】

* Yaofu: The style name of Shao Yong (1011-1077), a philosopher and poet in the Northern Song Dynasty (960-1127). He was an expert in the study of *The Book of Changes* but refused to take office and lived as a hermit during his lifetime.

284. 热中取静　冷处热心

284. Be sober-minded on the occasions of bustle and excitement, and preserve a positive attitude in times of dejection and desolation.

热闹中着一冷眼，便省许多苦心思；冷落处存一热心，便得许多真趣味。

【今文解译】 在热闹喧嚣的场合里若能冷眼以对，便可省却许多令人烦恼的事情。
失意落魄的时候若能保持积极的心态，便可获得许多真正的人生乐趣。

【English Translation】

If a man can observe the world with sober eyes on the occasions of bustle and excitement, he will be able to spare himself the trouble to deal with lots of annoying matters.
If a man can preserve a positive attitude in times of dejection and desolation, he will be able to enjoy inexhaustible true happiness in life.

285. 寻常人家　最为安乐

285. The most carefree life can only be found in an ordinary family.

有一乐境界，就有一不乐的相对待[①]；有一好光景，就有一不好的相乘除[②]。只是寻常家饭，素位风光，才是个安乐的窝巢。

【中文注释】 ① 相对待：相比较。
② 相乘除：相参照。

【今文解译】 有快乐的情绪就一定有不快乐的情绪，有欣欣向荣的景象就一定有衰败凋敝的景象。只有那些普通的家常便饭和俭朴的生活环境，才是真正的安乐所在。

【English Translation】

Where there is happiness there must be sorrow on the contrary. Where there is prosperity there must be a decline in opposition. It is only the homely fare and humble living environment that make people feel at paradise.

286. 乾坤自在　物我两忘

286. Untrammeled Nature makes man ignorant of the existence of the world and the self.

帘栊[1]高敞，看青山绿水吞吐云烟，识乾坤之自在；竹树扶疏，任乳燕鸣鸠送迎时序[2]，知物我之两忘。

【中文注释】 ① 帘栊：带帘子的窗户。

② 送迎时序：送别旧的时节，迎接新的时节。

【今文解译】 卷起帘子，打开窗户，看青山绿水间云蒸霞蔚的景色，才知道大自然是多么美妙自在。

竹林茂密，草木繁盛，听乳燕斑鸠交相鸣叫送迎时序，才领悟天地万物与我实为一体。

【English Translation】

Unfurl the bamboo blind and gaze out of the window at the clouds and mists rising and floating among the blue hills and green waters, and then you will acquire the splendor and liberty of Nature.

Behold the luxuriant bamboos and trees, listen to how the sucking-swallows and chirping turtledoves herald the coming and parting of the seasons, and then you will find the myriad things and you are one.

287. 生死成败　任其自然

287. Let life and death, success and failure take their own course.

知成之必败，则求成之心不必太坚；知生之必死，则保生之道不必过劳。

【今文解译】 有成功就会有失败，明白了这个道理，求取成功的心思就不会太决绝。

有生就会有死，懂得了这个规律，就不会在养生之道上耗费过多精力。

【English Translation】

When a man understands that every success is accompanied by failure, he will not be too crazy about success. And when a man realizes that every life must have its end, he will not tax too much of his mind and energy to the way of prolonging life.

288. 水流境静　花落意闲

288. However swift the water flows, its surroundings are quiet; however frequently the flowers bloom and fade, the scene remains leisurely and carefree.

古德①云："竹影扫阶尘不动，月轮穿沼水无痕。"吾儒②云："水流任急境常静，花落虽频意自闲。"人常持此意以应事接物③，身心何等自在！

【中文注释】 ① 古德：古代的高僧。佛教徒对有建树的佛家先辈的尊称。

② 吾儒：因为作者自己是儒家学者，所以称同道中人为"吾儒"。

③ 应事接物：待人接物。

【今文解译】 古代有位高僧曾经说过："翠竹的影子掠过台阶却扫不走灰尘，月光照在池塘里却激不起涟漪。"我们儒家的一位学者也曾说过："水流得再急，四周的环境却还是静悄悄的；花开花落再频繁，赏花人的意兴却依旧悠然自定。”为人处世若常能保持这样的境界，身心将是何等畅然自在啊！

【English Translation】

An ancient Buddhist monk of moral integrity once said, “The shadow of a bamboo flickering across the footsteps cannot erase the dust from them. The moonbeams reflected in a pond arouse no corrugation on the surface of the water.” While one of our Confucian scholars said alike in another way, “No matter how swift the water flows, so long as you have a peaceful mind, the surroundings will remain quiet. No matter how frequently the flowers bloom and fade, so long as you keep yourself at leisure, ease will stay with you.” If a person can constantly bear in mind this perception in his dealings with the world, both his body and mind will be in a state of blissful abstraction.

289. 自然乐曲　乾坤文章

289. Most wonderful are the melody and spectacle created by Nature.

林间松韵，石上泉声，静里听来，识天地自然鸣佩①；草际烟光，水心云影，闲中观去，见乾坤最上文章②。

【中文注释】① 鸣佩：古人身上佩戴的饰物，走起路来会发出撞击声。此处喻指自然界的声响。

② 最上文章：最好的花纹。此处指自然界中的景色。

【今文解译】山林中松涛声声，泉石间流水潺潺，静心听来，大自然美妙的乐韵油然荡漾在耳畔；草丛里烟霞迷蒙，水中央白云映照，闲中望去，天地间无处不在的大好景色尽收眼底。

【English Translation】

By listening in quietude to the appeal implied by the pines in the woods and the murmuring of spring water over pebbles, one can appreciate the exquisite melody composed by Nature.

By watching in idleness the mist rising from the thick growth of grass and the shadow of snowy clouds reflected on the surface of a lake, one can find the wonderful spectacles created by the Heaven and Earth.

290. 谿壑易填　人心难满

290. Gullies are easy to fill up, but men's desires are hard to fulfill.

眼看西晋之荆榛①，犹矜白刃②；身属北邙之狐兔③，尚惜黄金。语云："猛兽易伏，人心难降；谿壑易填，人心难满。"信哉！

【中文注释】

① 西晋之荆榛：西晋王朝变成荆棘丛生的荒凉之地，比喻西晋的覆灭。

② 矜白刃：矜，怜惜；白刃，锋利的刀刃，泛指战争。西晋亡于末代统治者愍帝向攻城之敌的投降，所以此处当指不肯用兵或不敢用兵。

③ 北邙之狐兔：出没于坟地的狐狸和野兔。北邙，山名，即邙山，在今河南洛阳东北，东汉北魏以来，达官贵人死后多葬于此，后来以北邙山泛指墓地。

【今文解译】

眼看江山就要不保，可西晋昏聩的王朝却不敢拼死抵抗；自己都快成坟堆里狐狸和野兔的美味了，心里却还舍不得黄金。俗话说："猛兽容易制伏，而人心难以降服；沟壑容易填平，而人心难以满足。"此话不虚！

【English Translation】

When the Western Jin Dynasty was about to become a land of briers and brambles*, its ruler still dared not use his armed forces to fight back. When his body was already doomed to be the delicacies for foxes and rabbits haunting the graveyards, he still grudged his gold. This is what called "Beasts of prey are easy to tame, but men's hearts are hard to control; gullies are easy to fill up, but men's desires are hard to fulfill." How true these verses are!

【English Annotation】

* A land of briers and brambles: Indicating the doom of the Western Jin Dynasty (265-317).

291. 心无风涛　性有化育

291. Get rid of the distracting thoughts from your mind and nurse the charity in the depth of your heart.

心地上无风涛[①]，随在皆青山绿水；性天中有化育[②]，触处见鱼跃鸢飞。

【中文注释】 ① 风涛：心里的起起伏伏。意指心里的杂念等。
② 性天中有化育：性天，自然本性；化育，万物的自然生育与成长。

【今文解译】 心中若无纷乱复杂的欲念，到哪儿眼前出现的都是青山绿水。
本性中充满对自然万物的爱，所见皆是鱼跃鸟飞的生动景象。

【English Translation】
If a person has no distracting thoughts in his mind, wherever he goes he would feel as if lingering in a wonderland of blue hills and green waters.
If a person has love for Nature in the depth of his heart, whatsoever he catches in sight is a lovely scene, where fishes are leaping and birds flying.

292. 贵贱高低　自适其性

292. Everyone should conform himself to his own nature, whatever his social status.

峨冠大带之士，一旦睹轻蓑小笠飘飘然逸也，未必不动其咨嗟；长筵广席[①]之豪，一旦遇疏帘净几悠悠焉静也，未必不增其绻恋[②]。人奈何驱以火牛[③]，诱以风马[④]，而不思自适其性哉？

【中文注释】 ① 长筵广席：形容宴请场面的豪华奢侈。
② 绻恋：羡慕之情。
③ 火牛：据《史记·田单列传》记载，战国时期齐国大将田单调集城中一千多头牛，角上绑兵刃，尾巴束苇灌脂。趁夜间，士兵点燃牛尾，火牛便疯狂地奔向敌阵，接着齐

军五千兵将一阵冲杀，燕军大惊而乱。“驱以火牛”指你争我斗，无所不用其极。

④ 风马：即风马牛。风，雌雄相互引诱之意。马和牛本不相配，却非要让其相互引诱，进行交配。“诱以风马”指为了荣华富贵而不择手段。

【今文解译】 头戴高帽、身穿华服的达官贵人，如果有一天看到头戴斗笠、身穿蓑衣的平头百姓那么逍遥自在无忧无虑，心中未必不会百感交集；习惯长筵广席的富人，如果有一天看到布衣人家那种窗明几净、悠闲恬静的生活状态，难保不会艳羡不已。世上的人们何苦还要无所不用其极地拼个你死我活，而不去过悠闲自得的生活以顺应自己的心性？

【English Translation】

One day when the magnate in high hat and broad girdles chances upon an ordinary guy who wears bamboo hat and palm-bark cape and see how free and unrestrained he is, the feeling of envy would somehow well up in his heart. One day when a wealthy man indulgent to extravagant eating and drinking happens to pass by a mean house and sees through the window how clean the table is and how leisurely and quiet the family life, he might somehow feel a pang of nostalgia. Why do people contest with each other so bellicosely and unscrupulously? Why do they not think about living a plain life by following their own bent?

293. 处世忘世　超物乐天

293. Rise above the world though you live in it, and you will enjoy the natural amusement.

鱼得水游而相忘乎水，鸟乘风飞而不知有风。识此可以超物累[①]，可以乐天机[②]。

【中文注释】 ① 超物累：意为“超脱外物的束缚”或“摆脱外物的拖累”。超，超脱，摆脱；物累，外物的束缚或拖累。

② 乐天机：乐，享受欢乐；天机，此处喻天趣。

【今文解译】 鱼儿在水中悠游而全然不知有水在一旁帮衬着，鸟儿在空中翱翔而全然不晓有风在左右托扶着。有了这种认知境界，人便可以超脱外物的束缚，尽享快乐的天趣。

【English Translation】

A fish swims in the water, yet it forgets the existence of the water. A bird flies on the wind, yet it ignores the being of the wind. Perceiving this enables us to rise above the strictures of worldly things and enjoy the natural amusement.

294. 盛衰无常　强弱安在

294. Prosperity and decline are not constant, nor everlasting are the strong and weak.

狐眠败砌，兔走荒台，尽是当年歌舞之地；露冷黄花，烟迷衰草，悉属旧时争战之场。盛衰何常？强弱安在？念此令人心灰。

【今文解译】 狐狸做窝的残垣断壁，野兔出没的荒楼废台，这些都曾是当年显贵们歌舞升平的地方；沾满夜露的黄花，烟雾笼罩的衰草，这些都曾是古代豪强逐鹿的战场。盛衰兴败何者能长久不变？！强弱胜负哪个能延续至今？！一想到这儿就不免心灰意冷。

【English Translation】

The dilapidated walls and houses where now inhabit the foxes and the abandoned stages and galleries where now haunt the rabbits used to be the places of singing and dancing in those days. The wilds sprinkled with chilly dews and the sere grasses draped in thick mist used to be the battlefields of old. Can the prosperity and decline be everlasting? And where are now the strong and the weak of the past? At the thought of these, one cannot help feeling dispirited.

295. 宠辱不惊　去留无意

295. Remain indifferent whether granted favors or subjected to humiliation and give no heed to whether demoted or promoted from the present post.

宠辱不惊，闲看庭前花开花落；去留无意，漫随天外云卷云舒。

【今文解译】　不要在乎荣宠与屈辱，尽可悠闲地观赏自家庭院里的花开花落。

不要介意官场的沉浮，尽可学做天上的浮云时而翻卷时而舒展。

【English Translation】

Remain indifferent whether you will be granted favors or subjected to humiliation, and just do it by leisurely watching the flowers in the courtyard, bloom and fade.

Pay no heed to whether you will be demoted or promoted from the present post, and just do it by casually following the clouds on the horizon, mass and scatter.

296. 高天可翔　万物可饮

296. The vast sky allows a soaring flight, and produces of Nature are open to all living beings.

晴空朗月，何天不可翱翔，而飞蛾独投夜烛；清泉绿草，何物不可饮啄，而鸱枭[1]偏嗜腐鼠。噫！世之不为飞蛾鸱枭者，几何人哉？

【中文注释】　① 鸱枭：鸟类的一科，头大，嘴短而弯曲，专吃鼠、兔昆虫等小动物，对农业有益。亦称“鸱鸮”。

【今文解译】　晴空万里，朗月高照，天空何处不能任意翱翔，可飞蛾却偏偏要扑向烛火；清泉流水，绿地芳草，哪一种东西不能饮食果腹，可鸱枭却偏偏爱吃老鼠的尸体。唉！世上的人们又有几个不像飞蛾鸱枭那样偏执偏行，愚蠢之极？！

【English Translation】

In the clear, moonlit sky, there is ample room for a soaring flight; yet the flying moth would just dart straightway onto the ignited candle. Everywhere are the limpid springs and green plants, none of them not edible; yet the owl would only prefer the putrid rats. Alas, how few are people who do not act like the moth and the owl!

297. 求心内佛　却心外法

297. Plead with yourself for enlightenment by shaking off the bonds of external things.

才就筏便思舍筏，方是无事道人；若骑驴又复觅驴，终为不了禅师。

【今文解译】　才登上竹筏就想到上岸后要舍弃竹筏，这才是不为外物所累的出家道人。
骑在驴背上却还想着再找一头驴，这样的人终究还是个尘缘未了的和尚。

【English Translation】

One that, just having embarked on a bamboo raft, deliberates to abandon it after crossing the river is called a true Taoist priest who knows how to shake off the bonds of external things.
One that, while already riding a donkey, is still thinking of seeking another to ride can only be counted as a Buddhist monk who hasn't finished the dusty affinity.

298. 冷情当事　如汤消雪

298. Handling affairs with a cool mind is like thawing the snow by pouring hot water on it.

权贵龙骧，英雄虎战，以冷眼视之，如蚁聚膻，如蝇竞血；是非蜂起，得失猬兴[①]，以冷情当之，如冶化金，如汤消雪。

【中文注释】 ① 猬兴：刺猬的刺竖起来。与前句中的“蜂起”近意，比喻“多”。

【今文解译】 有权有势的人，像龙一样傲视众物；好战的英雄豪杰，像猛虎一样相互争斗。如以冷静的眼光旁观，这些人都只不过是一群聚在一起啃食腥膻之物的蚂蚁和争相竞吸动物鲜血的苍蝇。

人世间的是是非非不计其数，得失多寡之争比比皆是。如以超脱的眼光看待，这些形形色色的纷扰现象，最终都会像被投进了熔炉的金属和被沸水淋过的冰雪那样，消失得无影无踪。

【English Translation】

The powerful and influential assume majestic airs like dragons; the warriors of heroism fight against each other like tigers. If you look upon them with cool eyes, they are all no different from the ants gathering around putrid carcasses or the flies swooping toward bloodstained filth.

Contentions over right and wrong are as chaotic as the bees rising in swarms; debates on gain and loss are as countless as the spines of a hedgehog. If you deal with them with a cool mind, they will all vanish like the metal melted in furnace or the snow thawed out when hot water is thrown on it.

299. 物欲可哀　性真可乐

299. It is lamentable to be trammeled by material desires but joyful to preserve the genuine character.

羁锁于物欲，觉吾生之可哀；夷犹于性真，觉吾生之可乐。知其可哀，则尘情立破；知其可乐，则圣境自臻。

【今文解译】 受制于物欲的困扰，人会觉得自己很可悲；悠游在纯真的本性中，人会觉得自己很快活。知道受制于物欲的困扰很可悲，对尘世的迷恋之情也就可以马上破除了；知道悠游在纯真的本性中很快活，圣人的境界自然也就可以达到了。

【English Translation】

When we are trammeled by material desires, we would feel that life is lamentable. But once we are free from restraint and have our genuine character well preserved, we would feel that life is brimming with joy. Now that we know clearly the lamentation of being trammeled by material desires, the mundane feelings can be dispelled immediately. And now that we know clearly the joy of preserving the genuine character, the realm of holiness can be reached naturally.

300. 胸无物欲　眼自空明

300. As soon as you cast aside the material desires, your eyes will be brightened up.

胸中既无半点物欲，已如雪消炉焰冰消日；眼前自有一段空明，时见月在青天影在波。

【今文解译】 一切物欲都去除掉了，心里就会有一种炉火消融了雪、阳光晒化了冰的感觉。

当人的心胸变得空明时，眼前的景物就会像空中的明月映照在水面那样清晰。

【English Translation】

By the time when all the material desires are dispelled from your breast, it is as if the snow has been melted by stove fire and the ice thawed out by the sunlight.

By the time when your mind has become open and bright, the scene before you will be as clear as the moon hanging in the sky and its beams reflected on the water.

301. 林岫江畔　诗兴自涌

301. Amidst the forests and hills or beside the rivers and lakes, the exalted, poetic mood will spring up of itself.

诗思[①]在灞陵桥[②]上，微吟就，林岫便已浩然；野兴在镜湖[③]曲边[④]，独往时，山川自相映发。

【中文注释】 ① 诗思：作诗的情思。

② 灞陵桥：灞陵，古地名。本作霸陵。旧址在今陕西省西安市东。汉文帝刘恒葬于此，故称。三国魏改名霸城，北周建德二年废。后人提及“灞陵”二字，多指往事不堪回首之意。史籍中并无“灞陵桥”一说，而只有灞桥，疑是作者误用典故或后人讹传所致。灞桥，桥名，在西安市东，跨水作桥。汉人送客至此桥，折柳赠别（古代文学作品中的柳枝作为赠别之物就源于此）。唐宋明清各代的文人墨客常在作品里直接引用“灞桥”二字，多指送别或送别时的忧伤。

③ 镜湖：古代长江以南大型农田水利工程之一。在今浙江省绍兴市会稽山北麓，与曲娥江相接。东汉永和五年（公元140年）在会稽太守马臻主持下修建。以水平如镜，故名。

④ 曲边：曲娥江边。

【今文解译】 古人送朋友至灞桥，总会因为作别而诗兴大发，微吟片刻就能成诗，甚至连周遭的山林都会跟着感慨万千。

游兴大发时，独自去往会稽山北麓的镜湖旁和曲娥江畔，远山近水交相辉映一览无余，心中自是陶陶然。

【English Translation】

It is on Ba Bridge* where the persons in parting would mostly fall into an exalted poetic mood. The lines murmured out on this bridge would permeate the forests and hills or thereabout with the artistic breath of poetry.

It is beside Jinghu Lake* and the Qu'e River where a person lingering about by himself would be mostly aroused to a feeling of wilderness. Though with no one in company, the brilliance enhanced between the mountains and the rivers would still make him quite intoxicated.

【English Annotation】

* Ba Bridge: Lying in the east of today's Xi'an, it used to be a place where the local people bade farewell to their relatives or friends during the Han Dynasty (206BC-AD220). When literally used, it simply signifies as: "To reflect on the past events is a thing unbearable to one's heart." The very allusion often used

to air the sadness in parting can be attributed to Ba Bridge.
* Jinghu Lake: Adjacent to the Qu'e River, it is located in the northern end of the Kuaiji Mountain in today's Shaoxing City, Zhejiang Province, where used to be one of the major irrigation works in ancient China (around the year of 140). The surface of this lake looked like a mirror, so named. The Chinese character pronounced as "jing" stands for "mirror" in English.

302. 伏久飞高　开先谢早

302. The longer the bird rests in concealment, the higher it flies; the earlier the flower blooms, the sooner it fades.

伏久者①飞必高，开先者②谢独早。知此，可以免蹭蹬③之忧，可以消躁急之念。

【中文注释】 ① 伏久者：长时间蛰伏的鸟。
② 开先者：先开放的花。
③ 蹭蹬：遭遇挫折，不得意。

【今文解译】 鸟儿蛰伏久了，出了巢就会一飞冲天；越是先开的花，谢得也就越早。明白了这个道理，就可消除怀才不遇的幽怨，也可省却急功近利的焦躁。

【English Translation】
The longer the bird rests in concealment, the higher it flies. The earlier the flower blooms, the sooner it fades. Realizing this may help us avoid the depression of being frustrated for our talents and banish from our minds the irritable thoughts to seek quick success and instant benefits.

303. 花叶徒荣　玉帛成空

303. The flourishing flowers and leaves are nothing but brilliance in vain; the multitude of wealth is only a brief dream of grandeur.

树木至归根，而后知花萼枝叶之徒荣；人事至盖棺，而后知子女玉帛之无益。

【今文解译】 树木到了叶落归根的时候，才知道花团锦簇、枝繁叶茂其实只是一时的荣华。
人到了盖棺定论的时候，才明白子孙绕膝、金玉满堂其实是那么徒劳无益。

【English Translation】
Only by the time when the leaves fall to settle on their roots can the trees realize that the flourishing branches and flowers are nothing but brilliance in vain.
Only by the time when the lid is placed on a man's coffin can people understand that the multitude of offspring and wealth is good for nothing.

304. 真空不空　在世出世

304. To preserve internal emptiness does not mean to expel all the sensations; only by living in the mundane world can one transcend it.

真空不空①，执相②非真，破相③亦非真，问世尊④如何发付⑤？在世出世⑥，徇欲⑦是苦，绝欲亦是苦，听吾侪善自修持！

【中文注释】 ① 真空不空：佛教用语。摒弃所有的杂念使心不为任何外界事物所迷惑，但又不致一无知觉。
② 执相：只看到事物的表象。
③ 破相：看破事物的表象。
④ 世尊：佛教创始人释迦牟尼。
⑤ 发付：打发。如何发付也即“如何是好”之意。
⑥ 在世出世：要想超脱于世俗就离不开身处世俗。
⑦ 徇欲：追求物欲。

【今文解译】 摒弃心中的杂念以求不为外物所迷惑，并不等于非要将一切都看空；光执着于事物的表象是看不清事物本质的，即使看清了事物的表象也不等于发现了事物的本质。请问世尊该如何解释个中佛理？
身处俗世但又不囿于俗世，一定要有超脱世俗的信念；追求物质欲望是痛苦的，而杜绝所有的物质欲望也是痛苦的。真正要想做到身处俗世而又不囿于俗世，需要我们在自己平时的修为上狠下功夫。

【English Translation】

To preserve internal emptiness does not equally mean to expel all the sensations from the mind. One can never obtain the true essence of a thing if only clinging to its appearance; nor necessarily can he do so even if seeing it through. Ask the Buddhist patriarch what to help, and the answer will stand as: "Only by living in the mundane world can one transcend it." It is painful to strive for the worldly desires; so is it to give them up. What we should do is to school ourselves to moral refinement.

305. 欲有尊卑　贪无二致

305. The respected and the humble are different in desires, but are much the same in cravings.

烈士[①]让千乘，贪夫争一文，人品星渊[②]也，而好名不殊[③]好利；天子营家国，乞人号饔飧[④]，分位霄壤也，而焦思何异焦声？

【中文注释】 ① 烈士：此处指侠义之士或大丈夫。

② 星渊：一个是天上的星辰，一个是地上的深潭，两者差别很大。下文中的"霄壤"与此同义。

③ 不殊：与……相比没有区别。

④ 号饔飧：为乞讨早饭和晚饭而号叫。

【今文解译】 豪侠可以为节义而将千乘之国礼让于人，小人可以为一文之利而与人争得面红耳赤。这两种人品虽有天壤之别，但是豪侠的好名之心和小人的好财之念本质上却没有区别。

当天子的统管国家大事，做乞丐的沿街乞讨。这两种人的地位和身份虽然相去甚远，可是天子管理国家大事时的殚精竭虑和乞丐沿街乞讨时的哀号声，又有什么两样呢?！

【English Translation】

A straight, high-minded person may decline the benefit equivalent to a state of a thousand chariots, while an insatiable person would even enter into rivalry with others over the profit of a single cent. Their characters are as far apart as heaven and earth, but their cravings for fame and wealth are more or less the same.

Every day, the emperor attends to myriads of state affairs, while the beggar only cries out for leftovers. Their positions are also as far apart as heaven and earth, but is there any difference between the emperor's deep concern for state affairs and the beggar's piteous crying for leftovers?

306. 覆雨翻云　不介于怀

306. Take no heed to the changes of the world, however frequent.

饱谙世味，一任覆雨翻云，总慵开眼；会尽人情，随教呼牛唤马①，只是点头。

【中文注释】 ① 随教呼牛唤马：不管别人怎么称呼叫唤，哪怕再不入耳也不予计较。这是一种超脱。语自《庄子·天道第十三》中老子对孔子的一段话："夫巧知神圣之人，吾自以为脱焉。昔者子呼我牛也而谓之牛，呼我马也而谓之马。"

【今文解译】 饱尝人间酸甜苦辣的人，在面对世事的反复无常时，总懒得睁眼去看一看。

阅遍人情世故的人，即使被人当作牛马一样叫唤，他们也只是点点头而已。

【English Translation】

A person who has weathered many storms would disdain to open his eyes to heed any of the possible changes that take place in the world.

A person who has seen through the fickleness of human nature would only give a nod heedlessly even if he is called a cattle or a horse.

307. 前念后念　随缘打发

307. The distracting thoughts, previous or present, are better to be dismissed as circumstances would allow.

今人专求无念，而终不可无。只是前念不滞，后念不迎，但将现在的随缘打发得去，自然渐渐入无。

【今文解译】　今天的人们专注于心无杂念，可终究无法企及这样的高度。其实，只要不让先前的杂念在脑子里滞留，把未来将来的杂念拒之门外，然后再把现在还在作怪的杂念随缘打发了去，人也就自然而然地一步步进入了没有杂念的境界。

【English Translation】

Today's people are keen on banishing the distracting thoughts from their minds, but finally fail to succeed in doing so. The right way to do it is, first, not to hold the previous distracting thoughts at heart; next, to turn down the rising of the new ones; and then, to dismiss the present ones as circumstances would allow. That way, the realm free of distracting thoughts can be reached naturally and gradually.

308. 偶会佳境　自然真机

308. A casually grasped apprehension leads to the realm enjoyable, and a thing arising in accord with Nature bares its mystery.

意所偶会便成佳境，物出天然才见真机。若加一分调停布置，趣意便减矣。白氏①云："意随无事适，风逐自然清。"有味哉！其言之也。

【中文注释】　① 白氏：唐代诗人白居易。

【今文解译】　不经意间悟到的意境才是最美的，自然生成的事物才是最有机趣的。若稍微有一点人为的安排布置，意趣也就减却许多。诗人白居易曾有过这样的诗句："意随无事适，风逐自然清。"妙啊！它说的就是这个意思。

【English Translation】

A casually grasped apprehension leads to the realm enjoyable, and a thing arising in accord with Nature bares its mystery. If they are adorned or arranged artificially, even a bit, the flavor will decrease. Bai Juyi* once wrote in one of his poems, "Man's mind will be in a right state only if it attempts nothing. The breeze will be fresh when it follows its own bent." It is worthwhile to ruminate over the lines. What described therein just hits the said point.

【English Annotation】

* Bai Juyi (772-846): A poet and official of the Tang Dynasty (618-907).

309. 性天澄澈　何必谈禅

309. A pure-natured person needn't explicate the Buddhist tenets.

性天澄澈，即饥餐渴饮，无非康济身心；心地沉迷，纵谈禅演偈，总是播弄精魂。

【今文解译】 一个本性澄然的人，饿了就吃渴了就喝，纯粹只是为了维持身心健康的需要。

一个心思沉迷的人，纵然整天吃斋念佛，也总是在白白耗费自己的精神魂灵。

【English Translation】

A pure-natured person eats when he is hungry and drinks when he is thirsty. What he does is just to secure the health of his own body and heart. As for an addicted person, even if he can explicate the Buddhist tenets, he is only toying with his own mind and soul.

310. 人有真境　即可自愉

310. In everyone's heart there is a wonderland, leisurely and comfortable.

人心有个真境，非丝非竹[①]而自恬愉，不烟不茗而自清芬。须念净境空，虑忘形释，才得以游衍其中。

【中文注释】 ① 非丝非竹：没有丝竹乐，即现在人所说的不听音乐。

【今文解译】 每个人的心里都有一个极乐世界，即使没有音乐伴奏也照样能自娱自乐，即使不焚香不煮茗也一样清香如许。保持心境的纯净和空灵，排除烦恼，放松身体，非此不能无忧无虑地悠游于这个极乐世界之中。

【English Translation】

In everyone's heart there is a wonderland. It is full of ease and comfort even without melody of string and flute, and of delicacy and fragrance even without faint scent of incense and tea. So long as one can purify his mind by doing away with the distracting thoughts and make his heart and body free from restraint, he will pass his days in it at liberty.

311. 幻以求真　雅不离俗

311. Truth cannot but be obtained through illusions, nor can but nobility be derived from vulgarity.

金自矿出，玉从石生，非幻无以求真；道得酒中，仙遇花里，虽雅不能离俗。

【今文解译】 金子从矿砂冶炼出来，美玉由石头切割而成。这说的是：真实产生于虚无。
道理可在酒杯里求得，神仙可于花丛中遇见。这说的是：高雅离不开凡俗。

【English Translation】

Gold is panned out from ore and jade carved from stone. This is to say that truth cannot but be obtained through illusory exteriors.
The mysteries of the Way can be probed in wine cup and the legendary immortals be met with amid flowers. This is to say that a person is unable to separate himself from the mean world no matter how noble and graceful he is.

312. 俗眼观异　道眼观常

312. View with a mundane eye, things are different one another; but with a super-mundane eye, all the same.

天地中万物，人伦中万情，世界中万事，以俗眼观，纷纷各异，以道眼[1]观，种种是常。何须分别？何须取舍？

【中文注释】　① 道眼：此处喻“超越世俗的眼光”，与前句中的“俗眼”形成对应。

【今文解译】　天地间各种生物，人际间各种情感，世上各种事物，若以凡俗的眼光看，它们各不相同，若以脱俗的眼光看，它们都是没有区别的。何必非要分得一清二楚，厚此薄彼？！

【English Translation】

There are myriads of things between the heaven and earth, myriads of emotions in the human relations and myriads of affairs in the world. If we view them with a mundane eye, they are quite different one another; but if with a super-mundane eye, they are all in common. What's the need to distinguish between them, and to like or dislike?

313. 布被神酣　藜羹味足

313. Even a quilt of coarse cloth can bring a sound sleep and a scanty meal produce sufficient flavor.

神酣，布被窝中，得天地冲和之气；味足，藜羹饭后，识人生淡泊之真。

【今文解译】　睡觉香的人，即使身上盖的只是粗布棉被，也可吸收到天地间的和顺之气。
胃口好的人，即使吃的只是粗茶淡饭，也能够体会到生活简朴的真正滋味。

【English Translation】

So long as you are a man of easy sleep, even if wrapped in a quilt of coarse cloth, you can still extract the harmonious essence of the heaven and earth. So long as you are a man of good appetite, even if fed with a scanty meal, you can still appreciate the true subtlety of a simple life.

314. 了心悟性　俗即是僧

314. A layman is called a monk if he can discard the worldly desires and realize the essence of the Way.

缠脱只在自心，心了则屠肆糟廛居然净土。不然，纵一琴一鹤，一花一卉，嗜好虽清，魔障[1]终在。语云："能休尘境为真境[2]，未了僧家是俗家。"信夫！

【中文注释】 ① 魔障：佛家用语。恶魔在人们心中所设的障碍。
② 真境：此处指真正的极乐世界。

【今文解译】 摆脱俗欲还是为俗欲所累，全然取决于一个人的内心，内心摆脱了俗欲，纵然是屠户酒肆也会变成极乐净土。否则，纵然是琴鹤为伴，花卉满园，嗜好高雅，内心的魔障也还是去除不了的。俗话说："能休尘境为真境，未了僧家是俗家。"此言说得极是。

【English Translation】

To be fettered by or to be free from the worldly desires is merely up to what approach one takes. If one can discard the worldly desires from within, even a slaughterhouse or a wine shop will become the Pure Land; if one can not, even with an elegant hobby to have a lute or a crane for company, or raise flowers and grasses for self-amusement, the barrier in the heart set by a monster is still there. It is as an old saying which goes, "Only when a person has discarded the worldly desires can he enter nirvana. A monk who hasn't done so is the same as a layman." What a truth!

315. 万虑都捐　一真自得

315. Clear off all the worldly vexations, and one will feel quite oneself.

斗室中，万虑都捐，说甚画栋飞云，珠帘卷雨[①]；三杯后，一真[②]自得，唯知素琴横月，短笛吟风[③]。

【中文注释】 ① 画栋飞云，珠帘卷雨：指装修华丽的豪宅。
② 一真：即"真一"，道家用语。此处指真正的自我。
③ 素琴横月，短笛吟风：吹笛弹琴，吟风弄月。

【今文解译】 身处狭窄的陋室里，一切烦忧都烟消云散，谁还会去惦记富贵人家的雕梁画栋？！
三杯酒下肚，我仿佛找到了真正的自我，此时只知道在月光下抚琴，微风中横笛。

【English Translation】

Take a self-reflection in a tiny hovel and then I find that all the worldly vexations disappear, thereby realizing how worthless it is to admire the magnificent mansions with painted rafters and pearl-studded curtains.

After three cups of wine I feel quite myself, only left to think of the melodies of lyre and piccolo chiming with the moon and the soft breeze.

316. 性天未枯　机神触发

316. The instincts of all nature never wither and the tendency of life stops at nothing.

万籁寂寥中，忽闻一鸟弄声，便唤起许多幽趣[①]；万卉摧剥[②]后，忽见一枝擢秀[③]，便触动无限生机。可见性天[④]未曾枯槁，机神最易触发[⑤]。

【中文注释】 ① 幽趣：隐藏在心底的优雅趣味。
② 摧剥：凋零衰败。
③ 擢秀：花朵开放争艳。
④ 性天：此处指自然的本性或万物的本性。
⑤ 机神最易触发：此处隐含生生不息之意，喻万物的生

机无处不在，随时随地都可见可闻。

【今文解译】 万籁俱寂之中，忽然听到有一只鸟儿在鸣叫，心里顿时充满了幽雅的趣味；所有的花花草草都凋谢后，忽然看到还有一株花绽放在枝头，免不了被大自然的无限生机所感动。可见动植物的天性是不会轻易枯寂的，大自然的勃勃生机是无处不在的。

【English Translation】

When all the sounds are hushed, I suddenly hear the crying of a bird, and it arouses my numerous elegant innermost feelings. When all the flowers are withering up, I am amazed to find one of them is still in full bloom, and it evokes boundless vitality deep in my heart. This leads me to believe this that the instincts of Nature never wither and the tendency of life stops at nothing.

317. 把柄在手　收放自如

317. Obtain a firm hold so as to feel free whether to be restrained or unrestrained accordingly.

白氏①云："不如放身心，冥然任天造。"晁氏②云："不如收身心，凝然③归寂定。"放者流为猖狂，收者入于枯寂。唯善操身心者，把柄④在手，收放自如。

【中文注释】 ① 白氏：唐代诗人白居易。
② 晁氏：北宋文学家晁补之。
③ 凝然：凝神。
④ 把柄：把持，把握。

【今文解译】 白居易说："不如放开自己的身心，任由大自然在冥冥之中将我造就。"而晁补之则说："不如收起自己的身心，全神贯注地让自我回归寂静和安定。"放任往往使人张狂，而收敛又往往使人枯寂。只有善于调节自己身心的人，才能较好地把握二者之间的平衡，真正做到收放自如。

【English Translation】

Bai Juyi wrote in a poem, “Better be unrestrained so as to let the body and mind be molded by Nature without being noticed.” But Chao Buzhi* said otherwise, “Better be restrained so as to let the body and mind return to ease and quietude in a concentrated way.” It seems to me that the unrestrained are apt to become arrogant and conceited, while the restrained are apt to become dull and lonely. Only those who make themselves master of their bodies and minds are able to obtain a firm hold, thereby feeling free whether to be restrained or unrestrained accordingly.

【English Annotation】

* Chao Buzhi (1053-1110): A man of letters and official in the Northern Song Dynasty (960-1127).

318. 造化人心　混合无间

318. Nature’s creation and human feelings often blend as one.

当雪夜月天，心境便尔澄澈；遇春风和气，意界亦自冲融。造化人心，混合无间。

【今文解译】 每当夜雪飞舞，月光融融，人的心境就会变得清澄明澈；每当春风和煦，气候温润，人的意兴就会变得淡然恬适。大自然的造化和人们的心理感受，此时是紧紧融合在一起的。

【English Translation】

Every time when I gaze on the flying snow by night or on the moon hanging in the sky, my heart would turn out to be extremely pure and clear. Each year when spring comes and its breeze brings in warmth, my heart would be overflowing with joy and cheerfulness. What a splendid moment at which Nature’s creation and human feelings are blending as one.

319. 文以拙进　道以拙成

319. It is only on the basis of plainness that progress can be made in writings and accomplishment be effected in moral cultivation.

文以拙①进，道以拙成，一“拙”字有无限意味。如桃源犬吠，桑间鸡鸣②，何等淳庞！至于寒潭之月，古木之鸦，工巧中便觉有衰飒气象矣。

【中文注释】　① 拙：质朴。

② 桃源犬吠，桑间鸡鸣：这是东晋诗人陶渊明所著《桃花源记》描述的世外桃源景象。

【今文解译】　文章讲求朴实无华才能有进步，美德讲求诚实无欺才能修成，这两句话的意味深长无比。犹如桃花丛中有狗叫，桑树园里有鸡鸣，那是何等的醇厚质朴啊！至于寒潭冷月、枯木老鸦之类的辞藻，虽然工整对仗，但却充满着衰颓的气息。

【English Translation】

It is only on the basis of plainness that progress can be made in writings and accomplishment be effected in moral cultivation. The word “plainness” contains countless meanings. So natural and unaffected are the sounds such as the barking of dogs in peach blossoms and the crowing of cocks amidst white mulberries*. Whereas, so decadent are the descriptions such as the moon’s reflection in the cold pond and the crows on the old trees, though literally quite exquisite.

【English Annotation】

* Peach blossoms and white mulberries: The very scenery of a peaceful, happy and beautiful place isolated from the world and suffering no disaster or war, depicted by Tao Yuanming of the Eastern Jin Dynasty (317-420) in *The Story of the Peach Blossom Valley*. It is also known as Shangri-la.

320. 以我转物　大地逍遥

320. A good control over exterior things breeds boundless freedom and unrestrainedness.

以我转物者，得固不喜，失亦不忧，大地尽属逍遥；以物役我者，逆固生憎，顺亦生爱，一毛便生缠缚。

【今文解译】 由自己驾驭外物来做的事情，得手了没什么可高兴的，失手了也没什么可不高兴的，得失尽在两可之间。
由外物驱使自己来做的事情，受挫时就怨天尤人，顺利时就爱不释手，细小的变化都会使身心受到困扰。

【English Translation】
Those who are able to control and govern exterior things will not gloat over what they've gained, nor grieve about what they could not. Persons of this nature would be in no sense affected and restrained from without.
Those who are controlled by exterior things will easily become resentful when frustrated, and can't stop loving them when they are going well. Even a small shift as thin as a hair can worry and bind such persons.

321. 形去影去　心空境空

321. When the shape is removed, its shadow disappears; when the heart is made void, its surroundings become void, too.

理寂则事寂，遣事执理者，似去影留形；心空则境空，去境存心者，如聚膻却蚋。

【今文解译】 一件事情的事理要没了，事情也就不复存在了；想要放过事情但又纠结于事理，就好比保留物体却要去除影子。
心里的杂念要没了，环境也就干扰不了人了；改变环境但又不去除心里的杂念，就如同用腥膻之物来驱赶苍蝇。

【English Translation】
When the grounds for a thing are extinguished, the thing itself becomes extinguished. If a person leaves aside the thing but still hangs on its grounds, it is as stupid as trying to erase the shadow by not removing the shape.
When the heart is made void of the mundane thoughts, the surroundings breeding them will also become void. If a person intends to dismiss the surroundings by not having his heart made void, it is as ridiculous as trying to drive away the black flies by assembling carrion before them.

322. 处世任事　总在自适

322. In dealing with the world or doing something, one should always suit them to oneself.

幽人[①]清事总在自适。故酒以不劝为欢，棋以不争为胜，笛以无腔为适[②]，琴以无弦为高，会以不期约为真率，客以不迎送为坦夷[③]。若一牵文泥迹[④]，便落尘世苦海矣！

【中文注释】 ① 幽人：幽居者，幽居之士；隐士。
② 笛以无腔为适：吹没有腔孔的笛子以求自适。此处比喻吹奏笛子不在于笛子是否精致或笛声是否悦耳，而在于吹笛子的人能否从中得到乐趣，陶冶性情。下文的“琴以无弦为高”与此同理。
③ 坦夷：坦诚直率；不做作。
④ 牵文泥迹：拘泥于世俗的繁文缛节。

【今文解译】 幽居之士做清雅的事，总能以淡然的态度自适其性。故而他们的做派是：喝酒不以劝酒为欢畅，下棋不以争胜为目的，吹笛不以笛声悦耳为适意，弹琴不以琴声动人为高雅，见面不以是否相邀为真诚，宾客往来不以是否迎送为自然。如果这些事都刻板地按着俗套去做，一准会费心费力，苦不堪言！

【English Translation】

When engaged in elegant things, the recluse would prefer to follow his own bent. So what he advocates are: to drink wine, it is more pleasant not to urge or be urged to do so; to play chess, it is more brilliant not to contend for rivalry; to pipe the flute, it is more joyful to pipe it for self-appreciation; to play the lute, it is more graceful to play it as an improvisation; to have a meeting, it is more forthright and sincere to have it by chance; and to entertain guests, it is more natural and candid for not particularly rendering welcome and seeing-off. If he rigidly adheres to any of the conventional patterns in doing these things he will surely fall into the sea of bitterness.

323. 思及生死　万念灰冷

323. Think about life and death, and all the thoughts and ambitions will be blasted.

试思未生之前有何像貌①，又思既死之后作何景色②，则万念灰冷。一性寂然，自可超物外而游象先③。

【中文注释】 ① 像貌：模样。
② 景色：景象，情形。
③ 游象先：超逸于创造万物的上帝产生之前。典自老子《道德经》的"吾不知谁之子，象帝之先"。

【今文解译】 试想一下自己生前是啥模样，死后又将是什么情形，人就不会有那么多贪欲了。坚守自己的本性，心无旁骛，人就可以超然物外，不受任何羁绊了。

【English Translation】

If you can imagine what you were like before you were born and what you will be like after you die, all the covetous thoughts in your mind will be blasted. So long as you can stick to your true nature, you will certainly transcend this mundane world and feel as if you were roaming in another world before the existence of God*.

【English Translation】

* Before the existence of God: this phrase is attributed to Lao Zi who wrote in his Tao Te Ching, "I don't know where it (referred to the Tao — tr.) comes from. It seems to have appeared before the existence of God."

324. 福祸生死　须有卓见

324. There needs supreme wisdom to understand happiness and calamity, life and death.

遇病而后思强之为宝，处乱而后思平之为福，非蚤智也；幸福而先知其为祸之本，贪生而先知其为死之因，其卓见乎。

【今文解译】 身体染上疾病才懂得健康十分宝贵，遇到了动乱才明白平安无事是一种福分，这算不得什么高明。

追求幸福而先知道幸福只是祸患之源，贪恋生命而先明白生命的尽头就是死亡，这才是真知灼见。

【English Translation】

It cannot be called foresight if one realizes how precious health is only after taken ill, and appreciates the blessings of peace only after being in unrest.

It is called supreme wisdom if one seeks happiness and in the meantime understands that happiness is the source of calamity, and prays for longevity and in the meantime knows that life is the inevitable course to death.

325. 妍丑胜负　今又安在

325. Where now are the beautiful and ugly on the stage or the victory and defeat on the checkerboard?

优人[①]傅粉调朱[②]，效妍丑于毫端[③]，俄而歌残场罢，妍丑何存？弈者争先竞后，较雌雄于着子，俄而局尽子收，雌雄安在？

【中文注释】 ① 优人：演戏的人，旧时俗称戏子。

② 傅粉调朱：化妆打扮。

③ 效妍丑于毫端：用手中的化妆笔在脸上画出美与丑。

【今文解译】 演员涂脂抹粉，用彩笔在脸上描摹美丽与丑陋，不一会儿歌舞结束，卸妆离去，美丽与丑陋又在哪里？

弈者针锋相对，用棋子在棋盘上杀得天昏地暗，不一会儿胜败落定，局尽子收，胜者和败者又在哪里？

【English Translation】

Actors and actresses put on makeup to reproduce the beautiful and ugly on the stage. But after a while when the performance is over, where now are the beauty and ugliness?

Chess players apply stratagem and arrange layout to contend for the upper hand on the checkerboard. But after a while when the game is over, where now are the victory and defeat?

326. 风花竹石　静闲得之

326. The wind, the flowers, the bamboos and the rocks are only enjoyable at tranquility and leisure.

风花之潇洒，雪月[①]之空清，唯静者为之主[②]；水木之荣枯，竹石之消长，独闲者操其权[③]。

【中文注释】　① 风花、雪月：常用以描写四时的自然美景。典自“春有百花秋有月，夏有凉风冬有雪”。
② 唯静者为之主：意为“只有心静的人才能受享”。为之主，即成为受享的主人。
③ 独闲者操其权：意为“只有悠闲的人才能领略”。操其权，即掌握领略的权利。

【今文解译】　微风中的花朵潇洒自在，雪夜里的月亮空灵清澈，这样的风光只有心静的人才得以受享。
流水边树木的荣枯交替，竹林间石头的此消彼长，这样的景致只有悠闲的人才得以领略。

【English Translation】
It is only the tranquil-hearted person who is able to appreciate the grace of flowers casually flickering in the soft breeze and the crystal rays of the moon on a snowy night.
It is only the leisurely-minded person who is in a position to drink in the flourishing and decaying of the trees fringing the rivulet and the growth and decline of the bamboos among rocks.

327. 天全欲淡　人生至境

327. It is the acme of human life to keep the nature intact and get along with few desires.

田夫野叟[①]，语以黄鸡白酒则欣然喜，问以鼎食[②]则不知；语以缊袍短褐[③]则油然乐，问以衮服则不识。其天全[④]，故其欲淡。此是人生第一个境界。

【中文注释】 ① 田夫野叟：泛指乡下的种田人。
② 鼎食：泛指美味。古代只有帝王之家和达官贵人才能享用鼎这种代表身份的器皿，用鼎烧煮或盛放的食品也即山珍海味。
③ 缊袍短褐：指平民百姓穿的粗布衣服。缊袍，用碎麻片做成的长袍；短褐，用褐布竖裁做成的短而窄的衣服。
④ 其天全：其自然本性未受外界不良影响。

【今文解译】 跟村夫谈论黄鸡白酒，他们就劲道十足；跟他们说起山珍海味，他们则全然不知；跟他们谈论粗布麻衣，他们就喜形于色；跟他们说起黄袍朝服，他们则丝毫没有概念。天性未被熏染，欲望当然也就淡泊。——此所谓人生第一境界。

【English Translation】

When talking about water-boiled chickens and sorghum liquor, the country folks will beam with joy; but when asked about a feast served with tripod cauldrons, they have no idea at all. When talking about floss-padded robes and cutty sarks, they will be wreathed in smiles; but when asked about brilliant court dresses, they are left at a complete loss. From this we see that it is by virtue of the intactness of their natural characters that they can get along with few desires. This is so called the first acme of human life.

328. 观心增障　齐物剖同

328. To undertake self-examination is to add more barriers to self-cultivation; to integrate the myriad things is to disintegrate the organic whole.

心无其心[①]，何有于观[②]？释氏[③]曰：“观心者，重增其障。”物本一物，何待于齐？庄生[④]曰：“齐物者，自剖其同。”

【中文注释】 ① 心无其心：心无杂念。前一个“心”指人的内心，后一个“心”指心中的杂念。
② 观：观心，即观察自己的心性。佛教主张的修为之法。
③ 释氏：释，释迦牟尼。释氏，泛指佛教或佛教僧人。

④ 庄生：庄子，名庄周，战国时期宋国人。中国著名的思想家、哲学家。

【今文解译】 心里若无私欲杂念，人又何必要闭门观心？佛家学者说："观心多了反而会增加修行的障碍。"
世上万物本是一体的，有什么可划一的？庄子说："着意划一反而会把本属一体的东西拆散了。"

【English Translation】

If a person has no selfish desires or distracting thoughts in his heart, will it be necessary for him to undertake meditation on himself? The Buddhist said, "He who meditates on himself is simply adding more barriers to his self-cultivation."
All things on earth are an organic whole, what is the need to integrate them? Zhuang Zi* said, "If a person intends to integrate the myriad things on earth, it is no more than disintegrating the organic whole."

【English Annotation】

* Zhuang Zi (c. 369BC-286BC): Named Zhuang Zhou, he was a native of the State of Song in the Warring States Period (475BC-221BC). Born into a declined noble family, Zhuang Zi received relatively high education as a teenager, but suffered when growing up with his state subjugated and family wrecked.

329. 悬崖撒手　苦海离身

329. Rein in at the brink of the precipice so as to avoid falling into the sea of bitterness.

笙歌①正浓处，便自拂衣长往②，羡达人撒手悬崖③；更漏已残时，犹然夜行不休，笑俗士沉身苦海。

【中文注释】 ① 笙歌：合笙之歌。也可指吹笙唱歌或奏乐唱歌。
② 拂衣长往：起身整衣然后离开。
③ 撒手悬崖：这里指见好就收、意志力强的意思。

【今文解译】 歌舞表演正入高潮时便整衣离去，这样能见好就收的豁达之人实在是令人称羡。

夜深人静了却还在为名利四处奔走，这样身沉苦海的鄙俗之人实在是可笑至极。

【English Translation】

The person, who can leave the theatre without the least hesitation just when the show of dancing and singing is at its height, is an enlightened man who knows how to stop at the right time. Such a man deserves to be admired.

The person, who is still busy rushing about for fame and wealth even late at midnight, is a mean fellow who is deeply submerged by the sea of bitterness. Such a fellow is destined to be held up to ridicule.

330. 修行绝尘　悟道涉俗

330. To conduct self-cultivation, it is best to cut loose from the worldly affects; to perceive the way of the world, it is best to merge into the world of mortals.

把握未定①，宜绝迹尘嚣②，使此心不见可欲③而不乱，以澄吾静体；操持既坚④，又当混迹风尘⑤，使此心见可欲而亦不乱，以养吾圆机⑥。

【中文注释】 ① 把握未定：尚无能力把握自己。此处指内心的修炼还未到家。

② 绝迹尘嚣：远离世俗社会。

③ 不见可欲：见不到可以引起欲念的事物。

④ 操持既坚：意为“能很好地把控自己”。

⑤ 混迹风尘：投身纷杂的社会。

⑥ 养吾圆机：修养自己圆通的灵机。结合前文内容，此处可理解为“更加自如地应对这个复杂的社会”。

【今文解译】 一个修炼尚未到家的人还是远离尘嚣为好，这样可以使自己不会因为受到外界诱惑而妄动，保持内心的澄净与安宁。

一个已经修炼到家的人则应多出去走走，要有意识地在充满诱惑的环境里磨炼自己的自持能力，以养成圆通的灵机。

【English Translation】

When your virtue and ability are not yet well cultivated, you'd better sever yourself from the clamor of the world so as to avoid confusion by letting your heart stay out of desirable objects. This will help to purify your innate nature. Once your virtue and ability are fully cultivated, you may venture yourself into the world of mortals so as to learn how to dispel confusion by having your heart to brave out external temptations. This will help to perfect your cultivation.

331. 人我一视　动静两忘

331. Regard the multitude and yourself as one and let both quietude and clamor fade into oblivion.

喜寂厌喧者，往往避人以求静。不知意在无人便成我相[①]，心著于静便是动根。如何到得人我一视[②]、动静两忘的境界?

【中文注释】 ① 我相：佛教用语。比喻执着于自我。
② 人我一视：对待别人和自己都一样。

【今文解译】 喜欢安静不喜欢喧闹的人，往往刻意避开人群以求得安静。殊不知这种做法只会导致自我封闭，而一心想求得安静本身就是躁动的根源。如此怎能达到人我一视、动静两忘的境界?！

【English Translation】

Those who prefer quietude to clamor tend to seek solitude by keeping themselves away from the multitude, hardly realizing that to stay clear of the multitude is nothing but the presentation of autism, and that to set their hearts on seeking solitude is only the root cause of agitation. How can they come up to the point of regarding the multitude and themselves as one and letting both the quietude and clamor fade into oblivion?

332. 山居清洒　入尘即俗

332. When dwelling in mountains one feels fresh and relaxed but becomes vulgar when returning to worldly society.

山居胸次清洒[1]，触物皆有佳思：见孤云野鹤而起超绝之想[2]，遇石涧流泉而动澡雪之思[3]，扶老桧[4]寒梅而劲节挺立[5]，侣沙鸥麋鹿[6]而机心[7]顿忘。若一走入尘寰[8]，无论物不相关，即此身亦属赘旒[9]矣！

【中文注释】 ① 胸次清洒：胸中清新洒脱。

② 超绝之想：超然一切的念头。

③ 澡雪之思：此处指洗涤心中杂念的想法。

④ 老桧：类似松柏的老树。

⑤ 劲节挺立：坚贞的情致。

⑥ 侣沙鸥麋鹿：与沙鸥和麋鹿为伴。沙鸥，一种经常栖息于沙洲、飞翔于江海之上的水鸟；麋鹿，一种哺乳动物，俗称四不象。

⑦ 机心：机诈之心。

⑧ 尘寰：尘世。

⑨ 赘旒：旗帜上装饰用的飘带。喻多余之物。

【今文解译】 人住在山林里，心胸清新洒脱，所见所闻都能勾起美好的联想：看见一片孤云或者一群野鹤就会有超然物外的想法，路遇山谷岩石间流动的清泉就会有荡涤俗欲的想法，抚摸苍劲的松柏和耐寒的冬梅就会节义凛然，和沙鸥麋鹿一起玩耍就会忘记诡诈的心思。此时他若回到纷扰的社会，且不说外物与其无关，即使他的身体也成了多余的摆设。

【English Translation】

Dwelling in the mountains makes one feel fresh and relaxed. Whatever he chances upon will engender elegant associations: when he catches sight of a solitary floating cloud or hovering wild cranes, there would emerge in his mind the thought to cherish soaring aspirations; when he comes across the murmuring streams in the valley, there would appear in his mind the notion to dismiss all vulgarities; when he caresses an old pine or a winter plum tree, there would arise in his mind the determination for unyielding integrity; and when he has sand-pipers or elks for company, all the cunning schemes in his mind would vanish instantly. But if he returns to the dusty world at this moment, not only the external things but also the flesh of his own body would become as worthless as the superfluous ribbons of a flag.

333. 野鸟作伴　白云相留

333. So long as your mind is set at leisure, even the wild birds and white clouds will come to accompany you.

兴逐时来，芳草中撒履①闲行，野鸟忘机时作伴；景与心会，落花下披襟兀坐，白云无语漫相留②。

【中文注释】 ① 撒履：脱掉鞋子。
② 漫相留：漫，意即不要或者无须。相留，意即挽留或者邀请。

【今文解译】 兴致来的时候，不妨脱掉鞋子到芳草地里去走走，这样的时刻，野鸟也会忘了可能被捕捉的危险而前来与你做伴。
当好景遇到好心情的时候，花雨下独自披着衣服静坐观赏，这样的时刻，白云也会径自悬停在你头顶上不肯离去。

【English Translation】

When the fit is on you, you may well take a stroll barefooted in the field of fragrant grasses. At such a joyful moment, even the wild birds will forget the danger of being captured and fly clapping their wings to play along with you from time to time.

When your heart blends with the scene of fallen petals, you may well sit alone with a robe draped on your shoulders. At such a leisurely moment, even the white clouds will waft silently from afar and linger round over your head without invitation.

334. 念头稍异　境界顿殊

334. A minor shift of mind can immediately bring about a quite different world in front of our eyes.

人生福境祸区，皆念想造成。故释氏云：“利欲炽然即是火坑，贪爱沉溺便为苦海；一念清静烈焰成池，一念警觉航登彼岸。”念头稍异，境界顿殊。可不慎哉?

【今文解译】　人生的福祉和灾祸全在于一念之间。所以佛家有言：“名利心太重就会跌入火坑，贪嗔爱恋太甚就会掉进苦海；而一个清醒的念头可以使火坑变成碧池，一个警觉的念头可以帮人脱离苦海。”念头稍有不同，境遇就大不一样。能不慎重吗?!

【English Translation】

The happiness and sadness of a man are both decided by the mind he has. That is why the Buddhist said like this, “When greed rages like fire, it becomes a fiery pit. Overindulgence in avarice leads the way to the sea of bitterness. But a moment’s clear-mindedness enables one to turn the fiery pit into a cool pond, and a flash of alert can help him cross over the sea of bitterness.” Thus we understand that a minor shift of mind can immediately bring about a quite different world in front of our eyes. We cannot be too careful!

335. 水滴石穿　瓜熟蒂落

335. A stone can be worn away by drops of water; when a melon is ripe, it falls off its stem.

绳锯木断，水滴石穿，学道者须加力索[①]；水到渠成，瓜熟蒂落，得道者一任天机[②]。

【中文注释】　① 须加力索：必须下功夫探索。

② 一任天机：道家的一种世界观。意为：“要让天下万物都随着它们的自然本性去发展，不要人为地去改变它们。”

【今文解译】 绳子能把木头锯断，流水能把石头滴穿，学道之人如果不下死功夫就不能得道。

水到之处会形成沟渠，瓜果熟透了会从藤上落下来，得道之人遇事要顺其自然。

【English Translation】

A wood can be cut off by sawing with a rope; a stone can be worn away by dripping water. Enlightened by this, those who intend to learn the Way must constantly exert themselves to do so.

When water flows, a channel is formed; when a melon is ripe, it falls off its stem. So those who have comprehended the Way should not intervene but should let things follow their natural bent.

336. 机息有风月　心远无喧嚣

336. The mind free of intrigues and maneuvers brings natural subtlety; the heart far apart from the mundane world has no room for distractions and confusions.

机息时，便有月到风来①，不必苦海人世；心远处，自无车尘马迹②，何须痼疾丘山③。

【中文注释】 ① 月到风来：月光照我身，和风拂我面。此处喻心情疏朗。

② 车尘马迹：此处指尘世间的喧嚷躁动。

③ 痼疾丘山：执着于远离尘世的深山老林。痼疾，久治不愈的病。此处喻执着、偏执、迷恋等。

【今文解译】 机巧杂念平息时，心里自然就会有清风明月，因而也就不用在人生的苦海中挣扎了。

心思远离尘世时，人自然也就没了外界的烦扰，何苦还要躲进深山老林里修行养德。

【English Translation】

By the time when the intrigues and maneuvers in the mind have subsided, the subtlety of natural elegance will emerge of itself, so there is no need to linger and struggle in the sea of bitterness.

By the time when the heart has been kept far away from the hubbub of the world, its distractions and confusions will disappear of themselves, so there is no need to go and live as a recluse in the caves for personal cultivation.

337. 生生之意　天地之心

337. Boundless vitality of myriad things is the fruit of the charity of Nature.

草木才零落，便露萌颖①于根底；时序虽凝寒，终回阳气于飞灰②。肃杀之中，生生之意常为之主，即是可以见天地之心。

【中文注释】 ① 萌颖：新出的嫩芽。

② 飞灰：古代一种测定节气的土办法，即将芦苇烧成灰放在竹管里置于封闭的户内，等到冬至来临时，竹管里的灰就会慢慢向管外移动，最后随着空气飞扬开来，以此测定气候的由暖转寒。

【今文解译】 树木才开始凋零，其根部就已露出新芽；寒冬虽未过去，但暖春一定会随着季节的转换缓缓而至。萧条衰微的景象中，常常蕴含着主宰事物发展的勃勃生机；大自然哺育万物的鸿恩大德，由此可见一斑。

【English Translation】

Just when the trees and weeds wither, their roots begin shooting out new buds. Although it is cold at the moment, the warm season will return for sure when the reed ashes* fly from the pipes.

Even if the world is in a bleak box, there still remains in concealment the boundless vitality that dominates the way myriad things are going. It is from this that we perceive the charity of Nature.

【English Annotation】

* Reed ashes: The powder that remains after reed plants have burnt. In ancient China, people usually put reed ashes in bamboo pipes and kept them in a sealed room to ascertain the changes of climate. When the Winter Solstice came, the piped reed ashes would move out and fly up with the air here and there. By observing the flying of the ashes, people would know that there was

a change of season.

338. 雨后山清　静中钟扬

338. After a shower of rain the hills look so fresh and so melodious sounds the bell tone in stillness.

雨余观山色，景象便觉新妍；夜静听钟声，音响尤为清越。

【今文解译】　雨后观赏山峦秀色，便觉得景象异常新鲜明丽。夜里静听寺庙钟声，便觉得声音尤为清脆悠扬。

【English Translation】

Watch the hills after a shower of rain, and you will find that the view at your sight is exceptionally fresh and elegant.

Listen to the bell tone in the still of night, and you will find that the sound you pick up is especially clear and melodious.

339. 雪夜读书　神清气爽

339. Reading a book on a snowy night helps to refresh the spirit and comfort the heart.

登高使人心旷，临流使人意远。读书于雨雪之夜使人神清，舒啸于丘阜之巅使人兴迈。

【今文解译】　站在高处使人心旷神怡，面对流水使人意境深远。在雨雪之夜捧书研读，人会觉得神清气爽；在山丘顶上放声长啸，人会觉得意兴豪迈。

【English Translation】

Ascending a height makes one feel relaxed and joyful. Standing on the brink of a stream gives magnificent rise to one's thoughts.

Reading a book on a rainy or snowy night helps to refresh the mind. Shouting heartily at the peak of a hill enables one to arouse the boldness.

340. 万钟一发　存乎一心

340. The value of a thing, big or small, is decided by the conception of value.

心旷，则万钟①如瓦缶②；心隘，则一发似车轮。

【中文注释】 ① 万钟：此处喻巨大的财富。
② 瓦缶：古代平民用来装酒的瓦器，多被形容为不值钱的物品。

【今文解译】 心胸旷达的人，即使面对万千财富也如同面对瓦罐那样不为所动。
心胸狭隘的人，即使一根毫毛在他眼里也如同车轮那么巨大无比。

【English Translation】

To a person who is broad-minded, even a tremendous wealth is as worthless as a crock. But to a person who is narrow-minded, even a single hair seems to be as big as a chariot wheel.

341. 以我转物　驾驭欲念

341. Control the external things and be master of your internal desires.

无风月花柳不成造化，无情欲嗜好不成心体①。只以我转物，不以物役我，则嗜欲莫非天机②，尘情即是理境③矣。

【中文注释】 ① 心体：有灵魂的躯体。
② 天机：大自然的规律或奥秘。
③ 理境：理性范畴。

【今文解译】 没有风花雪月就不成其所谓大自然的造化，没有七情六欲就不成其所谓人的心性。只要能做到我控制外物而不是外物控制我，风花雪月就无不都是自然的机趣，七情六欲又何尝不在理性的范畴之内。

【English Translation】

Without the wind, the moon, flowers and willows, Nature will not be its self any more. Likewise, without emotions, desires, addictions and predilections, man's temperaments are no longer what they should be. If a person can control external things rather than be controlled by them, not only his pleasure-seeking longings are considered congenial to the mystery of Nature, but also his mundane feelings and affections agreeable to rational faculty.

342. 就身了身　以物付物

342. Understand your true self through meditation, and let things go in accord with their natural bent.

就一身了一身者，方能以万物付万物；还天下于天下①者，方能出世间于世间。

【中文注释】　① 还天下于天下：道家的一种治国理念。典自庄子的“爱以身于为天下，则可以寄天下。”意思是“将天下托付给爱天下如同爱自己生命的人”。而接下来的“出世间于世间”则是佛家的一种劝世思想。本意为：“超脱世俗离不开接触世俗。”或为：“要想真正超脱世俗，就得先了解世俗，看破世俗。”

【今文解译】　只有自己对自己了悟了，才能让世间万事万物都按其自然本性和规律发展。

只有将天下托付给爱天下如同爱自己生命的人，才能看破并最后超脱世俗。

【English Translation】

Only when one could understand his true self through meditation can he let things go in accordance with their natural bent. Likewise, only when one could entrust the world to another who would cherish it as his life can he free himself from the mundane affairs.

343. 抱身心忧　耽风月趣

343. Just as beware of untoward happenings to the body and heart, so try to understand how to take the pleasure to enjoy the mysteries of Nature.

人生太闲，则别念窃生；太忙，则真性不见。故士君子不可不抱身心之忧，亦不可不耽风月之趣。

【今文解译】 生活过于闲逸，杂七杂八的念头就会悄然滋生；生活过于忙碌，纯真的本性就会被泯灭。所以，有德的君子不可忽略自己的身心健康，也不可没有吟风弄月的雅兴。

【English Translation】

Living too idle a life will give secret birth to the crooked thoughts in the mind. Living too busy a life will lead to the loss of a man's true characters. Therefore, a scholar of high virtue should not neglect untoward happenings to his own body and heart on the one hand, nor should he fail to know how to take the pleasure to enjoy the mysteries of Nature on the other hand.

344. 一念不生　处处真境

344. Banish the distracting thoughts from your mind, and you will find paradise everywhere.

人心多从动处失真[1]。若一念不生，澄然[2]静坐，云兴[3]而悠然共逝[4]，雨滴而泠然[5]俱清，鸟啼而欣然有会[6]，花落而潇然[7]自得。何地非真境？何物无真机？

【中文注释】 ① 从动处失真：在内心躁动的情况下失去自然本性。
② 澄然：清澈透明。此处喻心无杂念。
③ 云兴：云彩飘荡。
④ 共逝：一起飘向远方。
⑤ 泠然：形容声音清越。此处喻心灵变得清澈。
⑥ 有会：领会相通。
⑦ 潇然：悠然自得的样子。

【今文解译】 一个人多在心浮气躁的时候失去自己的本性。如果心无杂念，平静如水，那么，当他遥望云彩的翻卷心就会随之而远逝，看见雨水的淅淅沥沥心就会变得清澄明澈，听到鸟儿的啾啾声心就会欣然与其共鸣，观赏花朵的飘落心就会变得洒脱自如。普天之下，何处不是人间仙境，何物不是生机盎然？

【English Translation】

People are liable to lose their true characters when agitated by impulse from within. If a person can banish all the distracting thoughts from his mind and sit in silence with an unaffected heart, then, when watching the floating clouds, he will feel himself wafting off with them; when beholding the pure raindrops, he will feel his heart being cleansed and refreshed; when listening to the chirping of birds, he will feel his heart becoming cheerful and apprehensive; when gazing on the falling of flowers, he will feel quite unfettered and self-composed. And so, is there any place not thought as an earthly paradise? Or, is there anything not containing natural exuberance?

345. 顺逆一视　欣戚两忘

345. Extend equal treatment to both fortune and adversity, and remain unswayed by either joys or worries.

子生而母危，镪积①而盗窥，何喜非忧也？贫可以节用②，病可以保身，何忧非喜也？故达人当顺逆一视③，而欣戚两忘④。

【中文注释】 ① 镪积：积累财富。镪，古人用来串铜钱的绳索，后泛指金钱。

② 节用：勤俭节约。

③ 顺逆一视：对顺境和逆境一视同仁。

④ 欣戚两忘：对高兴的事和不高兴的事都不耿耿于怀。

【今文解译】 婴儿降生之时母亲却面临危险，财富积累多了盗贼就盯上了，谁能说这是喜而不是忧？贫穷可以教会人节俭，疾病可以提醒人注意身体，谁能说这是忧而不是喜？所以，通达的人应当将顺境和逆境同样看待，既不要见好就喜也不要见坏就忧。

【English Translation】

When a child is given birth, the mother faces danger. When more of your wealth has been accumulated, it attracts the wicked intention of robbers. How can such happenings be simply called joys rather than worries? Poverty enables a person to cultivate thrift. Illness enables a person to pay attention to preserving his health. How can such cases be simply called worries rather than joys? Therefore, an enlightened man should extend equal treatment to both fortune and adversity, and remain unmoved by either joys or worries.

346. 空谷巨响　过而不留

346. The whistling wind blowing through an open valley leaves no sound behind when it passes.

耳根①似飙谷投响②，过而不留，则是非俱谢③；心境如月池浸色④，空而不著，则物我两忘。

【中文注释】 ① 耳根：佛家用语。佛教中有“六根清净”之说，六根即眼、耳、鼻、舌、身、意。耳根指对声音产生知觉。

② 飙谷投响：狂风吹过山谷时发出的巨响。

③ 谢：消失。

④ 月池浸色：月光映照在池塘的水面上。

【今文解译】 耳朵听东西就像狂风呼啸着吹过山谷，风过去了风声也就消失了；风与风声是这样，人世间的是是非非又何尝不是如此。

心境就像月光洒在池水上，月亮隐去了池水上的月影也就不在了；如果心境能够像池水一样，做到物我两忘也就不难了。

【English Translation】

When the wild whirlwind blows through an open valley, it makes deafening sound. But as soon as it passes no more sound is left to be heard. If our ears could act like the valley, the arguments over right and wrong will disappear of themselves.

When the moon casts its beams in a pool, it forms a beautiful reflection on the surface of water. But as soon as it moves away no traces can be marked again. If our hearts could act like the pool, neither the external things nor the self will disturb us.

347. 世亦不尘　海亦不苦

347. The world is not a land of pomp and vanity, nor is the human life a sea of bitterness.

世人为荣利缠缚，动曰："尘世苦海。"不知云白山青，川行石立，花迎鸟笑，谷答樵讴。世亦不尘，海亦不苦，彼自尘苦其心尔。

【今文解译】 世人都为名位利禄所累，所以动不动就说："人生犹如苦海。"殊不知天地之间还有飘浮的白云、青葱的山峦、汩汩的流水、挺立的涧石、迎风招展的鲜花、欢唱的鸟儿，以及山谷里回荡着的樵夫歌声。由此可知，人间并不是尘世，人生也不是苦海，所谓的尘世苦海皆由世人不能自拔的名利心所致。

【English Translation】

As people are ensnared in the bonds of fame and gains such as glory, splendor, wealth and rank, so at every turn they complain, "The world is like a sea of bitterness." What a pity that they do not know that the white clouds surrounding the green hills, the streams flowing among the towering rocks, the flowers blooming with the singing of the birds and the song of the woodcutter echoing in the valley are all fantastic scenes of the world. Actually, the world is not a land of pomp and vanity, nor is the human life a sea of bitterness. The reason why people lodge such a complaint is just because they are unable to extricate their hearts from material ensnarement.

348. 花看半开　酒饮微醉

348. To enjoy flowers, it is best to enjoy them when they are in half bloom; when drinking wine, drink only until you are tipsy.

花看半开，酒饮微醉，此中大有佳趣。若至烂漫[1]酕醄[2]，便成恶境[3]矣。履盈满者[4]宜思之。

【中文注释】 ① 烂漫：花朵盛开。
② 酕醄：烂醉如泥的样子。
③ 恶境：恶劣的境地。
④ 履盈满者：泛指功成名就的人。

【今文解译】 赏花最好待到花朵半开，饮酒最好饮至微醉，这样才能体会到赏花饮酒的最大乐趣。如果等到花瓣尽开再去赏花，酒喝到酩酊大醉才肯罢休，那就根本没有乐趣可言了。功成名就、志得意满的人可要好好思考一下这个问题。

【English Translation】

To enjoy flowers, it is best to enjoy them when they are in half bloom. When drinking wine, drink only until you are a trifle tipsy. This is the gateway to the profound enjoyment. Once the flowers bloom in full and you drink yourself drunk as a jellyfish, adversity will supervene. Those who are at the zenith of their fortunes should take this into careful consideration.

349. 坚守故我　不受点染

349. Keep your nature intact by remaining unspotted by the mundane affairs.

山肴[1]不受世间灌溉，野禽不受世间豢养，其味皆香而且洌。吾人能不为世法[2]所点染，其臭味[3]不迥然别乎？

【中文注释】 ① 山肴：指可食用的山中野生植物。
② 世法：世俗所遵循的礼法。泛指各种俗事俗物。
③ 臭味：气味。此处指人的气质或气宇。

【今文解译】 山里的野菜野果并未经过人工的培植，野生的禽兽也未经过人工的喂养，可是它们的味道却是那么清香醇厚。如果有谁能做到不为世间的俗事俗物所影响，他的气质就一定和别人的不一样。

【English Translation】

Edible wild plants in the mountains are not irrigated artificially, nor are wild birds fed within a fence. Yet they are all savory and palatable. If we remain unstained by the worldly affairs, our makings would be definitely different from those of others.

350. 玩物自得　不在物华

350. To ride a hobby is not to enjoy the superficial brilliance, but to attain enlightenment from it.

栽花种竹，玩鹤观鱼，亦要有段自得处。若徒留连光景，玩弄物华，亦吾儒之口耳[①]、释氏之顽空[②]而已。有何佳趣?

【中文注释】 ① 口耳：此处口耳指“口耳之学”。语出《荀子·劝学》：“小人之学也，入乎耳，出乎口。”谓只是耳听口说的学习。后用以指道听途说的肤浅之学。
② 顽空：佛教用语。指一种无知无觉的、无思无为的虚无境界。

【今文解译】 尽管只是栽花种竹，玩鹤观鱼，但也是要从中有所感悟的。如果只是一味地流连于眼前的景致，玩赏景致表面的华美，岂不流于儒家所不齿的浅薄无知和佛家所不屑的虚无顽空了吗?！还有何乐趣可言!

【English Translation】

To cultivate flowers and plant bamboos or to sport with cranes and raise fish, one should have them done to meet the purpose of attaining enlightenment from them. If he does them only for the purpose to enjoy instant amusement or superficial brilliance, then all he does will be no more than what the Confucians call the fragmentary hearsay knowledge or what the Buddhists call the inanity. How could a meaningful delight be expected therefrom?

351. 清名沦丧　生不如死

351. A depraved person would be better off to die than to live.

山林之士，清苦而逸趣自饶[①]；农野之人，鄙略[②]而天真浑俱[③]。若一失身市井驵侩[④]，不若转死沟壑，神骨犹清。

【中文注释】 ① 逸趣自饶：安闲自得，情趣丰富。
② 鄙略：地位低，见识少。
③ 天真浑俱：本性中质朴的东西全都保留着。
④ 市井驵侩：市场里唯利是图的奸商。驵侩，马匹交易的中间人。

【今文解译】 隐匿山林的居士，生活虽然清苦却安闲自得，情趣沛然；乡野田间的农夫，人虽卑微而且见识也少却质朴无华，本性纯然。一旦他们丢弃这些优点转而变成市侩了，还不如死在沟壑里，以留个灵魂和肉体的清白两全。

【English Translation】

A recluse in the mountains lives a Spartan life, but still he is fully contented with the elegance of carefreeness. A country fellow looks vulgar and outlandish, but still he keeps his nature intact. Should they ruin their pure virtues and become like horrid men in the market, they would be better off to go and die in the wild valley, thereby preserving the purity of their souls and bodies.

352. 着眼要高　不落圈套

352. Be far-sighted and high-minded so as to avoid falling into a snare.

非分之福，无故之获，非造物之钓饵，即人世之机阱[①]。此处着眼不高，鲜不堕彼术中矣。

【中文注释】 ① 机阱：设有简易制动装置的捕兽陷阱。此处喻害人的圈套。

【今文解译】 不是自己应享的福分以及无缘无故得到的好处，这两样东西即使不是造物主抛出的诱饵，也一定是世人设下的陷阱。此时若不能明察秋毫，有所警觉，很少有人不落入圈套中去的。

【English Translation】

Fortune undeserved and gain unearned are either the bait set by the Creator or the trap purposely laid by the world of mortals. Not a few people who happen upon them, if not vigilant enough, will fall into the snares.

353. 根蒂在手　不受提掇

353. Stick to the crucial points by not being manipulated by the outside force.

人生原是一傀儡①。只要根蒂②在手，一线不乱，卷舒自由，行止在我，一毫不受他人提掇③，便超出此场中矣！

【中文注释】 ① 傀儡：木偶；木偶戏。
② 根蒂：比喻事物的根基或基础。此处指拴在木偶上的绳索。
③ 提掇：提拉。此处喻来自外部的牵制或干扰。

【今文解译】 人生本来就是一场木偶戏。只要牢牢把握住牵动木偶的绳线，线与线之间保持有序不乱，放松或收紧、行进或停止皆由我掌控，丝毫不受他人的掣肘，就不仅能演好这场戏，而且还能另有所获。

【English Translation】

Man's life is similar to a puppet show; so long as you hold the strings in your hands, keep them in good order, roll them back and forth freely, act as you will and go without the least manipulation from outside, you will certainly accomplish more than you perform for.

354. 无事为福　雄心冰融

354. To be involved in nothing is happiness in which ambitions vanish like the melted ice.

一事起则一害生，故天下常以无事为福。读前人诗云："劝君莫话封侯事，一将功成万骨枯[1]。"又云："天下常令万事平，匣中不惜千年死[2]。"虽有雄心猛气，不觉化为冰霰[3]矣。

【中文注释】 ① 劝君莫话封侯事，一将功成万骨枯：奉劝各位不要再谈什么封官授爵的事了，将军的战功可是用无数人的白骨堆出来的。

② 天下常令万事平，匣中不惜千年死：为了使天下能永葆和平，即使将征战用的刀剑放在匣中一千年让它锈蚀腐烂掉，我也在所不惜。

③ 冰霰：下雨时，雨滴落到地面之前，遇到冷空气而结成半透明的小冰珠。

【今文解译】 有事就总会有弊处，所以天下的人都把不卷入什么事情当作是一种福分。古人有诗云："劝君莫话封侯事，一将功成万骨枯。"还有诗云："天下常令万事平，匣中不惜千年死。"读了这些诗句，即使再大的雄心壮志，也会像阳光下的冰霰一样，不知不觉地化为乌有。

【English Translation】

When something happens, there must be disadvantages. So, many people often take it as happiness for not being involved in anything. I once read a poem written by an ancient, which goes, "Please bid no more words about being conferred a title, just realize that the military exploit of a general costs numerous lives." And, "For the sake of an everlasting peace of the world, I would by no means grudge encasing my sword for a thousand years." Upon reading these lines, even a gallant guy could not help throwing his ambitions into thin air, like the ice melting in the sunshine.

355. 茫茫世间　矛盾之窟

355. The vast world is like a den of motley crowd.

淫奔[1]之妇矫而为尼[2]，热中之人激而入道。清净之门，常为淫邪之渊薮[3]也如此。

【中文注释】 ① 淫奔：自西周起，男女缔结婚姻必须经过"父母之命，媒妁之言"。在宗法制下，由父母家长决定子女的婚姻大事，通过媒人的中介来完成，否则即是非礼非法，称为"淫奔"，不为宗族和社会所承认。
② 矫而为尼：因矫情而皈依佛门，削发做起了尼姑。
③ 渊薮：人或事物聚集的地方。

【今文解译】 不守礼法与人私奔的女人因矫情而削发为尼，热衷功名利禄的人因一时意气而当起了道人。佛寺道观本都是清净之地，竟也常常成为藏污纳垢的去处。

【English Translation】

An immoral woman becomes a Buddhist nun simply out of pique. A man who has been hankering after fame and wealth all the time retires to a Taoist temple just because of an offhand radical thought. Generally, both Buddhist and Taoist temples are places far away from the worldly hubbub, but now they are often usurped to shelter the immoral and countenance the accursed.

356. 身在事中　心超事外

356. When engaged in something one should let his heart stay aloof from it.

波浪兼天，舟中不知惧，而舟外者寒心[1]；猖狂骂坐[2]，席上不知警[3]，而席外者咋舌[4]。故君子身虽在事中，心要超事外也。

【中文注释】 ① 寒心：此处喻害怕。
② 骂坐：多指酒席间借酒泄愤而破口骂人。
③ 不知警：喻没有丝毫警觉。
④ 咋舌：形容吃惊的样子。

【今文解译】 行船于滔天的波浪里，船上的人毫无惧色，反而是岸上的人看了提心吊胆；席间有人大放厥词，同桌的人不觉得什么，反而是邻桌的人听了瞠目结舌。所以，君子置身事中时一定要有超然事外的心态。

【English Translation】

When the billows dash against the sky, the persons inside the boat remain unruffled, but those outside are seized with terror. When one shouts abuse at a feast, all the rest sitting around the same table are not alarmed, but those in the neighborhood are left speechless with astonishment. Thus we realize that when engaged in something, a gentleman should let his heart stay aloof from it.

357. 不减求增　桎梏此生

357. Those who do not seek to save the troubles but strive to increase them instead are simply fettering themselves.

人生减省一分，便超脱一分。如交游减便免纷扰，言语减便寡愆尤①，思虑减则精神不耗，聪明减则混沌可完②。彼不求日减而求日增者，真桎梏此生哉！

【中文注释】 ① 寡愆尤：寡，少；愆尤，责备或埋怨。

② 混沌可完："混沌"又作"浑敦"，也即《庄子·应帝王》中所说的中央之帝。南海之帝倏和北海之帝忽经常在混沌的领地见面并受到很好的款待。为了报答混沌的友善，倏和忽决定为混沌凿出七窍，使之视听饮食方便。于是，他们每天给混沌凿一窍，结果刚到七天，就把混沌凿死了。此处指避免弄巧成拙。

【今文解译】 人的一生总是少一事就多一分超脱：少一些交际应酬，就可以少一些外界的纷扰；少说一些话，就可以少一些别人的怨尤；少一些思虑，就可以少耗些精神；少卖弄些聪明，就可以少一些弄巧成拙。不想着每天少一些反而想着多一些事情，这样的人生真就像套上了枷锁一样！

【English Translation】

The more we save ourselves troubles, the more we are free from vulgarity. For instance, by reducing social intercourse and entertainment, we will be able to turn away unnecessary external disturbances; by talking little, we will be able to avoid possible offences; by moderating contemplations, we will be able to spare our energy and strength; and by playing lesser petty tricks, we will be able to refrain from becoming the objects of ridicule. Those who do not daily seek to save the troubles but instead strive to increase them are simply fettering themselves.

358. 满腔和气　随地春风

358. Fill the heart with auspiciousness, and wherever you go you will have the spring breeze for company.

天运①之寒暑易避，人世之炎凉难除；人世之炎凉易除，吾心之冰炭②难去。去得此中之冰炭，则满腔皆和气，自随地有春风矣。

【中文注释】 ① 天运：天体的运转。此处指自然界季节的变化。

② 冰炭：像冰和炭一样不能相容。此处指自己内心的欲念与世之常理的冲突。

【今文解译】 四季变化带来的严寒与酷暑容易应对，而人与人之间的世态炎凉却难以排解；人与人之间的世态炎凉容易排解，而人内心那些与世道格格不入的私念却难以平复。平复了内心的私念，则满腔都是祥和的气息，到哪儿都如春风拂面。

【English Translation】

It is easy to shun the cold and the heat as the seasons take turns, but not easy to eliminate the fickleness of the world. Even if easy to eliminate the fickleness, it is still not easy to expel from the heart the selfish thoughts incompatible with the way of the world. If a person can expel the selfish thoughts, his heart will be filled with auspiciousness and peacefulness; and wherever he goes, he would feel the spring breeze caressing the face.

359. 嗜欲无碍　纯朴就好

359. Personal addictions and desires bring no harm so long as they are kept in a simple and honest way.

茶不求精而壶也不燥，酒不求洌而樽也不空，素琴无弦而常调，短笛无腔而自适。纵难超越羲皇①，亦可匹俦②嵇阮③。

【中文注释】 ① 羲皇：伏羲，传说中的古代皇帝。
② 匹俦：媲美之意。
③ 嵇阮：嵇康和阮籍。嵇康，三国魏思想家、文学家，服膺老庄，自称“老子、庄周，吾之师也”。强调精神上的自我修炼，主张心无是非。阮籍，三国魏诗文作家，魏晋玄学清谈中的一位重要人物。两人皆为“竹林七贤”之一。

【今文解译】 喝茶不求茶叶有多好，只要茶壶里有水即可；喝酒不求酒有多好，只要酒杯始终都不空着；弹琴不求琴弦有多好，只要弹者能常娱其心；吹笛不求腔孔有多好，只要吹者能自适其性。所有这些，即使不能与上古时的伏羲比谁更朴实，至少可以和竹林七贤中的嵇康和阮籍比一比谁更洒脱。

【English Translation】

To drink tea, it does not matter how fine the tea is; what matters is to ensure that the teapot is never dry. To drink wine, it does not matter how mellow the flavor is; what matters is to ensure that the wine cup is never empty. A coarse lute, even without refined strings, can still play a melody to satisfy itself. A simple flute, even without proper holes, can still pipe a tune to compose itself. All these are rude but honest traits. Although they may not be as admirable as those in the epoch ruled by Emperor Fu Xi*, they are at least comparable with those in times of Ji Kang and Ruan Ji*.

【English Annotation】

* Emperor Fu Xi: A legendary ruler in ancient China. At his age, people were thought to be pure in nature and simple in mind.

* Ji Kang and Ruan Ji: Two of the “Seven Worthies of the Bamboo Grove” in the Three Kingdoms Period (220-280). Ji Kang (223-263), a thinker and man of letters in the State of Wei, esteemed Lao Zi and Zhuang Zi as his teachers

and advocated personal moral cultivation. Ruan Ji (210-263), a writer of poems and senior military officer of the State of Wei, pursued the philosophy combining the doctrines of Taoism and Confucianism.

360. 万事随缘　随遇而安

360. Comply with fate and Nature in doing everything and accommodate yourself to circumstances.

释氏随缘①，吾儒素位②，四字③是渡海的浮囊④。盖世路茫茫，一念求全则万绪纷起⑤，随遇而安则无入不得⑥矣。

【中文注释】 ① 释氏随缘：释氏，即释迦牟尼。缘是佛教讲求的一种冥冥之中的自然境界，具有命中注定之意。随缘就是顺其自然，因势而为。

② 吾儒素位：吾儒，即我们儒生（因作者推崇儒学之故）；素位，此处指坚守本分、本性等。

③ 四字：即“随缘”和“素位”。

④ 浮囊：一种简易的渡水器材，多由兽皮或畜皮制成。

⑤ 万绪纷起：此处指杂乱的想法或外界不计其数的诱惑。

⑥ 无入不得：所到之处，都能自得其乐。

【今文解译】 佛家讲求的是随缘，而儒家在意的是素位，这四个字是为人处世的秘诀，像渡海用的浮囊。人的一生前路茫茫，如果什么事都想做到尽善尽美，必定会有数不尽的烦恼与诱惑；遇事如能安然以对，那么所到之处就都乐在其中了。

【English Translation】

What Buddhism is particular about is to accord with the factors that condition a situation, and what Confucianism emphasizes is to be content with the present status and environment. These two stresses amount to a pneumatic float with which people cross the sea of life. The roads of the mundane world are boundless and indistinct. If a person intends to seek completion and perfection from them, he will soon find himself lost in countless vexations and temptations. But if he is ready to accommodate himself to any circumstances he would meet, then no matter where he is, he won't fail to find happiness and contentment.